THE REPLACEMENTS

A FRACTURED FAMILY FAIRY TALE

Written By
CYNTHIA A. KING

Copyright © 2025 by Cynthia A. King
All rights reserved.
ISBN: 979-8-89324-341-3

No part of this book may be reproduced, stored in a retrieval system, or transmitted in any form or by any means—electronic, mechanical, photocopying, recording, or otherwise—without prior written permission of the publisher, except for brief quotations used in reviews or articles. The opinions expressed by the Author are not necessarily those held by the Publishers.
The information contained within this book is strictly for informational purposes. The material may include information, products, or services by third parties. As such, the Author and Publisher do not assume responsibility or liability for any third-party material or opinions. The publisher is not responsible for websites (or their content) that are not owned by the publisher. Readers are advised to do their own due diligence when it comes to making decisions.
Published by Franklin Publishers
Printed in the United States of America
For permissions, inquiries, or additional copies, contact:
Franklin Publishers
www.franklinpublishers.com

To Kathy, my fellow misery sister.

Table of Contents

Prologue..7
Chapter One - Grey and Val..9
Chapter Two - Val 23
Chapter Three - Grey and Val..38
Chapter Four - Val and Grey 54
Chapter Five - Val and Grey 68
Chapter Six - Grey and Val..85
Chapter Seven - Val and Grey..107
Chapter Eight - Val and Grey...117
Chapter Nine - Grey and Val..127
Chapter Ten - Val and Grey...133
Chapter Eleven - Val and Grey...148
Chapter Twelve - Val...172
Chapter Thirteen - Grey and Val..175
Chapter Fourteen - Val..192
Chapter Fifteen - Grey and Val..232
Chapter Sixteen - Grey and Val..252
Chapter Seventeen - Val..278
Chapter Eighteen - Grey..301
Chapter Nineteen - Grey and Val...322
Chapter Twenty - Val..334
Chapter Twenty - One - Val...349

Prologue

VAL

"MOM," her oldest daughter Astrid asked, "where are we going again?"

"Will you stop asking me that? You know where we're going. Your grandmother's funeral. Your Gramma Wilson. You kids were just with her last summer. You stayed there summers after Dad and I split up," Valerie said, sitting on a bench in the park. She needed a break from packing for the trip, and this seemed to be the best option.

"But why are you going? She's your ex-mother-in-law. I can understand why we should go. But you?"

"That's what happens when you grow up in a small town. Everybody knows everybody else. Besides, I loved her, and I'm sad."

"Well, I don't know anybody, and neither does Ingrid. Fiona doesn't either." The mention of Fiona caused Valerie to take a look at her sleeping three-year-old in the stroller. At rest, she was an angel. Awake, Fiona was a wild-haired, bright-eyed, moving mass of kinetic energy, atoms pinging around at full speed.

She operated just as well in stealth mode, so anything of value must be out of reach. Her latest trick was to go through any unattended purses, take lipsticks, and hide them.

"What about your father? Shouldn't his children come and pay their respects to his mother? Besides, it's the right thing to do."

"Him," Astrid said in a tight voice. "Like he'd go out of his way for us."

"That's between you two. I told you a long time ago not to expect people to give you what they don't have. Saves a lot of time as far as being disappointed," Valerie said and returned to the book she was reading.

She couldn't focus on the words on the page; the thoughts in her head wouldn't lay dormant. Gramma Ellin. She and her husband Dave did such a good job picking up their son and Valerie's ex-husband Greg's slack. That lady knew the meaning of rising above your circumstances, your lousy marriage, and your boozehound of a husband. She never once questioned Valerie's side of the story. It was with her full endorsement that Val left. Valerie felt like she left the scene of an accident without calling 911 and never looked back. She reluctantly went back in her mind to those days, those days of high school when the horizon seemed so clear and adulthood so far in the future it wasn't even worth a thought.

One

GREG AND VAL

GREG WILSON WAS THE MAN. The star quarterback who took the team to the state title and was crowned the Homecoming King at halftime. Tall, handsome, and brimming with youth and vitality, old people wanted to stand next to him, hoping some of it would spill over onto them. Greg had beautiful blond curls and cerulean eyes. Valerie once told him that was the color of his eyes, something she learned in art class. He just laughed and said blue WAS blue.

Everyone wanted to hang around with him and be his friend. He was the guy who put a live goat on the opposing team's football field before a big game. Everyone knew he did it, but nobody could prove it. The farmer who owned the goat was pissed he had to come into town to pick it up. They won that day, 21-0. He could out-drink anyone; he was the life of every party he attended. Even if there was a hint of him attending, people showed up.

How she ended up dating him was a mystery. They were on complete opposite poles of the spectrum. She was studious and smart. In her free periods, she went to the Art room or the library, and the teacher in charge always allowed her to go. Valerie's point about how anybody could get any work done in a study hall filled with a bunch of loudmouth jocks was valid. There was a sub one day who wouldn't let her leave, so she was forced to sit as far away from them as possible and work on her essay about Lord of the Flies.

Valerie wanted to compare it to high school, with the jocks as the hunting party, with Greg Wilson as the main guy. She would be Martin, trying to maintain order and some sense of civility. Valerie had her head down, wondering who would be Piggy? Simon? A knock on the table forced her to look up. It was Greg Wilson looking down at her with those blue eyes and a big smile. Valerie was momentarily stunned.

What does he want, she thought. He just looked down on her and said nothing.

"Yes?" she asked, more shocked than impressed it was him. "What do you want?"

"To see what you're doing," Greg said.

"Writing a book report for English."

"Yeah, but it's not due until Friday. It's only Tuesday."

"So? I like to get in front of things. I'm not a wait-until-it's-due kind of person. How do you know it's due on Friday?"

"Because I'm in your English class."

Valerie sat back and looked at him again. "Oh, okay. I guess you are," she said as she lowered her head to her paper. Instead of realizing she had dismissed him, he sat down. She glanced up at his muscular forearms covered with white-blonde curly hair. Look away, Val told herself. Look away.

"What book?" Greg asked. He had his arms on the table, and Valerie couldn't help but stare at those curly, blonde-white hairs that covered his muscular arms. She wondered if he did that on purpose.

"The Collective Works of William Shakespeare."

"That sounds way too hard. Why choose that?" Greg looked puzzled that someone would do more than the bare minimum to satisfy an assignment.

"It probably does sound too hard to somebody who has never read it. The beauty of his use of language, the deep context of relationships, of love and loss. Its romance and subtlety would be lost on someone who only reads comic books."

He pointed at the book in her hand. "You're not reading Shakespeare. It wasn't on the reading list. You made all that up."

"Guilty," she said with a shrug.

"What book are you reading for your essay?" Greg asked.

"Lord of the Flies."

"What's it about?"

"It's a lot like high school," she said and tapped her pen rhythmically on the table.

"How come you didn't pick Catcher in the Rye?" he asked. "That's what I picked."

"Because I've already read it a couple of times," Val said, still looking up at him. She found his blue eyes hypnotic and hard to look away from. No wonder every girl in the school is crushing on him, Val thought.

"You'd read a book twice?" he asked incredulously, thinking, This girl is nuts.

"If it's good, yes," she said, still puzzled by what he was still doing there.

"What's it about?"

"Don't you know? I take it you haven't started reading it yet." Look away from his eyes, she told herself. Look away from his eyes.

"No, I told you it's not due until Friday. I was hoping you were reading it so you could write the book report for me," Greg said.

"Oh, well. You lose." Valerie broke free from his eyes and put her head down, again ignoring him.

"No, you lose. I was going to pay you fifty bucks." He got up and knocked on the table. "Goodbye, miss-nose-always-in-a-book-front-row-sitting Valerie Reynolds," Greg said as he walked away, back to the corner of the room the Neanderthals claimed as theirs.

A few days later, in English, instead of going down the row that brought him the fastest way to his desk, he cut over, so he deliberately passed by her desk. He didn't say anything. He just rapped his knuckle on her desk. Valerie looked up, and he was smiling at her as he walked by. She didn't smile back, but she didn't frown, either.

Valerie looked, well, stunned. He noticed her. Greg took that as a good sign.

Later that day, during study hall, the regular teacher was back. Valerie got a hall pass to go to the art room. She gathered together her things and left the room.

She was halfway down the hall when she heard a voice telling her to wait up. Valerie turned to see who it was. It was Greg Wilson approaching her at a slow jog.

"You sure walk fast, probably because you're tall. You take bigger steps," he told her and asked, "Where are you going so quickly?"

"The Art room." She shrugged. "Why are you following me? Where are you going?"

"The hall pass is for the bathroom, but it didn't specify which one. I think I'll walk you to the Art room and use the one down there."

Valerie shrugged again and kept walking.

"What do you do in the Art room?"

"What do you think? Art. What do you do in the bathroom?"

Greg laughed. "You don't want to know. But it's nice to know you have a sense of humor."

"Is it now?" Valerie said.

She went into the art room without saying goodbye. Greg stood for a second and watched her back walk away. She confused him. Everyone in school, girls and guys, teachers even, were drawn into his orbit. Greg couldn't help it. It happened as far back as preschool. Kids would argue about who got to sit next to him at circle time. Greg always took it for granted. That was just the way it was. He never had to actively seek out friends, people were always nearby who just waited for an opportunity to hang out with him.

Valerie didn't seem impressed by him at all. It wasn't that she was playing hard to get. He could tell when a girl was doing that. It was more out of sight, out of mind. Greg didn't like the fact that he thought about her way more than she thought about him. When most girls looked out the window and daydreamed, sooner rather than later, he crossed their minds. When Valerie daydreamed, he wouldn't be surprised if it was a foreign concept to her, but if she did, she was probably thinking about Shakespeare or Van Gogh. He went back to study hall, where all the girls secretly lusted over him, the guys all shoved over to create room for him, and all was right with the universe. His universe, anyway.

They had lunch in the same period. Valerie always sat with two girls, Emily Flynn and Kylie Hernandez, or Kylie Flynn and Emily Hernandez; he wasn't sure which name belonged to which girl. He always sat in the same spot with a rotating group of guys. He never noticed Valerie in the lunchroom before. He never noticed her at all, and suddenly, it seemed she was everywhere he looked. Had she been there all along, not even a blip on his radar, and he failed to notice her? Why did she suddenly appear out of seemingly nowhere, and why am I so preoccupied with her? he wondered.

He decided Valerie would notice him, whether she wanted to or not, but he wasn't sure. This uncertainty was a feeling he found unfamiliar. The only people he could discuss this with were his brother Jason, who was away at school, his father, who hadn't dated in about fifty years, or his sister, Caroline. His sister was two grades below him, but he figured she at least thought like a girl.

Greg caught her one afternoon when she was in her room and not on the phone, a very rare occurrence. Caroline was on it ninety percent of the time, the coiled cord disappearing under her closed door. He knocked from the doorway. Nobody was allowed in her room unless invited. She looked up from what appeared to be her Advanced Algebra textbook, grateful for the distraction.

"Caroline, do you have a minute?" Greg asked after he knocked.

"What do you want?" she said, immediately suspicious of his motives. He was remotely more interesting than Advanced Algebra, which was the only reason she considered talking to him at all. She was so sick of being Greg Wilson's little sister. Caroline looked forward to next year when he'd have graduated and gone to college. She'd have two years of high school, not living in his shadow. Two years of people not wanting to be her friend because maybe he'd be home when invited over to her house.

"Are you going to invite me in?" he asked before he crossed the threshold.

"Is this going to be that lengthy a conversation? You need to come in here to talk about it?" Caroline asked, now mildly curious.

"Caroline, don't bust my balls over this. I just wanted some input as to the workings of the female mind. Last I knew, it said female on your birth certificate, despite looking like a twelve-year-old boy."

"You can't talk to someone like that and expect her to be hospitable, let alone let you in her room. You want to talk to me, not the other way around."

"Okay, I apologize." Greg started over. "Caroline, would you please help me? I need some assistance, and I was hoping I could ask you a few questions about girls."

"Girls? You want to ask me about girls? You managed to get this far without my advice. Why now?" She thought a minute and looked him in the eye. "You want to talk to me about girls or a girl? A specific girl?"

"I've got to hand it to you, Caroline. You're a lot smarter than I've ever given you credit for."

"Thank you. You're the last person to figure it out. Now, about this girl. This specific girl. What's the problem? It has to be big if you want to talk to me about her. Does this girl have a name? Do I know her?" Caroline fished for details while she marked her place in her textbook.

"Her name's not important. The problem is, she has no idea I'm alive. How do you impress a girl who thinks you're just a big dumb jock? Usually, being a big dumb jock is enough." He still stood in the doorway.

"Now I have to know her name," Caroline said. "I want to know what girl is apparently immune to your charms. Who is she?"

"You don't know her. Everything she's interested in, I know nothing about. I guess you'd call her an intellectual. She fucking likes Shakespeare. She's not a cheerleader. She knows nothing about sports. She actually wants to study during study hall. A lot of the time, she asks to be excused so she can go to the library during study hall because we're too loud. I'm stumped. I don't know what to do."

"I have a few thoughts. A couple of good ones, but I'm not saying a word until you tell me her name."

"You won't know her. I guess her name doesn't matter. Valerie Reynolds."

"Nope. Doesn't ring a bell." She got off the bed and went over to her bookshelf. Caroline thumbed through a few books and said, "Aha!" She pulled last year's yearbook off the shelf, sat back down on her bed, and held the yearbook close to her chest.

He made a grab for it. "I didn't know you had one of those."

"No way," she said, hugging it tighter. "There's a lot you don't know because you are so self-absorbed you don't pay attention to anybody but yourself. Your grade?" she asked him, and Greg nodded. She went through last year's junior class and found her. Caroline gave him the yearbook and pointed at a girl. "Her?"

"Yeah, that's her. I think that's her. I've never seen her smile before, but that's what she'd probably look like if she smiled."

"She's never even smiled at you? Boy, that is some tough sledding," Caroline said. "But I have a few ideas. Does she have any friends?"

"Friends? Probably." He shrugged.

"No wonder she wants nothing to do with you. You don't know anything about her. Her friends? Are you in any of the same classes?"

"Uh, English, but she sits up front. She doesn't hang around with anybody. She just comes and goes and doesn't seem to walk or wait for anybody special. Oh, and lunch. I see her at lunch sometimes."

"That's good. Who does she sit with at lunch?"

"A couple of girls, the same two, so they must be friends. I think."

"Jesus, Greg. Your observation skills suck. You'd be worthless as an eyewitness. The two girls, do you know either of them?" Caroline probed further.

"Yeah. One's a redhead with a million freckles. I think her name is Emily. And the other one's brown. Her name is Kylie, I think."

"Brown? She's brown? Very good, Greg," Caroline said sarcastically. "The redhead? Emily?" His sister flipped a few pages. She stopped and pointed out a girl. "Her?" He nodded.

"Her name is Emily Flynn. I think I know the 'brown' girl." She flipped back a few pages and pointed at a girl. "Her?"

"Yeah, that's her. She's a real pretty girl," he said to his sister.

"Figures you noticed her. Her name is Kayla, not Kylie. Kayla Hernandez. Why aren't you interested in her?"

"I don't know. Usually, I like them good-looking, and Kylie is a stone-cold fox. Valerie's hot, too. She's the one that interests me."

"Kayla. She's the captain of the volleyball team. She'll kick your ass if you don't get her name right."

"Okay, duly noted. We know she has a couple of friends. So what?"

"God, you really are a dumb jock. Use her friends to get to her. If there's a party, invite them. They'll make her go. Girls always travel in a group for safety reasons. Flirt with them and ignore her. Do any of your friends like these girls? Have them conveniently cross paths. What else does she do?"

"She goes to the Art class in her spare time," he offered.

"Perfect. Sign up for it as an elective. Or find out when her class is and see if they have room for you now and enroll."

"Art?" he said painfully, like he found the idea on par with home economics, something his mother used to do with his aunts, another girlie thing he had no use for.

"Well, look, genius. You're not going to find her waiting for you on the fifty-yard line. Be glad she's not in drama or choir because those really are painful."

She paused a second. "Wait a minute. You're not going all out to get this girl precisely because she's not into you, and you want the pleasure of dumping her after she's hooked? It's not retribution for having to devote all this time and energy to land her so you can put her in the win column. Is your ego doing all the thinking or your dick? Because I'll write a note about the insincerity of your affection and stick it in her locker. Don't think I won't if that's what you're doing," Caroline said, and the tone in her voice left no room for doubt.

"Look. I don't know what I'm doing," Greg admitted. "I just know when she looks at me, it's like she's looking right through me, and I don't like it. I think about her all the time." Caroline looked at him.

"I feel for you, brother. You got it bad." Caroline said, secretly pleased at his difficulty.

"But I don't even know her. It makes no sense at all," he whined.

"Hey, the heart wants what the heart wants."

"That's fucking Shakespeare, is it?"

"I don't know. Joy Behar, The View," she said.

"Don't ever read Shakespeare." He made her swear. "It's pretty, the iambic pentameter and all. That's the rhythm. It gets you in the mood because it's all romantic and stuff. Guys use that to get girls into them."

"What the fuck are you talking about? Do you even know Romeo and Juliet die in the end?"

"They do?" Greg asked. "At least some action happens, but you have to wait until the end? That's stupid. You've got to read all that other shit to get to the good part? I'll pass."

Greg spent a few days thinking about his sister's advice, mostly while looking at the back of Valerie's head in English. She was tall, so most of it was visible. Valerie had such pretty hair; today she wore it in a braid. He studied her brown hair, but it wasn't really brown. He noticed some streaks of blond among the brown, but the brown, in reality, was deep chestnut. Greg looked at her hair woven among itself. He didn't even realize there could be that many shades of brown, and they were all wrapped up in that braid. A braid so thick it could rival Rapunzel's; it resembled the kind of rope used to tie a boat to a pier. He wanted to reach out and grab hold of it in the worst way; once he got that close, he would never let it, or her, go.

"Mr. Wilson? Care to join us?" Ms. Malinkowski asked. He knew she caught him spaced out. He had to think of something quick.

"Sorry, Ms. Mal. I was thinking about this week's game, and my mind wandered off. I won't do it again."

"See that you don't." Greg may have been a big dumb jock, but in being one, many people let him get away with things others didn't.

Being an intellectual didn't get you out of shit, but being an athlete sure did. In fact, Greg could see no purpose in being overly smart. It's not like you grow up and sit around, have a few beers, and talk about Gandhi, for Christ's sake, he thought. He knew he should do something at lunch. What, exactly, wasn't very clear.

Greg ate his lunch and secretly kept an eye on her. He stood up. "I'm still hungry," he announced to his friends. "I'll be right back." He went through the line again, and this time, Greg picked out three ice creams, those little tubs with wooden spoons attached. The cafeteria policy was one ice cream per student, but once again, his jock status circumvented any penalty deviating from the norm. He was the big man on campus, the quarterback. The cafeteria ladies weren't above his charm and let him eat as much as he wanted. He had to keep up his strength if they expected to win. Greg thanked them profusely and exited the line. Greg headed towards the table where Valerie sat with her friends, right at the end. He walked up to where they were and stopped. Greg looked at the three ice creams.

"Geez, will you look at that? They gave me three," Greg announced and turned towards the three girls. "Here," he said, "have some ice cream," and he proceeded to give Emily and Kayla the two extras.

"Thanks," Emily said, a bit shocked the star quarterback gave her ice cream. Kayla was not so easily impressed. She pointed at the third ice cream in his hand.

"Didn't you forget one?" She pointed at Valerie. "Hers?"

"Oh, no, this one's mine. I heard your friend is lactose intolerant," he said as he walked away.

"You're lactose intolerant? I never knew that," Kayla asked.

"Me either," Emily said.

"I'm not," Valerie said, an edge in her voice. "He made that up."

Greg went back to his table and sat down. He glanced over to where the girls sat. They looked liked they were having a heated exchange, probably over him, his ego said. Maybe his sister was smarter than he thought. Greg watched them talk. They finished, grabbed their things, and left. "Which one?" asked his best friend, a wide receiver named Evan.

"What?" said Greg.

"Which girl has your attention?" Evan questioned.

More like I don't have hers, Greg thought. "She doesn't have my attention. Yet," Greg answered.

"It's not the redhead, is it? I have fantasies of playing connect the dots with all those freckles," Evan confessed.

"No. Not her, and not the other one," was all Greg elaborated.

Greg's next opportunity came during study hall. He heard Valerie ask for a pass to the library, and after she left, he went to the teacher and requested one, too. The teacher looked at him as if he were asking for a ticket for the next moon launch.

"The library?" she said in disbelief.

"I have to find Valerie. I was going to ask her for our Global History notes. I lost mine, and we have a test tomorrow. She left before I had a chance to ask if I could borrow hers." That sounded like him losing his notes. The teacher believed it and wrote him his pass.

Greg went through the library door and immediately scanned the room, but he couldn't find her. He figured she would be the furthest away from the door, and he wasn't wrong. Valerie was at a table in the back, with her back towards the room.

Greg kind of snuck up on her and decided this was too obvious a tactic. He was on the other side of the last bookshelf. He pushed a book off the shelf on the other side, and it hit her in the back.

Valerie looked around, confused, but saw nothing amiss, and she put it back. He waited about five minutes and did it again, this time hitting her in the shoulder. Greg used those quick foot drills from football to slide two stacks back from where he stood when he pushed the book. He peeked through the books and watched her check out where somebody who would push books at her needed to stand, but there was no clue as to who it was. Valerie went back to her seat and continued working. Greg went back a third time and pushed a book from the upper shelf, only it was higher and heavier than he realized. It hit her in the head. Greg didn't move and allowed her to catch him this time.

"What is wrong with you?" Valerie asked, pretty pissed off. He had a chance to look, really look at her. As much as her hair was every conceivable shade of brown, her eyes were the same. Amber, auburn, all colors of brown, like they were lit from inside. They were bright and pretty, with little speckles of gold in them, too. Her face was made up of strong features, but somehow looked delicate instead of sharp.

Greg decided to go the big dumb jock route. "I'm really sorry. I was trying to be funny."

"Funny? Giving me a concussion is funny?"

"No, it's not, and I am sorry." Greg decided to go the humble big dumb jock route. "I just wanted to talk to you. But you scare me. I'm afraid you'd tell me to get lost. So I decided to act like a fifth grader, but looking back on it, I probably should have picked a different way to get your attention."

"How about 'hello'?" Valerie asked him. "Wait a minute. Back up. You're scared of me?"

"Yeah. I figured I'd have one chance with you, and hello wouldn't cut it."

"You're probably right. You've got my attention. Now, what do you want?"

"Do you mind if I sit down?" She shrugged her shoulders and took a seat. He sat across from her. "Have you ever gone to Homecoming?"

"What?" She sounded like the question annoyed the hell out of her. "No. Once, maybe. Freshman mistake."

"I figured as much. You're a senior. This is the last chance to ever go to one. I was hoping I could talk to you about the game."

"The game? What game?"

"The football game. I was hoping you'd be interested in going to the game. Maybe if you saw me do something I'm good at, you wouldn't think I'm such an ass."

"Isn't there a dance, too?" She raised a brow.

"Look. Don't get me wrong. I'm not asking you out on a date. I'm not asking you to go to the dance with me. I'm asking you to watch a football game, that's all. Bring your friends. You don't even have to wave to me. Just watch the game. Stay until half-time. I don't care. It's the only way I can think of to redeem myself."

"Redeem yourself from what?"

"Look, I know in your eyes I'm nothing but a big dumb jock. I feel the need to show you I may be a big dumb jock, but at least I'm good at being a big dumb jock. Maybe first impressions count, but maybe second or third impressions could count a little, too. Does that make any sense to you?"

"Yes, sort of. I don't understand why what I think matters to you, but if the weather's okay, I'll go. Emily and Kayla are going. I suppose I could go with them, once again, weather-dependent. I'm not going to sit in the rain to watch a football game, not even if Joe Namath himself is playing."

Greg smiled. "That seems reasonable. You know who Joe Namath is?"

Valerie smiled back. "Maybe I'm not the brainiac you think I am, first impressions and all. I'll try to make it to the game."

He made her smile, he thought to himself. It was even prettier in real life.

***

Two

VAL

FRIDAY WAS A WONDERFUL FALL DAY, the perfect night for the homecoming football game. The sun was out, the air as crisp as a fresh apple. Instead of the last class of the day, they had an assembly in the gym. Valerie forced herself to attend. She went to the one her freshman year and found all the Who-Hah Who-Rah irritating as hell. Valerie skipped the next two years, hiding in the girls' locker room, only to find herself going through it in her senior year.

Valerie decided to look at it from a dispassionate anthropologist's point of view; at least she could observe the festivities but not participate. She sat with Emily and Kayla, who were both possessed by the school spirit. The cheerleaders and mascot came into the gym, whooping and hollering and trying to whip the crowd up into a frenzy. Everyone was stomping on the bleachers, and the gym got louder than Valerie ever heard it. She found herself caught up in the moment, laughing and pounding along with everybody else.

When it was determined the place couldn't get any louder, the football team came busting out of the locker room, and the place went nuts. The whole team created the gym, with the cheerleaders and mascot, so loud it sounded like a freight train coming through. Valerie couldn't help but look at the players in search of Greg. After all, he was the one that talked her into going to all this bullshit. He was with all the other players, feeding off the energy of the crowd, when she noticed a blond cheerleader go over to him and jump in his arms. Greg held onto her tight, and whether he got carried away with the intensity of the crowd or him glad to see her, he kissed her. A full-on, in-love kiss. It wasn't the other way around. Greg kissed her. All her suspicions of him evaporated. What did he need her for? He already had a girlfriend. Valerie felt a weird pang of an emotion she never gave credence to: jealousy.

After the team came out, the pep rally ended. Kids filed out of the gym, buoyant by a noise that carried them out of the building. Everyone made plans to meet there later, before the game. After she saw Greg and his girlfriend, she saw no reason why she should go to the game.

Valerie tried to tell her friends she would pass on the game, but they wouldn't let her. She hadn't shared why she wanted to go, and she didn't share why she changed her mind. Emily and Kayla wouldn't allow her to not go. Instead of taking her home, they went to Emily's and ordered pizza. When it came time to leave, they did a makeover on her. Valerie had skin like porcelain; putting makeup in the right place and emphasizing the right spots was the hard part. She let them put some curls in her hair, making it even more voluminous.

"Why are you in such a funk? What happened?" Kayla asked.

"Nothing happened. I just reconsidered. It looks like a bore."

"You're hurt," Kayla said. "I saw you see him with his girlfriend. So what? Fuck him. He's not ruining our night. Let's finish off the pizza, go to the game, and see what's all this madness around football. It can't be that stupid."

"I think it is. Stupid. Really stupid," Val answered.

"I don't care. You said you'd go with us, so you're going. And you're going to look like a girl having a good time. A girl having a great time. A girl who looked like she's having the best time ever," Emily said.

They didn't do too much to her face, just a swash of blush. They accented her eyes by smudging some charcoal, that made them seem bigger. She wouldn't allow false eyelashes, but they put enough mascara on her lashes that they stuck together anyway.

They went to the game; it's easy to be a fan when you're winning on a perfect fall evening. It was a beautiful night with a full moon. Every once in a while, a gust of wind would stir the dead leaves up in a whirl.

It was a perfect night for the quarterback and the head cheerleader to be crowned Homecoming King and Queen. Valerie watched the ceremony. That pang of jealousy didn't occur, so she felt nothing as she saw the two of them crowned king and queen. She felt a little something, but not enough that it deserved a name.

The game ended; the home team beat the opposition by fourteen points. Nobody left. There was a tradition of throwing the winning football into the crowd. It would happen again, like it always did after the game. The crowd stayed and waited to see what the quarterback, Greg Wilson, would do.

Greg threw the football, a perfect spiral, like it was shot out of a cannon, aimed directly at Valerie's chest. She could hear the sound of her father's voice in her head saying, "Whatever you do, don't lose the ball," when it hit her right in the chest. Valerie didn't catch it so much as to trap it against her body with her arms. She bobbled and almost went down, but stood firm at the ricochet. Valerie took the ball, and he watched as she triumphantly held it over her head with both hands.

Valerie saw relief flood his face. Any other girl would flub it, and that would be part of her charm, but the girl who caught the football he threw to her like she was a dude was awe-inspiring and a little scary. This would be one memory forever burned in his mind.

In that one moment, right before he threw the ball at her, the blond cheerleader and everything else faded away. Greg looked for her. He deliberately combed the crowd, looking for her. Valerie saw him seek her out. When their eyes locked, he gave her a look she didn't understand. Was it because he chose to throw the ball to her? Did her catching it mean anything? It was too deep a look to process at the moment; right then, a group of guys saw her and yelled, "Over there! Get the ball!"

Valerie held it firmly, thinking, Don't lose the ball! Don't lose the ball! She was ready when some kid tackled her. He knocked her, and she banged the side of her face on the metal seat of the bleacher. When he released his hold on her to grab the ball, she rolled off the bleacher and onto the ground underneath. Valerie still had the ball, and she heard a commotion above her. The guys who wanted the ball were yelling, "Where is she? Get the ball!"

Some parents witnessed her catching the ball and the kid tackling her. They stepped in, trying to break up the boys and stop them from trying to steal the ball.

Valerie heard yelling and arguing above her. She knew they would figure out she fell off and come down looking for her, so she got on her hands and crawled out. She kept the ball on the ground under her in case someone jumped on her. Val crawled out, the argument above her caused enough of a distraction to give her time to escape. She came out among a mob of people, mostly their legs.

Some older man, either a parent or a teacher, saw her on the ground and started yelling, "Help, she's hurt!" He asked her if she could stand. Valerie could, but a couple of people had to help her up because she wouldn't let go of the ball. People surrounded her, keeping the boys at bay. The athletic trainer drove his golf cart over to make sure she wasn't hurt. He had her sit in the cart so he could evaluate her. He looked at her and snapped his fingers in front of her face.

"Hey! Hey! You still with us?" She nodded. "You need to let go of the football. It's the only way I can check you out." She still held it tightly to her chest. Valerie would only release it if the trainer promised he'd give it back. Emily and Kayla saw her with the trainer and came over.

"What are you, nuts? I can't believe you still have the ball," Emily said excitedly. "Are you hurt? You must have fallen ten feet from the bleachers. I can't believe that kid tackled you!"

Valerie checked out fine. The trainer wanted to drive her to the car so they could put the ball in the trunk and put an end to this foolishness. Her friends hopped on and allowed the trainer to take them to the car, and Kayla put the ball in the trunk. She got back on, and the trainer dropped them off at the front entrance, assuming they were going to the dance. They thanked him for the ride.

"No problem. You," he said, pointing at Valerie, "no more football unless you're wearing pads. You're a very lucky girl." He drove off, back towards the field.

"I can't believe that just happened to you. Are you sure you're all right? You probably don't want to go to the dance now," Kayla said.

"I think I do. This homecoming bullshit makes me curious about what's going to happen next."

The crowd from the game started to arrive. They stood outside for a while and watched kids enter. Once they decided enough people were there, they went inside. There were disco balls shining in pieces all over the gym. There were synchronized lasers, and the bass line just throbbed.

The DJ was a senior they recognized, so the music was loud and current. Teachers were on grind patrol. Any kids caught in any simulated sexual acts were kicked out. Humping got you a warning, and the second time, kicked out. The adults didn't bother with the mosh pit. The last time they tried to break it up, a teacher caught an elbow and needed stitches. It was engaged at your own risk, and the teachers chose not to.

Emily and Kayla went out on the dance floor; the days of waiting for a boy to ask you to dance were long gone. If a girl was out there dancing and a guy wanted to dance with her, he started dancing with her and her friends. If she were interested, she'd kind of break off from her friends and pay attention to the guy. If they got too close, the grind police stepped in.

"Come on," her friends said. "Dance with us. You wanted the whole homecoming experience. You have to dance." Valerie decided they were right. She followed them out and danced. Val danced until she was hot and sweaty. Guys moved in and out of their circle, but she never made the move to someone specific, so they came and went.

After about an hour, they decided to go out and get some air. Once out, if you went to your car, you weren't allowed back in, so you were limited to a small area in the front. Valerie leaned against the brick wall of the school when the football team arrived. They went home to shower and change; that explained their late arrival.

Still pumped up from the win, they were loud, and the cheerleaders even louder. Valerie and her friends watched the team enter. Greg's friend Evan grabbed Emily by the wrist and said, "You need to come in and dance with me."

She said okay and went inside.

Valerie watched the rest of the guys come in. Greg came in with the last of them but was laughing and joking, looking elated, with his cheerleader on his arm. His eyes didn't search for her. She told Kayla she was going to call her mom for a ride home; she was feeling kind of sore.

"You stay and make sure Emily's all right. Just because he scored on the field doesn't mean he gets to score with her." Valerie told her.

"That's fine. I'll keep my eyes on Emily. I don't blame you for wanting to leave. Does the arrival of Homecoming King and Queen have anything to do with it?" Kayla asked.

"What? Who?" Valerie's confusion about them reassured Kayla her friend wasn't crushing on the most popular guy in school. Valerie used the pay phone to call home to ask her mom to come to pick her up.

"Do you want me to wait with you? Are you going to be okay if I leave you here alone?"

"I'll be fine. I live like ten minutes from here. She's coming," Valerie told her. "Make sure you give me back my football."

"Yeah, yeah, yeah. I won't lose the ball," Kayla promised and went inside.

A little while later, Greg approached Kayla. The little rah-rah probably went to the ladies' room, so he had a few minutes, Kayla thought.

"Hi, uh, Kayla." He was unsure he got her name right, but he must have; she didn't correct him. "I'm looking for your friend. Do you know where I can find her?"

"Well, that one's over there with your friend, and the other one is waiting for her ride home out front."

"Is she okay? Your friend. That girl. Did she get hurt?"

Kayla shook her head. "She's okay."

"Thanks," Greg said and ran for the front door, but Valerie was gone. Kayla stood back and watched him go look for Valerie. *Maybe I've got it wrong, she thought. It looks like he has a thing for her, not the other way around.*

Her mom came right along; Valerie gently sat in the front seat. After she pulled out of the school and onto the road, she spoke to her daughter.

"How was homecoming? Did you have a good time, honey? You seem a little off. Did something happen?"

"Oh, Mom, you wouldn't have believed it even if you were there." She explained the night in great detail, barely pausing to catch her breath.

"That's one for the books, for sure," her mom said, "it still doesn't explain why you're so sad."

"Why do you think I'm sad?"

"You are, aren't you? I'm your mother. You develop a six sense about things, I guess. You know when your child has a problem before they do. Is that the right word? Sad?"

"I suppose that is the word, sad. It's as good as any other," Valerie turned her body towards to door, away from her mom.

"Maybe if you tell me about it, we can find the right word. Is it about a boy?"

"Why would you say that?" Valerie bristled. Her mother came too close.

"I only have one question. I know it's not your grades. You just got them last week, and they were fine. You don't have a job, so it's not your boss. You don't play sports, so it's not your coach, and you got the homecoming ball, so you should be overjoyed about that, but you're not. The only thing left is a boy. Did I come close?" her mom asked.

Too close. I need to get a life, Valerie said to herself. To her mother, she said, "Yeah, it's about a guy. Something happened I don't understand. He acts weird around me. He pays attention to my friends but not me. He's in my study hall. If I get a pass to the library or the Art room, he gets one for the bathroom and follows me around. Tonight, he looked for me to throw the game ball on purpose, but then he walked right by me into the dance with his girlfriend. What's your opinion on that?"

"Boys are strange, that's true, but not very complicated. It sounds to me like he's trying hard to get your attention. The hall passes, the game ball, and he wants your attention. The question is, why? What's he going to do with it? He already has a girlfriend. Is he a real pig that just wants anything with boobs, and he decided he liked yours? The girlfriend. Is he the kind of guy that cheats?"

"No. That's the thing. I fill no need in his life. He's worshipped and adored because he's the star football player. He doesn't lack female attention. He has his girlfriend and any other girl he wants. He doesn't want to copy my homework. I don't have anything to offer that he doesn't already have. I wish he'd just leave me alone."

"If that's what you want, tell him so."

"That's my problem. I don't know what I want."

"I think his plan's worked so far. He's gotten your attention."

"So, what's next?"

"Let's just wait and see. Think of him as an annoying fly. He's only bugging you because he can. Avoid him as much as possible; don't be so predictive."

"What does that mean? Is that even a word?"

"Predictable. That's a word. The word," her mom decided. "It might be, or I might have made it up. What I mean is, don't do the same thing the same way all the time. Take different stairs. If you always sit in the same spot in the library, sit somewhere else. See if you can't eat lunch at a different time or in the girls' locker room. Switch things up. Get lost. How he responds will tell you a lot."

"That would mean I cared about what he thought, and I'm not sure I do. I just think he'll get bored and bother someone else. I hardly live a life that somebody would find interesting."

"That's up to you. Don't be surprised if he moves on. Boys that age have the attention span of a flea."

It moved faster than either one thought. He came over the next day and knocked at the door. Valerie's mom answered the door and saw a tall, very handsome young man. "May I help you?" she said.

"Hello, Mrs. Reynolds. My name is Greg Wilson, and I was hoping to speak to Valerie. Is she home?"

"Hello. Val's out back playing with the dog. If you walk around the house on the left, you can let yourself in through the gate."

"Thank you, Mrs. Reynolds." Greg walked around the left side of the house. He came to the gate but didn't let himself in. He watched her throw a stick at a huge dog. Valerie tossed the stick, and the dog chased it.

Greg yelled at her, "Hey, that's the best you can do?" Valerie turned and saw him at the gate, stunned. She bent down to fix her laces to buy her enough time to get her game face on and stood up.

"What are you doing over there?"

"Waiting for you to invite me in," he said.

"Come on in."

Greg lifted the latch and entered. She turned back to the dog, picking up the slobbery stick. Valerie threw the stick again, not looking at him. Greg walked over and stood next to her. "You call that an arm? It's hard to tell which one's the stick," he told her.

"It's this one," she said, handing him the saliva-coated stick. He threw the stick a lot farther than she did. The dog brought the stick back to him. Greg threw it a few more times and sat down next to her.

"What brings you by?" she asked him.

"A couple of things. First, I wanted to apologize for throwing the ball so hard. I wanted to make sure you got it, and accuracy requires that kind of throw. It was only after I let it go I realized you don't play football and would have no idea how to catch it."

"But I did."

"You sure did. What happened afterward?"

"Some guys decided I didn't deserve it and tried to take it away from me. One guy tackled me, and while he was grabbing the ball, I slipped off the bleachers. While they were fighting up top, I crawled out, and some old guy helped me and kept them away until the trainer came over."

"I panicked," he confessed. "First, I nailed you in the chest with that rocket, then I saw that kid tackle you, and you went down. I couldn't see anything after that. I was too far away to do anything, and I couldn't get off the field to find you. By the time I got over there, the trainer had taken you away. I don't have your number, and it's not in the phone book, so I couldn't call. I remembered when you took the late bus, you got off here, so I figured I could at least try."

"The late bus? You took the late bus?"

"You stayed late every day you could, um, to do art. It was no big deal. I had to take it for football. It was easier than finding time in my parents' schedules for a ride."

Valerie remembered taking the late bus. They'd be home in plenty of time to start schoolwork and eat. It was a nice fifteen-minute break from the daily grind. His came to an end when his friends started driving. She took the late bus for two years. The portfolio she was working on was exhibited at the museum at the end of her junior year. Greg remembered she won something.

"Didn't you win some art competition?"

Valerie looked at him. Why would some jock know that? Had she been on his radar since tenth grade? Once his friends started driving, she never saw him again.

"Yes, I did. I'm surprised you know that."

"I know that because my sister won an award for something, and my parents made me go in support. You won like some big award. I vaguely remember you onstage."

"Yeah. My portfolio won the Central Region, and it went on to the state judging," she said, her eyes downcast, picking at the grass.

"Well, how did you do?" Greg asked. Competition, now that he could relate to.

"Better than expected. Out of fifteen, I came in third. I won a partial scholarship."

"Really? That's great. No wonder you spend so much time in the Art room. A scholarship," he admired. A win was a win, his sports training told him, and she was a winner.

"A partial scholarship to a fancy college in NYC. It wasn't much, and the cost of living there, plus what the scholarship didn't cover, it wasn't worth it. I'd be in debt till I was eighty. If it was a full scholarship, I would have taken it in a minute, but otherwise, it was unrealistic."

"Really? If you love art so much, you should go."

"That's the thing. I love art class. I'm pretty good, so it's easy to love something you're good at. I thought about just saying fuck it and going for it, but when I got to the state level, I saw the competition, and there were a lot of great people out there better than I was. Way better. I guess I didn't have the temperament, or ego maybe, to think I could make a living are it. Art for art's sake is great, but it won't put food on the table. I just didn't want it as much as these other kids. I wasn't that intense about it. You don't need a degree to pick up a paintbrush, so I decided it wasn't the right fit for me. I couldn't sit at a cafe wearing a black beret, drinking really strong coffee, and smoking French cigarettes without feeling like a phony."

"Kind of like Holden Caufield," he said.

She looked at him. "What does that mean?"

"All the phonies. What else did he call them? Dopes?"

Valerie looked at him, seeing layers to him she never knew were there. "Kind of."

He glanced at her. "I did read the book, you know. Or maybe the Cliff's Notes. But the kid had a lot of problems."

Here was this guy, the hottest guy in school, sitting in her yard, having an actual conversation. The one of a kind of intimate flow between two people is a rare, once-in-a-lifetime occurrence. It was scary. Valerie was petrified.

"Hey. Is something wrong?" Greg asked her.

"No, quite the opposite. Like two tons of love is gonna rain down like bricks on us."

"Oh," he said, at a loss for words.

Mrs. Reynolds opened the door and came out with a tray holding a pitcher of lemonade and two glasses. "I thought since neither of you have stopped talking all afternoon, you must be getting thirsty."

"Thanks, Mom!"

"Thanks, Mrs. Reynolds," Greg called up to her and got up to get the lemonade. He poured it into two plastic tumblers and gave her one. He took a sip and said, "This is real."

"Yup. My mom's secret recipe. Comes out of a can."

"What?" he said. He didn't get the reference. Greg sat there and enjoyed the conversation. There wouldn't be many more days like this as the weather got colder, but sitting here in the grass with her on a rare fall day seemed like the most normal thing in the world.

"What time is it?" Greg jumped up. "Oh, no, I've been here over five hours!"

She looked at him. "Don't let me keep you."

"No, that's not what I meant. I meant I'm sorry to take up all your time. I'm sure you have better things to do than talk about nonsense."

"Well, it wasn't a waste for me," she said, looked up at him, and smiled.

He suddenly dropped to his knees. When she looked up at him, he noticed the bruise forming by her temple. "You're hurt!" He knelt next to her and turned her face. He ran his hand gently along her hairline and discovered a lump. Her face was turning purple from her eyebrow to almost her jaw.

"Does it hurt? Do you need to see a doctor?" He asked.

"Just headache. It was worth it for my dad. He was proud I didn't lose the ball. The closest to another son he'll ever get."

"Is your father nuts?"

"Yeah. But in a good way."

"I didn't mean to take up your whole afternoon. You're just so easy to talk to. I didn't worry about offending you once," Greg confessed.

"Do you offend people often?" Valerie asked him.

"No, but I worry about it," he said.

"Well, don't. Do something more constructive with your time," she advised.

Valerie laid on her back and looked at the clouds. She found one shaped like an elephant and pointed to the sky. Brutus thought they were doing something dog-related, like looking at a bone-shaped cloud, and came over and put his nose in Valerie's ear.

She screamed, "The dog had just put his tongue in my ear!" For some reason, Greg thought it would be funny if he stuck his tongue in her other one. She screamed again, and the dog laid on her; when she rolled out from under the dog, she rolled right into Greg. They were lip to lip for about ten seconds, and he looked so deeply into her eyes, it spooked her.

Nobody ever looked at her like that, and what he might see scared her. Brutus broke the moment. He put his big hairy paw on Greg because Valerie was his, after all. He partially stepped on her head. She still was laughing when Greg pulled her out from under the dog. Valerie sat next to him, closer this time. The dog sat down next to her. They were quiet for a bit, and she finally spoke.

"Look, Greg. It was awfully nice of you to stop by and see how I am, but I think you need to go. You have a girlfriend, and she might consider your concern, um, a bit excessive. I might consider your concern excessive if you show me any more of it. So you gotta go."

"I'd argue, but I'd be wrong. I'm not that guy. And you're not that girl." Greg stood up and extended his hand to her. Valerie took it and stood. He held on to her hand a few seconds longer than he should. He let go, and they walked to the gate.

"Thanks for coming over to see how I made out, but you can see I'm fine."

"You're finer than fine. It's probably too late, but some ice on that can't hurt. I'll see you in school. Oh, wait. Let me bring the lemonade back to the kitchen." Greg jogged over and put it on the table near the sliding glass door. Valerie thought she would never see youth at its peak like this ever again. Even tomorrow, he'd be too old. He was so comfortable in his own body. She could imagine Michelangelo stopping him in the piazza, demanding him to pose for David.

Monday at school, the rumor mill was running at full tilt. The bruise on her face confirmed her involvement in the post-game fiasco. She was called into the front office to "talk" about the event. Yes, she caught the ball, but she didn't see who knocked her down.

"Let me clarify that," she said. "I didn't see who tackled me or knocked me off the bleachers. Somebody didn't just bump into me."

The principal had two boys waiting outside. When she walked by them, they whispered, "You didn't blow us in, did you?"

"I didn't see you, or else I might have," she whispered back.

The other talk was about how Greg Wilson broke up with his longtime girlfriend, Casey Wembridge. The star quarterback went over to the head cheerleader's house Sunday night and told her he no longer wanted to be her boyfriend. It wasn't anything specific; he just didn't feel right tying her down when he had all these doubts. She cried and carried on how he couldn't break up with her. They were supposed to be together forever.

"See, that's it. You want forever. I'm too young for those kinds of promises. Maybe someday, but I can't promise anything like that now to anybody."

Casey was not going down easy. "Who is she? Who?"

Greg was confused. "Who is who?"

"You know. Who's the girl you're dumping me for!" Casey yelled, bursting into tears.

"I'm not dumping you. I'm telling you I can't give you what you want, and you're free to go find it. I don't have another girl. I don't want a girlfriend. I don't want you unhappy, and you would be if we stayed together. Trust me. My head's not where it needs to be right now. I'm questioning a lot of things in my life. I need some space. Please respect that. I'm trying to do the right thing here. Don't make it harder." Greg tried to sound sincere; he hoped she heard it in his voice.

"Get out of here!" Casey screamed, throwing her math book at him. "How dare you lead me on like this? How dare you pretend to be someone you're not! You'll be sorry! When you come crawling back, I won't be here!"

He saw his opening, and he took it. "I'm sorry, Casey. I really am, although I know you don't think so."

He started towards the door, and she freaked out, yelling and throwing things at him as he hurried out.

He started his car and backed out of her driveway. He wanted to see Valerie in the worst way. His situation didn't have anything to do with her, but the timing was sort of iffy. He didn't want to drag her through this mess, so he satisfied himself by driving by her house. There were lights on upstairs, and he wondered which room was hers.

Three

GREG AND VAL

GREG AVOIDED any contact with either Valerie or Casey. He didn't want Casey to think she was right in assuming there was another girl.

He didn't ask for a pass when Valerie left the study hall. Greg tried to avoid both of them. The closest he got to her was watching her as she walked away. He looked at Valerie's back a lot. She was tall and graceful. Greg thought her hands fluttered like little birds; she would make an excellent magician's assistant.

Valerie always wore black track pants or jeans and tee shirts. If it was cold, she put a denim jacket over the tee. She wore it like a uniform or some variation of it every day. Greg studied her back, trying to figure out if she wore that outfit to stay anonymous, to be overlooked on purpose. He saw her arms when she wore the tee shirts, and he liked how smooth her skin was and how delicate her wrists looked. When he went to her house, he remained a perfect gentleman, although it took all he had not to jump her bones.

Casey took the breakup hard. She swung daily from crying endlessly to furiously irate. She stalked him and had all her cheerleader friends follow him, too. Casey was convinced there was another girl, and she was determined to find her and rip her hair out by the roots.

Valerie and Kayla were in the women's locker room checking out her bruises. She ended up with a black eye as well as the other damage. Kayla felt the bump in her hairline and assured her it was going down. They were looking at Valerie's face in the mirror when Casey and three members of her cheer squad stormed in.

"You!" she yelled at Valerie.

"What?" Valerie said, confused.

"You're trying to steal my boyfriend!" Casey screamed.

"Maybe," Valerie said. "Who's your boyfriend?"

"Greg Wilson! The quarterback!"

Valerie looked at her like she was crazy. "Your boyfriend? The quarterback? Oh, the guy who threw the football that hit me right in the face, gave me a black eye, and knocked me off the bleachers? That guy? Yeah, he's a real catch. No. I think I'll pass."

Casey was loaded for a fight, but Valerie's version of what happened was believable, plus she had a black eye. Casey focused on his advanced chemistry lab partner. The poor girl had no idea how she got involved in the popular kids' drama. Nobody from that sphere ever acknowledged her existence except for Greg, and that was because he had to, although he did say hi to her outside of class. Casey had her up against her locker and screamed so loud she spent the afternoon in the counselor's office. Her parents were called in, as well as Greg, to settle Casey down.

Valerie and his lab partner were not the only two girls she raged on. Casey's behavior was unacceptable, and she would lose her spot on the cheer squad if she didn't stop. The involvement of the adults really quieted her down. Now, she would go off in a corner and weep. Her girlfriends all gathered around to console her, and Casey found this attention more comforting than yelling at random girls.

Casey stopped her harassment of the other girls. She realized that what really bothered her was that he broke up with her. It wasn't the loss of Greg's love and affection she missed, and she did miss it, but she took him for granted. He was more like a prop for her most popular status or a loyal golden retriever. Greg was nice and treated her fine.

Greg was always around when she needed him and was happy to help her. He was the male version of her, or who she wanted the world to perceive her. Who was he to dump her? If anybody got dumped, it should be him. Casey's ego hurt more than her heart. Besides, she could snag another guy to worship and adore her in a snap.

Thursday was a study hall day, and Valerie got a pass for the library. She decided to take her mom's advice and sit somewhere else, so she sat off to the side. Valerie saw him go to the back, where she usually sat. She watched him look for her. He must have only had a bathroom pass because he didn't stay. She laughed to herself.

Friday at lunch, they ate in the girls' locker room; and she took different stairs to get to class. Valerie even skipped English. She took the bus home, she was one of the few seniors who did. Most caught rides with friends or had their own cars, but taking the bus home didn't bother her.

Valerie walked from the corner and saw Greg's car in her driveway. She knocked on his window and startled him. He rolled the window down and asked if she had a minute. She nodded her head, and he popped the lock for her to get in the passenger side. Val got in and asked him, "What's up?"

"What's up? Where have you been?" Greg asked her, either concerned or annoyed, or both.

"School. Why? Where have you been?" Valerie said, nonplussed.

"I haven't seen you. You weren't in the library. You didn't go to lunch. You weren't in English. Are you okay? I was worried," Greg said, concern laced his voice.

"Yeah. I've been trying to avoid your crazy girlfriend. She almost physically assaulted me in the bathroom."

"My crazy EX-girlfriend. I broke up with her on Sunday."

"How come?" Valerie asked him.

"I met another girl. She has a better dog. Casey has a poodle."

"Oh. Another girl? You're a busy guy."

"Not really. I spent a whole afternoon with her, and when I got home, I wanted to call her because I missed her and had a hundred other things I wanted to tell her. I couldn't keep talking to her if I had a girlfriend, so I broke up with her. I'm not into her anymore, like I am this new chick. I figured the new girl wouldn't think very highly of me if I was a cheater, so I am now unattached. I'm available. I'm interested. Are you?" he said with a smile.

"Well, I've got to say it sounds like a great position. I might be interested. How do I arrange an interview?"

"Come here, and I'll tell you."

She leaned over the console and put her face a few inches from his. They were silent as they looked at each other, the same way he looked at her on the football field. She looked back and him with a slight smile dancing on her lips.

"Make your move, sailor," she said in a husky voice. "My elbow is starting to hurt."

"We can't have that," he said and put his arms around her shoulders, pulling her over the console until she was practically in his lap. Greg looked at her and pulled her face to his. "You are so beautiful," he said before he kissed her. Her lips were so soft and lush, her mouth so inviting, he understood why cavemen clubbed women over the head and dragged them off to their caves.

When she kissed him back, it was so soft and barely a whisper, his breath caught in his throat. She went on the offense, her mouth taking possession of his. Greg was glad he was sitting because he couldn't feel his legs. Valerie kissed each lip separately and both together. It was like she had magic in her kiss. He wouldn't be surprised if she pulled a rabbit out of his mouth. Instead, she stole the breath from his lungs and the voice from his throat. Val pulled her lips from his and put that enigmatic smile back on her face. She raised an eyebrow and said, "Well?"

"Um, well, what?" he managed to get out.

"Do I get the position?"

"Baby, you get anything you want." Greg paused and checked the time.

"Oh, shit, I gotta go. I'm going to be late for practice!"

He helped her get back on the passenger side. Valerie opened the door and said, "See you around."

Greg knew he would be late, but he couldn't take his eyes off her until she went inside.

***

For the most part, their relationship wasn't apparent to most people. They didn't sit together in class. Valerie ate lunch with her friends; he, his. Greg occasionally gave her a ride home. They did their homework together sometimes, but he still had football practice, though the season was winding down.

Greg was on the basketball team, another sport in which he excelled, and the same with lacrosse in the spring. He chose not to pursue either his senior year. He had a football scholarship and didn't want to risk an injury, but he still had to hit the gym and keep in shape.

Valerie went with her friends to the last couple of games. The very last home game was senior night. All the seniors and their parents took the field at halftime. There were a lot of tears, and Greg was named MVP for the season. Valerie got all warm inside because he searched the stands for her and pointed at her with the trophy.

Soon, it was the end of the semester and final exams. They both did well. Winter break started, and she met his parents and his younger brother and sister. She introduced him to her parents and her older brother and sister, home from college. Her father was a jock from way back, and Greg's accomplishments were marked by her father reliving his glory days. They both tried very hard to be nice and polite in the presence of the other's family.

One night, Greg's family went to a holiday party, and they were alone. They never really tried to sneak away and be alone. They had some very intense make-out sessions, so intense it scared her. Greg was her very first steady boyfriend, and he knew she was young and inexperienced. He liked her enough not to push things. His family was out, and they were watching TV. They started out holding hands. He moved on to kissing that spot behind her ear that gave her goosebumps.

"Hey," he whispered in her ear, "can I ask you a question?"

"Sure."

"Why do you dress like that?"

"Like what?"

"Like an eighth-grade boy."

"Comfort, mostly. Why?"

"Because men are visual creatures, and I wondered if you did it so nobody would look at you that way. Womanly. Desirably. Sexually."

"Maybe a little, I guess. My philosophy has always been to keep your head down and stay off the radar. You can't do that in Daisy Dukes."

"I can understand that. What about me? I've felt you plenty of times, but I've never really seen you. The caveman in me wants a look. Do you trust me enough to show me?"

"Yeah, I guess I do."

"Come here, then." He sat on the couch and had her straddle him. He had her take the jean shirt, so she was just wearing her tee shirt. "Now kiss me."

She kissed him, and he started to squirm. Valerie reached down and pulled her shirt over her head. She sat up straight and let him look at her breasts in her demure white lace bra. Greg ran his hand over her bare skin. He stroked her back and stopped at her bra hook. He looked at her, and she nodded, and with one hand, he undid her bra. It slipped down her arms, and instead of being a shy, bashful girl, she put them on display for him.

She arched her back, put her hands on his shoulders, brought his face into the valley between them, and placed each of his hands on one globe of ripe, delicious flesh, and she laughed.

"Is the caveman pleased?"

Greg pulled his shirt off, and suddenly, it became paramount that every skin cell of hers came in contact with every skin cell of his. They rolled around each other, touching and feeling and licking. They were laughing and rubbing when he heard the garage door open.

"Quick! The bathroom!" Greg tossed her clothes to her and pushed her towards the door, grabbed his shirt, and put it on. She came out of the bathroom, said hello to his parents, and sat next to him on the couch. His parents went up to bed, and his brother wanted to watch TV. Greg tossed him the remote and said he'd give her a ride home now. She managed to hold it together and started laughing once they got in the car.

"What's so funny?"

"Your shirt. It's on inside out." Valerie laughed all the way home.

Christmas came and went. He gave her a gold bracelet, and she gave him a picture she painted. It was just Brutus lying in front of the fireplace. She used large brushes and bold strokes, but certain places were soft and elegant. As a joke, she gave him the stick he threw to the dog the first day he came over. Greg loved them both. He put the stick on a shelf in his room. Greg hung the painting, too, but said he would take it to his dorm room, and it would remind him of her while he was away.

Since he saw her topless, he was on a mission to see the rest of her naked. He told her the caveman inside him desired it, and he wanted to know what she thought about the idea.

"What does that mean? If you see me naked, what comes next? Are you going to pressure me to have sex?"

"No. I might beg, but the gentleman in me would keep the caveman in check, but men are visual," Greg said again.

"No, I'm not saying it right. Let me start over. You know you are my first steady boyfriend, and I've never done it before. I'm not against the idea, but it would have to be in the right setting. I'm just worried about what it will mean. Would you want to do it every time you see me? Will it be the center of our relationship? I'm nervous we're going to have this mad, passionate love affair right before we leave for school, and it will ruin the first semester for both of us. Instead of being open to new things, I'll be obsessed with when we'll be together again, and when we do see each other, is it going to be all about doing it?"

"Huh," he said. "Those are good questions. I know the teenage boy in me is saying, 'Hell Yes!' But the maturing male side of me is saying, 'Of Course Not!' What, there are six months until I leave. I can't promise I'm not going to try to get it in every time I see you. In my head, it will be the most incredible thing ever to happen to me, and if I have it once, I'm sure I'll want it again. Your point about going away and being able to leave it here is a good one. I don't want a picture in my head of you sitting in your dorm room when everyone else is out having fun because of your loyalty to me."

"What if you get the chance to backpack through Europe one summer, and you don't go because of your loyalty to me?" Valerie asked him. "I don't want you to miss out on anything. I don't want to miss out on anything, either. I love you, but I think we might be getting ahead of ourselves."

"You love me?" Greg asked, stunned.

"Oops, but yeah. It just occurred to me, but yes, I guess I do. We get along. We never fight, and we don't have to go anywhere to have fun. Everything seems to fit."

"You love me?" he asked again.

"Yes, I do. Don't make a big deal about it, or I'll never say it again," Valerie threatened.

"Do you expect me to say it back?"

"No. Not unless you mean it. Say it, don't say it, I don't care. That's part of what I'm talking about. It's too big to deal with now. We're too young to deal with it. Now is the time to explore new things and go to new places. Imagine a year from now, when your roommate asks you to spend the holidays with him in Hawaii. But you're having some internal conflict about me because you really want to go but are worried I'll be hurt. I don't want that for either of us. Or we're home, and all we do is fuck. I don't want that either."

"Obviously, you've thought about this a lot. What do you want?" Greg asked her.

"What do I want? Ideally, we play this out here, and when it's time, you go do your thing, and I do mine. If we see each other on breaks, that's cool. The romance goes on ice until we graduate college. If we end up in the same place at the same time, we go on. If we end up not in the same place, we still go on. Only our separate ways."

"That seems realistic and sensible. Is it feasible, though? Teenage hormones and all?" Greg said.

"I have no idea. But it's the only thing I can think of. Do you have any thoughts?" Valerie asked him.

"We don't break up? When we leave for school it's on pause? To be resumed at a later date? We can try. We can still see each other, right?"

"Yeah. But no obligations. If you make other choices, you make other choices. If feelings get hurt, they are going to get hurt anyway. At least we'll be four years more emotionally mature to deal with it. I hope. I just think we need to take the next four years to figure out who we really are, and being in love will get in the way."

"I agree. In theory. But let's go back to fucking. Can I be your first?"

"Sure," she said, like he wanted to borrow five bucks, "but not in the backseat of a car or a cheap motel, and not anywhere where our parents can walk in on us."

"I see. I have some work to do. But first, tell me you love me again."

"Why?" She laughed.

"So I can say it back."

It wasn't too long until the opportunity presented itself. His dad had a business trip in Florida, and his mother went with him to read magazines and sit by the pool. His sister was going to stay at her friend's house, and his brother was having a friend over to eat pizza and play video games.

They were at a Friday night basketball game, and they were beating the other team by a lot. Greg grabbed her hand at halftime and said, "Let's go." He drove over to his house and parked the car in the garage. Greg let them in the kitchen door. He said quietly, "Wait here."

Greg went into the family room and told his brother he was home and he'd be in his room. His brother didn't care. Greg came back and took her by the hand, and they went upstairs to his room.

Once inside, Greg kissed her with intent. He was hungry for her and kissed Valerie as if he was starving, and she was a hot fudge sundae.

"What's going on?" she said, giggling.

"Hush. No talking," he whispered. "Over here." Greg led her to the other side of the bed. He pulled out a bottle of Champagne and two glasses. He gave her the glasses to hold and popped the cork. Greg filled the glasses and put the bottle back in the ice bucket, which was just the bathroom wastebasket. He smiled at her, took one of the glasses, and clinked his glass against hers. "To you," he said and took a sip. Valerie took a sip and chuckled.

"Did you pop that cork so you can pop mine?" Valerie laughed quietly.

"If you want me to."

Valerie looked around the room. "What's all this?" She gestured to a blow-up mattress on the floor.

"Watch," he said and stood up. He went over and opened the blinds and shut the other light off. The only light was the moonlight streaming in the window. He sat on the mattress and invited her over.

"What's going on?" Greg didn't answer her but kissed her again and didn't stop until her body twitched reflexively.

"The caveman desires to see his conquest in the moonlight. With her permission, of course."

"When we get done, we'll see who got conquered."

They drank a little more Champagne. "Now," he said through his kiss. "The caveman wishes to admire his prize." He pulled her shirt off and removed her bra, running his hands over her body.

The moonlight bathed her naked body, highlighting some areas, others hidden in shadow. He was kissing her with a hot urgency he didn't know he possessed.

She pulled away, stood up, and dropped her jeans. Valerie wore a black thong. All the air left his lungs, and he hardly had enough to speak. She hooked her finger and went to remove the silky black triangle. Greg pushed her hand away and pulled her down into the moonlight.

"If anyone removes that, it'll be me, using my teeth," he told her.

Valerie stretched out, put her hands over her head, and looked at him. She watched him look at her.

Instead of feeling shy and bashful, she felt a certain power in her nakedness. Val stretched out further and tried to strike what she thought was an erotic pose, which consisted of sticking her boobs up. Her eyes never left his. Greg soaked it all in until he thought he would drown.

"Hey," she whispered. "Don't I get a view?" He stripped to his boxers and laid down next to her. She tugged the waistband of his boxers. "What's with these?"

"You want these off. Use your teeth," he said.

They lay facing each other. Greg started to kiss her, and she kissed him back. If he was in a hurry, she couldn't tell. He was kissing and touching Valerie when he rolled her on her back. He kissed her everywhere as he worked his way down her body. Greg took the thong in his teeth and tried to pull it down, but it took too long, so he pulled it off with his fingers. He leaned back and looked at Valerie in the moonlight. Her eyes glittered back at him. Greg told her she was the most beautiful thing he'd ever seen. He asked her if she wanted to stop. Her answer was to roll on top of him and grind her pelvis into his erection.

"I don't think so," she breathed into his ear. "Take those boxers off and touch me. See if I'm ready," she told him.

"Ooooh," he said. "A little bossy, are we?" Greg pulled his shorts off and put his hand between her legs. She was so juicy he almost lost it right there. He felt her warm wetness against his fingers. Greg wasn't sure if his hand was moving against her or she was moving against his hand, but it didn't really matter.

"Touch me," he asked her, his voice husky and low. Valerie took him in her hand. She threw her leg over him, and instead of rubbing against his hand, she started rubbing against him. He realized he better put a condom on; things were moving fast. He grabbed one from the windowsill and put it on while she watched. As she watched him, she put her hand between her legs and stroked herself like he did.

"Stop that," he ordered her. "It's time for me now."

Valerie rolled on her back and opened herself to him. She looked at him with a wicked look in her eye. "Come and get it," she said.

He positioned himself between her legs. "Get ready," he told her, plunging into her. The way she lifted her hips up to meet him and matched his push was too much for him, and he came. He pulled out before the condom had a chance to fall off. He looked at her and apologized.

"I guess it wasn't much for you, was it?" he said, his eyes looking down.

"This is what I was afraid of," she said.

"What is?" Panic was in his voice, thinking she was unhappy and wanted to stop.

"It was just enough to make me want to do it again." She kissed his throat. "And again." Kiss. "And again until I get it right."

"Don't worry. I'll help you get there."

Valerie eventually did get there with his help. Her fears came up against teenage hormones, and her fears lost. They were having sex whenever the opportunity presented itself. For spring break, his family went to Vermont to ski every year. He didn't want to go. Greg hadn't told his parents yet. He was thinking of using the excuse he couldn't get hurt skiing and jeopardize his scholarship when in reality, he didn't want to leave her.

"See, this is what I'm talking about. You don't want to go away with your family because you don't want to leave me. That's not right. You have to go because if you don't, I'll feel guilty that you gave up that trip for me. I don't want those feelings. I don't want you to miss things because of me. I was afraid of this. If you don't go, I can't see you anymore," Valerie said, looking out the window of his car.

Greg was stunned. "You're breaking up with me?"

"It's like I told you. You can't miss out on things because of me. If I'm always going to be your first choice, it's not a choice. I want you to go. If you don't go, your parents will blame me, and I don't want that. It's too much pressure on me. You're the first boyfriend I've ever had." She started to cry. "I don't know what to do."

"Hey, hey." He grabbed her hand. "It's okay. It'll be okay." He kissed her hand. "I'm worried if I'm gone, some other guy is going to carry you off to his cave, and I'll never see you again."

"What if you're at the grocery store, and when you give your money to the cashier, you feel a shock like lightning? You look her in the eye and see she's the one for you?" Valerie said. "How about joining a frat? You want to, but I think they're a bunch of douchebag bros? Or your friends want to go to Tampa for spring break, but my friends are going to Fort Lauderdale? What if?" Greg stopped her by kissing her quietly.

"I get it, I get it. You're right. Four years is a long time. Lots can happen. Then again, it's not that long. No matter what happens, I'll always love you. I believe you'll always love me. Four days for a ski trip or four years at college, I have faith we can survive. It doesn't matter. After it all, when we're on the same page at the same time, we'll take it from there." He kissed her again. "I'll go. I'll be open to everything. Don't worry about it. I'm not going to worry about some other guy. I'm going to focus on football. That's where I'm putting my energy, not worrying about you. No other guy is better for you than I am. It will all work out." Greg kissed her. "Let's not talk about it again."

***

After spring break, the seniors went into overdrive. Decisions needed to be made. Checks had to be written, and everyone wanted to know what everybody else was doing. Greg's decision had been made months ago, he had a football scholarship to a private school six hours west. Valerie chose a state school two hours east. They didn't discuss the eight-hour drive that separated them. Greg had to be there on August 1st. Valerie had a few more weeks.

They went to the senior prom. There was an all-night party afterward, and all the guys got totally wasted, as well as a few of the girls. Emily went with Evan. They had a thing, but it was casual and light. Kayla went with a long-time friend. The friends went in a group. Kayla and her date skipped the party; they went to the school-approved afterparty. To entice kids away from alcohol, they had great door prizes. Kayla won a Coach leather backpack.

Valerie drove Emily and Evan home in Greg's car. Those two had a bit of a buzz on and were laughing and joking in the back seat. She dropped them off. Greg drank a lot of beer and was passed out in the passenger seat. Valerie pulled into the driveway of his house.

The sun was coming up, and Valerie was exhausted. She was tempted to walk home and leave Greg where he was, but she thought, What if he choked on his vomit and died? She figured if his parents knew, then he was no longer her responsibility. She felt stupid ringing the doorbell at six a.m. in her prom dress.

They must have been asleep, it took them a while to answer the door. His dad answered the door, confused at Valerie's appearance.

"Valerie. Is everything okay? Did something happen to Greg?" Concern wiped the sleep from his eyes.

"Hi, Mr. Wilson. Greg is fine, I think. He drank too much, and he passed out in the car. I decided you should know in case you looked out the window and saw his car."

"You poor thing," he said. "Let me get my keys. I'll give you a ride home."

"That's okay, I can walk. It's not too far. Here are his keys," she said. Mr. Wilson took them from her and came outside in his bare feet. They walked to the passenger side of his car. Mr. Wilson looked at his son and then at Valerie. She shrugged. He opened the door and tried to wake his son. He shook him, and Greg came around. He opened his eyes and blinked a few times.

"Oh, hey, Dad. Whatcha doing here? Hi, Val. You look beautiful," he said, closed his eyes, and passed back out, his head lolling on his shoulder.

"Do you want me to help you get him in the house?" Valerie offered.

"Oh, no. I'm sorry he ruined your prom. I feel awful he did this to you," he said apologetically.

"The prom was fine. This"—She pointed at Greg—"happened at the after-party. Don't be too hard on him. I'm not the only girl having this conversation with her date's parents right about now."

"Thank you, Valerie. I'm glad you were there to make sure he got home okay," Mr. Wilson said. "Let me grab my keys, and I can run you home. And Valerie, Greg was right. You do look beautiful." She blushed.

"Why don't I jump in the backseat, and you drive? No need to go back inside and get your keys," Valerie suggested.

"If you don't mind, that would be great. I'll have you home in five minutes."

"Thank you, Mr. Wilson, that's nice of you to say, but I feel like eight miles of bad road. I'll get in the backseat, and you can take me home." He drove her home. Valerie didn't have her keys, so she leaned on the doorbell a bit until her mom woke up and let her in.

Her mom was curious as to why Mr. Wilson drove her home. "It's kind of early to drag your mom out of bed at six o'clock on a Sunday morning and not go to church. What happened?" Mrs. Reynolds asked.

Valerie explained everything in excruciating detail as her mom watched. "Well, I guess you'd call that a prom to remember," her mother said.

"To be perfectly honest, I'd rather just forget about it. Greg wasn't the only one who got wasted. All the guys did, except maybe Evan. They were so obnoxious I almost called a cab, but I didn't want Greg to drive, so I stayed."

"He's lucky to have you," her mother pointed out.

"Not for much longer. He leaves the last weekend of July, and we both decided that the next four years weren't about us. A long-distance relationship isn't an option."

"Did all that come from you?" Mrs. Reynolds asked.

"How can you tell? Because it did."

"I raised a smart girl."

"Yeah, thanks a lot for that. Instead of being a hopeless romantic, I am a practical realist. What a bore."

"I'm sorry, baby, but it will save you a lot of anguish in the future."

"I hope so. It's not doing me much for me now."

***

Four

VAL AND GREG

THE DAY AFTER THE PROM, Greg called Valerie and asked her to come by. When she got there, Greg brought her into the living room.

"What gives?" she asked. He didn't say anything. He just had her sit down. Valerie looked around and saw his parents and got nervous, looking at their somber faces. "I don't understand. What's wrong?"

His parents looked at him. "Greg has something to say," his mother said. Valerie looked at him.

"Um, Valerie, I just want to apologize for my behavior last night. You got all dressed up and looked so pretty, and I got smashed, and you had to drive me home, and my dad had to take you home. You deserved to be treated better than that, and I'm sorry. Really sorry," Greg said, embarrassed he had to have this discussion with Valerie in front of his stern-faced parents.

Valerie looked at all of them looking at her. "Apology accepted. It was no big deal. Like I told your dad, a lot of girls had to drive their dates home. All the guys got pretty wasted."

He looked at his mother. She nodded. "That's no excuse. You deserved better. It was terribly disrespectful, and I am so sorry," Greg finished.

"Mr. and Mrs. Wilson, this was the first time I ever saw him drink. It was an exception, not a rule. I think he regrets his actions now. It's okay. Really."

"You're a lovely girl, Valerie. You deserved better," Mrs. Wilson said. "A girl only has one senior prom. You should have better memories of it."

Valerie laughed. "We had a wonderful time at the prom. It wasn't until much later things went bad. Thanks for your concern. I think Greg learned his lesson." He shot her a look that said thank you.

"Greg, how's your stomach? Are you done puking? You can make it up to me by buying me an ice cream," Valerie said. He looked at his mother, and she gave him a slight nod, permission to leave. Greg grabbed his coat, and they went out the door. He got in her car and put his hand on her arm.

"Thank you, Val. Thank you."

"Look. I don't want to talk about this anymore. Your parents are way overreacting. Buy me a hot fudge sundae, and we're square."

Graduation came and went, and the parties, too. Kids were working summer jobs to get as much money as they could before they left for college. Greg worked a job landscaping and added a tan to his incredibly muscular physique. Valerie worked as a nanny for a couple of rich doctors. They paid her a lot of money to push a stroller and walk the dog.

They asked her to stay overnight for a few days, they wanted to go away for their anniversary. Valerie said she could but didn't realize it was Greg's last weekend in town. They weren't talking about each going their own way. It was going to happen whether they talked about it or not, so they didn't. After she put the baby to bed Friday night, he came over with a pizza.

"I didn't order a pizza," she said, "but you can come in if you promise to take your shirt off." He came through the door, put the pizza on the table, tossed his coat on a chair, and took off his shirt. She pulled hers off and met him in her bra.

"Hot delivery guy makes up for a cold pizza any day."

He took two steps and had her against the wall. "Don't give me any trouble," he said. "You'll only make it harder on yourself."

Valerie licked his neck and nipped at his ear. "How hard can you make it? Cause I can take it."

Greg picked her up and tossed her on the couch. He shut the inside lights off. The only illumination came from the streetlights outside. He undid her jeans and pulled them off her. Valerie looked up at him, dressed only in her underwear. Greg was silent as he pulled off his bottoms. He dropped his pants and pulled her off the couch onto the floor. He started kissing her, and she kissed him back, only harder and with more heat. He didn't think more heat was possible. Valerie pushed him on his back and leaned over him. She had never been the aggressor before. Tonight, she pushed and ordered him around. She kissed him all over his body. Every time he reached for her, she'd knock him back down. Greg had never seen her go this far, being in control. He liked her like this. Greg shivered and a thrill went up his spine. He reached for her, and she said no. Valerie was kissing him everywhere all at once, confusing his senses until he couldn't tell up from down.

Valerie pulled a condom out from under the couch, opened it, and put it on him. He almost lost it right there, but what really blew his mind was when she climbed on top and slid down until she could go no further. She ground herself into him and leaned forward. Her hair hung down, a curtain shutting out everything but their faces. She looked at him, moved against him, and told him to beg for it.

Every time he said, "Oh please, baby," she moved against him. The faster he said it, the faster she moved until he grabbed her hips and held them firmly against him while he came. His heart pounded so hard in his chest he thought she could hear it.

Valerie rolled off him and took care of the used condom. In a complete reversal, he was the one that clung to her afterward. Valerie held him, rubbed his back until he calmed, and made soothing noises until he stopped shaking. When they finally separated, she looked at him, and he had tears in his eyes. Valerie quickly gathered him in her arms and rocked him until he pulled away.

"Sorry," he said. "I guess I got overwhelmed by it all. I can't believe I'm leaving you. I can't believe in a week I'll be gone. Even if I stayed here, you'll be gone. It's all too much. Too much change at once."

"I know it's going to be hard, but maybe you'll be too tired from football to care that much. I'll cross your mind, but in a good way, like, 'Ain't that my girl. She could have picked anyone in the world, and she picked me.' I haven't thought about missing you because when I do, I feel like I can't breathe, like my heart is stuck in my throat, and I can't get any air. I don't want to think about it. I'm going to wake up in a strange place, and my best friend is eight hours away. I just plan on joining every club and taking extra classes, so I won't have time to miss you."

"You haven't told me any of this," Greg said. "I thought you were looking forward to it all, going away to a new phase in your life and leaving the old one behind."

"Sort of, but not like that. I do like new things and new experiences; I always have. I don't like leaving you at all. I just feel if we don't do it this way, we'll regret it in the future and might blame the other person as the reason they're not happy. You got old and missed your chance because the other person held you back. You have this gift, this ability to play at the college level, and it would be a sin to waste it."

"I'm glad you told me all this. I wasn't sure how you felt. I thought you were staying below the radar so I wouldn't notice when you left," Greg said. "Like you didn't want me to know and just crept away."

"No. That's just my style. I never wanted to call attention to myself or stick out, even when I was little. I always wanted to get lost in the mix. I still do. You're the star. You be the one that shines," Valerie said to him.

"Do you think you can keep your head down and stay below the radar for the next four years?" Greg sounded nervous.

"That's my plan, anyway. Why?"

"So no other guy will realize how totally awesome you are," he said with that pure teenage lust.

"I'll try my best. Look, the last thing I want is to deal with some scrub in my shit. Don't worry about it. I'm starving. Go get that pizza." He had to be there by Saturday, August first. They were leaving on Friday to move him in, so Thursday was the last time they would see each other for a while, maybe even not until Christmas. Greg took Valerie out to dinner on Thursday night. He was pretty depressed and sad. Valerie thought it was more than just her. He was going from a big fish in a small pond to a minnow among sharks.

"Greg, I think you need to get your head on straight." She moved his shoulder so her head rested on it. "You're looking at things the wrong way. You have to look at it like this: they recruited you. They offered a scholarship to you. They wanted you, so you must have the skills. You aren't leaving here. This will always be here. You didn't spend all this time and effort becoming a beast to hide in your dorm room."

"That is true, they want me. Maybe I'm obsessed with you leaving, so I don't have to think about me leaving. I am pretty nervous about being on a new team, about not fitting in." Greg confessed, self-doubt not a feeling he was familiar with.

"See, that's the thing. What you're worrying about is something you have rock solid. Muscle memory. Your body will know what to do even if you're scared shitless. Trust yourself. You got there because somebody saw something in you. You were just doing your thing, and they saw enough to want you. Trust them. Believe in yourself. You're good, and you have the stats to back it up. Yeah, you're playing a level up than you're used to. So what? You can handle it."

"You're right. If there's one thing I know, it's football. I'll be okay. I think I'm going to miss you most because you know what to say."

"Good. Don't be afraid, you got this. We'll call. We'll still see each other, just not as often or in the same state."

Dinner was fine after Greg talked it out. I am good. I do belong, he told himself. It would be hard, and that's good. Greg liked to work hard; it allowed him to get in a zone where no distractions from the outside world would impede his progress. He decided if he missed Valerie or home, he would hit the weight room.

Coming in as a freshman in a backup position, he doubted he'd play much. He had to maintain his abilities regardless, so he figured the weight room would be where he'd be if anyone wanted to find him. They would be leaving early in the morning, so he had to say goodbye to her tonight. They sat parked in her driveway and talked about it one last time. Greg would miss her terribly. Valerie always knew what to say to him to make him feel better.

"Look," she said, "I'm not leaving for three weeks. Call me. I'll help you adjust. You'll be in a good spot and not worry so much about me."

She kissed him goodbye. She got out of the passenger seat and walked to the driver's side, and he lowered his window.

"What?" Greg asked her. Val stuck her head in the window and kissed him again.

"That's for good luck, not that you need it. Knock 'em dead, you all-star, you," she said and walked to the door. Valerie waved to him as she went inside. Once inside, she ran to the front window and watched him drive away.

Greg didn't have as hard an adjustment as he thought. Valerie was right. If he only knew one thing, he knew football. He knew he wouldn't play soon, so he decided to impress the coaches with his work ethic. Greg lived and breathed football, and by the end of the day, he was exhausted. He didn't have the time to talk to Valerie as much as he thought. He did the first night, described what his first impressions were, and that he felt he'd be okay now that he was there.

"I don't know what I was afraid of," he said to her. "It's just football." The campus was a lot bigger than he thought. The football players sequestered all together in one section of the campus, left very little time to get out and socialize. Once his nerves settled, he got in the groove of things and wasn't unhappy. Sure, he missed Val, but even if she was here, he doubted he'd have any time to spend with her.

***

Valerie was having a much harder time adjusting. At home, she had two friends and never needed more. At school, she had nobody. Her roommate was an activist. You name a cause, and she got behind it. She was always coordinating protests. All kinds of characters were in and out of their room. Valerie didn't know what to do. Every time she went to her room, some stranger was on her bed. Sitting, laying down. Their heads on her pillows grossed her out.

Valerie asked if they could hold their meetings somewhere else. She blamed the room for being too small to hold all the people. Tricia, her roommate, would call Valerie names like a racist or a homophobe. She even called her a conservative. A capitalist. A republican. The first time she saw Tricia alone, Valerie was determined to set some ground rules, some boundaries, and try to get back her half of the room. It didn't go very well. Valerie decided she had to be blunt since subtleties went right over Tricia's head.

"Look, Tricia, keep your friends on your side of the room. I don't like some stranger with greasy dreadlocks putting his head on my pillow. Who knows when the last time any of these people took a shower was? I saw some girl I don't even know wearing my sweater on campus."

"You know, you're a real uptight bitch," Tricia said. "A real Miss Goody Two-Shoes. We're trying to save the whales, and you're upset somebody borrowed your sweater? How selfish can you be?"

"Fuck you," Valerie yelled at Tricia. "I'm selfish because I want strangers to stay out of my shit? How about you being a disrespectful, dirty pig? When was the last time you took a shower?"

"I'm done talking to you," Tricia said, put on her headphones, and pretty much dismissed Valerie. That infuriated her so much that she went over and ripped the headphones off Tricia's head.

"This isn't over!" Valerie yelled, threw the headphones in Tricia's lap, and stormed out of the room. She was going to take a walk to cool off, but when Valerie got to the front doors, she saw it was raining outside, but her jacket was in her room.

She went outside anyway. Valerie figured if she was all wet, nobody would know she was crying, and she started walking. Valerie ended up off-campus in an unfamiliar neighborhood. She was so upset. Val paid no attention to where she went, and she better get right before it got dark. She turned back around and tried to retrace her steps.

Valerie thought she had herself headed in the right direction; she heard someone yell, "Hey!" She glanced behind her but kept walking. Someone yelled Hey, again, only louder. She didn't bother to look. "HEY!" someone yelled right behind her.

Great, she thought. Another nutjob, and she spun around and yelled, "WHAT?"

It was a guy holding an umbrella. At her greeting, he took a couple of steps back. "Whoa. You walked by my house twice. I thought you might be lost."

"I might be, but I'll figure it out," Valerie said.

"At least take the umbrella."

"Too late. Already soaked." At this unexpected kindness from a stranger, she burst into tears. "Oh, God, no. No!" she yelled, mostly at herself for losing it in front of a stranger.

"Look, at least come sit on my porch and get yourself together." Valerie just stood there, crying. "Come on, it'll be okay." She stood, frozen in place and crying her eyes out. He reached out and touched her arm. "Here." He gently took her by the arm. "Come get out of the rain."

Valerie allowed him to lead her to his house. He sat her in a chair on his porch and went inside. He came back with a few towels, a roll of toilet paper, and a girl. Valerie sat with her face in her hands, crying. Somebody put a towel over her shoulders and gently patted her back. Soon, she was all cried out.

Valerie reached for the tissue and blew her nose. She cleaned her face and looked at them.

"Hi, I'm Tony, and this is my girlfriend, Lauren." The man talked in a quiet, soothing voice.

"Hi. You aren't going to kidnap me and sell me off into white slavery, are you?" She blew her nose again and said, "I'm Valerie. Valerie Reynolds." They looked at each other.

"No," he said, "why?"

"Because with the way my day is going, that would be an improvement," Valerie joked.

"Well, it couldn't have been that bad if you can joke about it," Tony said. Lauren came out with a glass of wine and gave it to Valerie.

"I'm not much of a drinker," Valerie told them.

"One won't hurt. It'll help warm you up. Are you a freshman?" Lauren asked her. Valerie burst out laughing. "That obvious?"

"Not really," Tony said. "We get lots of crying girls passing by here, but not usually in the pouring rain. Tell us what happened. Maybe we can help."

"Typical freshman roommate BS. My roommate is an activist. She'll protest anything, which doesn't bother me, but she holds all these meetings in our room. There are all kinds of weirdos in and out of our room, which I guess is okay, but these people are in my stuff. It's not wrong to consider a dirty, greasy guy you don't even know to be lying in your bed, his head on your pillow, out of bounds, is it? It's not wrong to be upset when you see some girl you don't know wearing your clothes around campus, is it? When I asked about it, she called me all kinds of names: a racist, a homophobe, a capitalist."

"She called you a capitalist? Them's fighting words." Tony laughed. "I know, right?"

"Are you loud? Do you have random men stay over? Do you pick up after yourself? Do you leave dishes with old food lying around the house? Do you respect communal areas?" Tony asked.

"No. I'm quiet, studious, and very respectful. Why?"

"This is a three-bedroom apartment. The third roommate ended up going to rehab, but he paid the first semester upfront, so we have an extra room if you want it. The only expense would be food and the internet. Do you have a meal plan?" Valerie nodded.

"You can eat on campus. So just the internet and phone. You have an extension in your room. Since it's a dial-up modem, we try not to tie up the phone. We usually make personal calls when nobody else is here. Sometimes we have Sunday dinners, but that's not too much."

"Why would you do that? How do you know I'm not a psychopath who would kill you both in your sleep?"

"We don't. It's a mutual risk. How badly do you want to get back at her?" Tony asked.

"I don't know. I'm not a vindictive person."

"Well, think about it. Our roommate, with the drug problem, left something behind. A bag of weed. The only reason we didn't smoke it is it's skunk weed and not worth the rolling papers, but if you want to hide it in your roommate's stuff, then report it. And the sketchy people she brought in, the stuff she had hidden, made you afraid of staying there. You have no confidence in the school's ability to keep you safe and found a place off campus. Demand your money back, threaten to go public. The university doesn't need the black eye a student making noise about feeling unsafe on campus would leave."

"Thanks, but I'm not sure. That sounds kind of extreme," Valerie said.

"Just think about it. Lauren, do you have a dry shirt Valerie could borrow? I'll give her a ride back to the dorm. She can take our number if she changes her mind," Tony said.

On the way back, she learned he was in the third year of architecture school, Lauren was in her third year of school to be a dietitian. Both were five-year programs.

Tony said, "We were freshmen once, and it's hard enough without a psychotic roommate, so don't be too hard on yourself." He dropped her off out front of her dorm and said, "You have our number. Call. Please. We'd be happy to help."

"Thank you. You and Lauren really helped me out today. You might be hearing from me," Valerie said gratefully.

When Valerie returned to her room, Tricia was gone. All of Valerie's things were messed up and out of order. Clothes that had been on hangers were now on the floor. Her books and papers were strewn about. The night table next to her bed had been disturbed; the lamp was on the floor.

The drawer was open, and her makeup bag was dumped out. Something was missing. Whenever she took a shower, she put her jewelry in one of the pockets of the cosmetics bag. The gold bracelet Greg gave her for Christmas was gone. That bitch stole my bracelet!

Tricia was lucky she wasn't there. Valerie saw red and would have strangled her. Instead, she took out her Polaroid and took pictures of everything, right down to her empty bag and missing jewelry. She called Lauren and asked if they were still willing to help her. Valerie didn't feel safe.

She wanted to crash at their place, come back the next day, hide the weed, and then raise holy hell about how she left yesterday, afraid for her safety.

"Yeah, sure," Lauren said. "Either Tony or I will be over to pick you up. The bed's already made, but bring your pillow and clothes for tomorrow. We can come to get the rest of your stuff later, after she gets busted. At best, they refund your money. If not, you get to live in off-campus housing, something they forbid freshmen to do."

Valerie waited out front; they didn't leave her out there for too long. Lauren picked her up and asked if she was hungry. Valerie had to think about it; she couldn't remember the last time she ate.

"Good," Lauren said. "Tony's made a big pot of spaghetti and meatballs. Well, it's vegetarian, but still, it's so good. We don't eat meat, but you can. Our routine is that Tony figures out the grocery list, and I do the shopping. He puts the receipt on the fridge and divides it into what each owes. We pay him our share. He puts the meal schedule on the fridge, and if he's not cooking or you don't like it, you get your own. Are there any specific things you like you buy, like cookies or yogurt? Usually, we do a big Sunday dinner, maybe invite a few friends, drink wine, and talk. If you want to do something else, do it. Everything is pretty loose. You'll find your place."

"I can't tell you how much this is going to help me. Even if you are a couple of serial killers."

"Don't ask what's in the meatballs," Lauren said, "or who. It may be why we need a third roommate. The old one is joining us for dinner, but not in the way you think." Both girls laughed as she pulled into the driveway.

Valerie stuffed her things into a garbage bag. She didn't want Tricia to know she'd been back; it would ruin her plan for tomorrow.

They entered the house, and the smell of the sauce made her stomach grumble.

Lauren showed her the third bedroom. It was the smallest, off the kitchen, but clean. A bed, a desk, and a dresser. The only thing she needed was lighting, and she ordered a couple of lamps to be delivered later that week. It was enough, just what she needed. She put the garbage bag in there, and she joined them in the kitchen. They handed her a glass of wine. "I'm a two-drink max, guys. My hangovers last for days," Valerie said.

"We don't drink a lot, but it's required for Sunday dinner. You can just have one more when we eat. That's not too much, is it?" Lauren asked Tony.

"No. It's just social drinking. We don't drink during the week, and a glass of wine now and again won't kill you."

"I'm down with that," Valerie said, "until my first hangover. Then we'll have to re-assess."

They were joined by a few neighbors, all upperclassmen, and all of them had some sort of roommate-from-hell horror story. They detailed the neighborhood for her, mostly college kids, but it did have times when young thugs targeted their area. They mainly caused a disturbance out front, and while the residents were dealing with the commotion, someone would sneak around the back and break in. They took mainly electronics, loose money, and small things they could sell or pawn. Valerie's eyes widened at the idea of living in a high-crime area.

"It's not that. After dark, drunk college students are easy to rob. Better safe than sorry. Once it gets cold, it's not a problem."

"I used to walk around campus after dark all the time. I had to do all my work in the library. I won't need to do that anymore, now I have my own desk, and my stuff won't go missing. I'm comfortable with everything. Just be smart."

"Exactly," said Tony. "As long as you don't wander around wasted, you'll be fine."

"Well, it was nice to meet everyone, but I'm exhausted. I need to go to bed now. Goodnight," Val said and went into the room that was now hers. She shut the door and was overwhelmed by her own space. She hadn't felt a sense of peace like this since she got here. She had a phone in her room, so she called Greg. Sunday evenings seemed like a good time for both of them. She called him, hoping he hadn't turned in for the night. He answered on the third ring.

"Hi, Greg. Am I calling too late? Are you asleep?"

"No, but where have you been? Is everything okay? I was worried about you," he said, concern lacing his voice. "Your roommate said you were gone."

"Today didn't start out that great, but it finished up okay. My psychotic roommate trashed my side of the room because I told her I didn't want her dirty friends on my bed. I met some people who had a spare bedroom. It's a few blocks off campus, but it's better than where I was."

"Wait a minute," Greg said. "Is it safe? I'm not sure it's a good idea to move in with some random people you just met."

"Isn't that what they do on campus, move you into a dorm room with some stranger? I feel safer here than I did there. I didn't want to tell you this, but she stole all my jewelry. She took the gold bracelet you gave me for Christmas."

"Wait. She stole your bracelet? I don't like it, Val. You should feel safe in your room. I can't believe she took your bracelet. Can't you report it or something?"

"Yeah, but it will be my word against hers. She'll be sorry she fucked around with me. I have a plan," she said and told Greg about it.

"If it works, that should be okay." He sounded hesitant. "Are you sure you want her mad at you? She sounds crazy. I'm not sure you want her as an enemy."

"I primarily want out of the dorms. Who knows what psycho they'll put me with next? I'm going to the RA, the Dean of Housing, the Dean of Student Affairs, and scream bloody murder about how they put me at risk. I took pictures of it all. I don't care if they give me a refund or credit. I'm not safe with all these strangers coming in and out. I'm not safe having to go to the library until midnight to study because my room is always full of these gross people." She changed the subject. "How are you doing, Greg? Are you adjusting okay?"

"You know, Val, what you said was right. It's all football all the time. The one thing I'm confident about is football. And you were right again; I am too tired to be neurotic about you, although I'm worried now about your crazy roommate."

"It will be fixed by this time tomorrow. I'll call you and let you know how it all worked out, but right now, you're too tired to talk. Go to sleep. I'll keep you posted. I love you, Greg, now goodnight."

"The same," he said that if other guys were around and might think he's a wuss. "Goodnight, Val," and he hung up.

Valerie was finally able to relax. Greg found his spot; she found hers.

Five

VAL AND GREG

VALERIE KNEW Tricia had a ten o'clock class and showed up at ten-thirty. Her side of the room was unchanged. She took the baggie of pot and threw it on Tricia's desk. Anyone who went to her side of the room would see it. It wasn't necessarily out in the open, but it wasn't hidden either.

"I need the RA! I need the RA! Somebody was in my room! They stole my jewelry!" Valerie screamed, doing her best to sound like a young, naive girl away from home for the first time. "Somebody help me!"

People who were in their rooms came out at the noise. They were met with a hysterical young girl. Somebody located an RA from another floor. The story she got from Valerie was she and the roommate weren't getting along due to all the traffic in and out of the room. Tricia was always organizing some protest or another, and many people on the floor could attest to the strangers going in and out of her room.

Valerie said she tried to talk to her yesterday, and Tricia told her to fuck off, so fearing for safety, she stayed with friends off campus, only to return to find her side of the room trashed and her jewelry stolen. The RA went to look at Tricia's side of the room and noticed the bag of weed. The RA asked Valerie if she'd ever seen Tricia do drugs.

"No, but I can smell it. My clothes reek of it. I wouldn't be surprised; some of her friends are pretty sleazy. I'm not staying another night here. She'll probably strangle me in my sleep. I'm leaving now and calling my parents. I'm going to the Dean of Student Affairs and whoever is in charge of student housing."

"I can't believe you risk us first-year students and let just anybody come and go! She stole my gold bracelet! I'm packing my things and calling my parents! My father will sue you!" Val kept yelling and grabbed her clothes, shoving them in her suitcase.

"Now, why don't you take a deep breath, and let's see what we can do to help you," the RA tried to say in a soothing voice.

"Help me?" Valerie cried. "You can help me by packing my clothes before that psycho comes back!" When she got everything packed, some kind people from her floor helped her bring her items downstairs. The RA kept trying to talk her down, trying to minimize what happened.

When she had all her stuff downstairs, everyone wandered off, and it was just her and the RA. The RA kept trying to make the situation less than it was, and Valerie tried to make it more. She started to raise her voice, something she knew would bug the RA.

"Look, you don't get it! Dozens of people told you about all the people going in and out of there. You saw what she did to my things, my schoolwork, and she stole my bracelet! A very valuable gold bracelet! And you found drugs! What more do you want? What more do you need? No wonder I don't feel safe here! And you want me to be responsible for it? What's your name and floor? I'm gonna report you, too. How dare you treat me like this!"

Lauren approached them while they were loudly discussing the situation. "You all set, Val? Tony's waiting out front. We can drop you off at the dean's office while we bring your stuff over. Give us a call, and we'll come pick you up when you're finished."

Val could see in the RA's eyes she was surprised that it had gotten out of hand so quickly. She was used to freshmen drama queens, and they'd stomp their feet and whine, but find all they wanted was a new room. But this girl wasn't playing. She had her exit planned, made other accommodations, and had a ride to the dean's office. She wasn't fooling.

Valerie helped Lauren bring her things out to Tony's car. She was tempted just to leave. She was removed from the situation and wanted to say, "fuck it," and go, but she figured she should follow it through. She walked over to the administration building and was surprised to find they were expecting her. The RA must have called ahead to do damage control.

The receptionist told her to have a seat, somebody would be out shortly. A few minutes later, an imposing woman who Valerie thought looked like Margaret Thatcher came out and called her back. She had her take a seat, introduced herself, and asked how she could help.

"I'm sorry to bother you," Valerie said, "but I had an issue with my roommate that came to a head over the weekend. Unfortunately, I felt my safety was in jeopardy and had to leave. I came home yesterday, and look what I found." She reached into her bag and showed her the pictures of her side of the room.

"This happened after I asked her to keep her friends off my bed. There are strangers in and out of our room all the time. I'm not saying she stole my things, but my jewelry is gone, including a valuable gold bracelet. I'm not going to say she does drugs"—Val took a dramatic pause—"but the RA found some on her desk. I hope you don't think I'm exaggerating, but how would you feel if you found one of her friends walking around campus wearing your clothes?"

The dean was very sympathetic, made noises of deep concern, and wanted to work towards finding an equitable solution.

"I'm sorry," Val said, "but this happened over the weekend, and I made arrangements to live with friends off-campus. I had no choice. I was very afraid of people I didn't know coming in or out. I felt my safety was at risk."

"Now, dear," she said, "let's just take a step back and see what we can do."

Valerie needed to bring out the big guns. She started to cry for real. "I don't know what can be done. I had to get my things out immediately and move. How can I feel safe living in a dorm after this? I had to miss a whole day of classes because of this situation. I can't move again. I can't fall behind in my schoolwork. I haven't even had time to tell my parents about it. My parents will flip out if they think I'm not safe."

Val reached out and took one of the lady's business cards off a pile she had on display at the front of her desk. "May I? My dad is going to want to know who I spoke to about this."

Once again, the woman tried to de-escalate the situation. "Now, I am sure we'll be able to solve this. Would you like to be placed in another dorm? I know we have no singles left, but maybe at the beginning of the next semester."

"Ma'am," Valerie said, "no disrespect intended, but I would like to stay where I am now. I need to focus on my schoolwork. I can't move again. It's too distracting. Let me stay where I am now through the end of the semester. I'll talk to my dad in the meantime."

Mrs. Thatcher was willing to let her stay where she was, however, she did need to talk to her dad. Valerie said he'd call her, thank you very much. He'd be in touch, and she let herself out.

The time passed, and it was Thanksgiving break. Greg was unable to come home; it was closing in on the end of the season, and there was plenty of football left to be played. The team had moments of brilliance, but overall, they needed a win, both for the record and post-season play. Greg was still the third of a three-deep QB roster.

He was noticed for his speed and his arm, and since they were weak on special teams, they put him in to return punts. In a total surprise to everyone but Greg, when he did get on the field, his first return was for sixty yards, and even though the offense made no progress, it set them up for a field goal.

Greg did it again in the fourth quarter, this time for forty-five yards that ended in a touchdown. It gave them a much-needed win. Greg was used to playing and winning, so he played on special teams for the rest of the season. It was too little, too late for a bowl bid, but Greg gave the team hope. The coaches had a big debate about where he should play. Being a wide receiver was an option, but the QB graduated, and because Greg could throw the ball as well as run it, they kept him as the backup quarterback, but used him when they needed some momentum on punt returns. He was able to come home at Christmas.

Greg and Valerie hadn't seen each other in months, and they were still as happy as ever. Time and distance did nothing to dilute their affection. His family was traveling over the holidays. He didn't have to go because he was only home for a few weeks. They spent whatever time they could in his room in a tangle of limbs and sheets.

It was almost harder to part this time than before; they knew what it was like to truly miss someone.

They returned to their respective schools and missed each other more than ever. Their spring breaks were at different times, so they wouldn't see each other until school officially ended for the year.

Most of Greg's first semester was spent on football, so it wasn't until after Christmas he had the time to experience college life. He had a great time. Greg still kept up with the weight room and conditioning, but he also managed to embrace the party side. There was so much to do if sports didn't consume all your time, and he tried to catch up as best he could. There were a couple of nights he couldn't remember how he got home, and a girl brought him to her place a few times, but he thought he passed out before anything happened. He stayed on campus during spring break, and Valerie went home during hers.

Something odd happened as Valerie studied for her finals. It was a letter from Greg. She opened it and almost fell off her chair. It was a picture of Greg, obviously asleep, and a girl in bed with him. He didn't have a shirt on, and apparently, she didn't either.

Valerie still stood by her opinion that was the point of college it was a place to learn and grow in all different directions. The picture seemed staged to her. She doubted he would send her a picture of him in bed with another girl; her only concern was how this chick got her address. Why was she sent this picture? She decided to trust Greg; she wasn't going to make a big deal about it. Valerie was going to send it back to him with no explanation. She went back to her books and forgot about it.

Right before she left for home, she got a message from him on her answering machine. It was a woman's voice. It said, "Hey, Greg, when are you leaving? I was hoping to see you one more time before you go." Once again, she fell back on 'what happened on campus, stayed on campus,' but this wasn't staying on campus. This was starting to fuck with her head, and if it happened again, she would be forced to change her number.

She was going to room with Tony and Lauren at their flat again in the fall, so she just brought a suitcase and a duffel bag home. She decided to take the bus. It seemed like the option that took the least amount of thought. She could take a cab when she arrived home. The bus got in, and she waited for her bags to be unloaded. As she stood there, somebody came up from behind her and whispered in her ear.

"Hey, gorgeous. Can I interest you in a lift?"

"Greg!" she screamed and threw her arms around his neck. "I didn't think you were coming until tomorrow!"

"I'm bringing my car back with me in the fall, so I flew in yesterday because I couldn't stand to be away from you one more minute. I have missed you so much, Valerie. It wasn't until I saw you there I realized how badly. I never want us to be apart again." His face was split by a huge grin. "Baby! You sure smell good."

She laughed at him. "Ew. You're nuts. I've been on that bus for hours. I probably smell like stale hamburgers and feet."

"As long as they're your feet, I don't care. Call your mom and tell her the bus broke down, and you can't get out until tomorrow morning. I've got us a room downtown tonight. We can go out to eat or have room service while we sit around and relax in our luxurious robes."

"Sounds wonderful." He carried her bags while she called her mom. He loaded her things and opened the door for her. He leaned over, kissed her, and shut her door.

"Man, I missed you," he said as he got in the car. It was a short drive downtown. He parked in the garage and got out of the car. He opened her door, took her by the hand, and headed toward the sky corridor that led to the hotel.

"Wait a minute," Valerie said, "I need my bag."

"No, you don't," he answered. "All you need is a toothbrush, and I have one in the room for you already."

He had checked in earlier. Greg had a vase of red roses waiting for her. The room was on an upper floor with a view of the city lights below. Valerie looked out the window and watched the headlights of the cars driving beneath them. He wrapped his arms around her.

"What do you want to do first?" he asked, licking her neck. She giggled in response.

"What I really want to do is take a shower and brush my teeth. Where's that toothbrush?" He pointed at a bag with a familiar drugstore logo.

"Hey, Greg. What's this?" She dumped the contents of the bag on the bed. Along with the toothbrushes and paste were a box of condoms and a tube of spermicide.

"You don't know what that is?"

"Yeah, I know what it is. I want to know why."

"We've been together for a while now, and I've always used a condom. I think I'd like to experience you, well, all of you. Maybe if you're afraid of getting pregnant, you won't have to be, and we wouldn't have to use those. Or else go on the pill."

"If you can help me understand something, I'd consider it," Valerie told him. "Sure. Anything. What do you want to know?" Greg asked.

Valerie pulled her bag out. She grabbed a few things. One was to the photo of Greg and that girl. "Who is she? How does she know who I am? Why did she mail this to me? How'd she get my address? And some girl left me a message on my machine, looking for you before you left, just a few days ago."

He looked at it. "Oh, her."

"Yeah, her." Valerie waited for his answer.

"All I can say is she's a football groupie. I got hammered one night and passed out. She climbed in, took that picture, and sent it to you. I don't know why other than to cause trouble."

"Okay, I believe that. What about the phone call? Who even knows who I am?" Valerie asked.

He looked her in the eye. "I wish I had an explanation that made sense, but I don't."

"So, if you tell me you've never had condomless sex, I could believe it?" Valerie asked him.

"Absolutely. You're the only one, Valerie. You'll always be the only one. I love you."

"I'm going to take a shower and think about it."

Valerie piled her hair on top of her head and let the hot water ease the tension from her neck and shoulders. Valerie turned the water off and stepped out into a nice, warm towel. Greg held it there to dry her off. After, he wrapped her in a thick Turkish terry robe.

"Would you prefer me for an appetizer or dessert?" he asked her.

"Both."

"Good answer."

Greg took off her robe, turned the bed down, and laid her on her back. Valerie smiled; she loved the way he looked at her when she took his breath away. He stripped and jumped in next to her. He was primed and ready to go.

"Sorry, baby, but I've been waiting for you all day."

"Well, you better bring me up to speed, then." It didn't take long to get them both on the same page.

He asked her if she wanted him to get up and get the condoms. "Nah," she said. "Let's try the other stuff and see if you can tell the difference."

Greg entered her slowly. "Oooh, yeah. Definitely. I feel like I'm home."

"I should probably get on the pill, but we don't see each other for long stretches, and I don't like the idea of being on it if I don't need it. What about a diaphragm?"

"This feels so good," he whispered in her ear. "Whatever you want, baby."

"Okay, I'll go to the doctor over break," Valerie whispered back.

He brought Valerie home the next day. Greg held her hand, rubbed her leg, and put his arm on her shoulder. He couldn't get enough of her. Greg stopped at her house, helped her get her things inside, and visited with her mom for a bit. They had a cup of coffee, and he talked about his first year of football and his adjustment to college life.

"What was the hardest thing about college?" her mom asked Greg.

"Honestly? Not having Valerie around. I love her. I missed her terribly. In fact, do you mind if I take her to breakfast? I'm sure you miss her, too. I'll bring her right back. I promise."

Valerie worked that summer as a nanny again; he worked as a carpenter's assistant. His family owned two development companies, one for commercial properties and the other for residential. Greg's major was engineering, and he hoped to work on the commercial side.

His father thought he should start in the company's equivalent of the mail room and work his way up. His dad believed you can't expect to be in charge if you don't know what you're in charge of, so he was going to be a grunt, work the construction side, and learn the business that way. Greg didn't mind at all.

He hung out with Valerie as often as he could. Her employers liked to take long weekends during the summer, and Valerie didn't mind working weekends. The baby was now a toddler and kept her on her feet more than last year. He also liked the stroller better, so she could keep him contained and amused while still walking the dog. She wrapped the leash around the stroller and gave him the end. "Hold the leash, Bennie. You're walking the dog now."

Laughing, he kicked his legs out and said, "Dog! Dog!" On weekends she worked, Greg came over and built things out of blocks with the little boy, Ben. Greg also bought two more boxes of wooden blocks, so their projects got larger and more complicated, and Greg never got mad when Ben knocked them over, something he enjoyed more than building.

Greg built a garage for Ben's truck. Ben loved that and would push his truck in and out for a while before destroying it, and he would look at Greg and ask him to do it again. Greg never lost his patience, leading Valerie to think he'd make a wonderful dad. Greg again had to report to football camp in August; he was leaving earlier than she did.

"I'm really going to miss you, Valerie. It's so easy to be with you, but we got through last year, and we'll get through this one, too. I wish you could come to see me play."

"Who knows," she said. "If you start as quarterback, I'll fly in for that one."

"Really?" He sounded so excited. "You would?"

"Yes, I would. It would be awesome to be there."

"I'm going to hold you to it. Right now, I have to practice tackling." He grabbed her and knocked her on the couch. "I'll let you sack me as much as you want."

***

Sophomore year had students suffering from various post-traumatic stress disorders. It was hard enough getting through their freshman year, only to go back and do it again. Just as tense, just as useless, and even more idiotic, stressful, and meaningless requirements clogged up their schedules and their brains.

People who were smart started to spread the workload into the fifth semester, opting to take a challenging course over that semester because it was too much during the year, but if it was the only course you took, it was manageable. Greg felt the same way. He came home later and reported earlier for football camp, and the time between their visits lengthened.

Junior year started the same as usual, only Greg evolved on the field. He was really at the top of his game, maturing as a man and a player. He was smart on the field. He practiced with dedication rarely seen, and he waited for his chance. The starting QB pulled a hammy and wasn't starting. Now it was Greg's turn.

Greg, excited by the idea of Valerie coming to watch him play, called to let her know. "Book your flight, Valerie. I'm starting this Saturday!"

"That's great news! What time?"

"Three p.m. My parents are driving in. Want to ride with them?"

"No, this is a special moment for them. What if I came on Friday, spent the night, and left after the game?"

"That would be fine if you want to spend the whole evening in bed. The day before we have a light practice, watch films, eat dinner, and rest up."

"I can do that and leave after the game, and your parents can spend time with you without me there."

"What do you mean? My family loves you."

"I know, but that's a long time to ride in a car with your own family, let alone people you aren't related to."

"But the morning of, I have to report at eleven. Will you be okay alone?"

"Yeah. I can walk around and check out the campus. I'll be fine."

"I can get you a special pass for seating, but you might sit with my parents," he said.

"Your parents are fine. I love them, but they are coming to see you, not me. Do you have a room where I can sleep? Don't you have a roommate?"

"I'll make arrangements for him to be elsewhere, but you know I can't have relations the night before. I need to be concerned with sapping my strength."

She laughed so hard she snorted. "Relations? Are you kidding me?"

"Can I trust you to keep your hands off me?" Greg asked.

"About as much as I can trust you," Valerie answered.

"Oh, good," he said happily.

She came in Friday evening, and he got done about eight. She managed to find the athletic complex and wandered around. The guard let her in to wait, and Greg came along.

"Here," he said and handed her a wrapped package.

"What's this?" she asked.

"Dinner. A sandwich. I spare no expense for my girl. Come on with me. I know I'm supposed to refrain from activities that can drain my strength, but there's no specifics about what I can do to you."

Later that night, he took her for a tour of the campus. He showed her the areas he never really spent much time in, the hallowed halls of academia. The medical school, the law school, all the highest of higher education.

His part of campus was the athletic complex. Tutors lived there and taught the kids who fell behind due to the commitment required to play collegiate sports. They went back to his room so he could rest up the night before his big moment. He wanted to celebrate her visit by falling asleep inside her, but she laughed and said no.

They violated policy by having sex anyway. Greg wanted to set the alarm for two a.m. and do it then and again when they woke up.

"Maybe, Greg. You have certainly packed on a lot of muscle. You are one fine hunk of man," she told him, running her hands over his body. "I understand the football groupies better. I might become one."

"You can't. You can worship only me."

"How many groupies are you allowed?"

"Now I'm the starting quarterback, I imagine I can have as many as I want."

Valerie looked at him, her expression said, "Wrong answer."

"Relax. I don't want any groupies. You are exactly what I want. No more, no less."

"Good answer," Valerie told him, snuggling into his chest. "If we can skip the two a.m., we can take it slow tomorrow morning, enough to settle your nerves but still leave enough gas in your tank to rock the stadium."

"You are the best girlfriend ever. I hope you don't fall for some Italian stallion and forget about me," he said about her upcoming spring semester in Italy.

"I'm only going to Italy for the art. I just want to see it all, to be where it was all created by the eye, with no computers or cheats, where they had to make the paint if they wanted to paint. Real old-school art."

"As long as you don't take off with some Italian guy named Art, we'll be good," he told her.

"His name would be Arturo, but you don't have to worry about it. I'm not into short, swarthy men. I want a tall, blonde, blue-eyed, all-American boy."

He squeezed her tight. "Say, man. You want an all-American man."

"I want a tall, blue-eyed, all-American man."

The distraction of Valerie and her garden of earthly delights didn't affect Greg's performance. She walked with him to where he needed to be at eleven. All she brought with her was a backpack; Greg carried it for her. She met a few of his teammates. They must have been offensive linemen because they were huge. He gave her a hug and kissed the top of her head. She figured any more PDA would be out of line with these guys.

"Wish me luck," he said.

"You don't need luck. You're the best," she answered. "Now go play and show off for your family," she told him. "I'll be sitting with them. I don't know what you guys do after a game, but I may have to leave before you're finished. If I'm gone, I may not have a chance to tell you this, but I'm real proud of you."

"Thanks, Val, I'm so glad you came. It means everything to have you here. If I don't see you, have a safe trip home."

"Well, right now, I have a whole bunch of tailgate parties to attend. Have a great game."

"Behave yourself," he said as he walked away.

Valerie had a few hours to kill, so she went into the parking lots and observed the pregame activities. People were so friendly; it was such a communal experience.

She had a burger with one group chili with another. She turned down offers of alcohol; many people were drinking before noon. She got in the school spirit and bought a jersey with his name on the back and put it on over her shirt.

Many people stopped her to comment on the quarterback who would return the school to its former glory and powerhouse of the conference. Not too much pressure, she thought. It didn't seem to ruffle Greg. Sometimes, his nerves and anxiety caused him to doubt his abilities, but he seemed to be beyond that and had everything under control. She went inside and found her seat. His family had already taken theirs. They were surprised to see her. They invited her to dinner and whatever else Greg had lined up for them, and Mrs. Wilson wanted to know where she got the jersey. They all wanted one.

"Somewhere at one of the tailgate parties. I wish I could be more specific, but there are so many out there. I imagine there must be a website. I think it's been licensed by the university." She glanced at the hem, searching for a label. She looked up. "I have a flight after the game, so I won't be able to join you after, but thanks for including me."

"How are you getting to the airport?" his mom asked.

"Cab."

"Oh no. We can give you a ride. Caroline won't mind."

"It will be better than waiting for a bunch of sweaty jocks to take a shower," Caroline said.

Greg had a decent showing. He threw one touchdown pass, scrambled when a play fell apart, and got the first down. He ran the ball in for a TD and set them up for two field goals. They won, and everyone was high on Greg's performance.

Dreams of a bowl bid next year didn't seem so far out of reach. He came over and talked to them.

Greg looked at Val's jersey and smiled. He had some post-game things to do and take a shower, so he'd meet up with them when he was finished. He thanked Caroline for helping Valerie. He said goodbye to Val, pleased he represented himself well in front of her. Greg kissed her on the head and headed into the locker room.

The rest of his family went to check out the campus. Caroline and Valerie found the car quickly. Greg got them a special parking permit, so it was nearby.

"So, Caroline, how's your first semester going?"

She was a freshman and going to a state school like Valerie. They had plenty of shared experiences, except Val's roommate's story trumped hers. It was about half an hour to the airport, so they had plenty of time to get to know each other.

"I like you," Caroline said. "He could pretty much have any girl, with his jock status and all. I'm glad he was smart enough not to blow it with you. Athletes tend to get swollen heads, and girls follow them around like they're rock stars or something. I guess I'd call what you guys have genuine."

"Yeah, Caroline. When we were freshmen, we sort of put the relationship on ice so it didn't interfere with what we wanted to do, like going abroad. Next semester, I'm going to Italy and then to an internship. So even if we went to the same school, we wouldn't end up seeing each other anyway.

"It's no strings attached. Suppose he falls in love with someone else, my loss. Works the same way for me, but I'm not interested in any emotional attachments. I think he's looking at it the same way, but every once in a while, I get these random photos and letters that make me wonder, but I just put it down to groupies. When I see him, he doesn't act guilty, so I guess all's good."

"What do you mean, random stuff?" Caroline asked. Valerie got out the photo that girl sent the letter.

"Aren't you pissed off? Who is that bitch?" Caroline asked, mad on her behalf.

"Greg said he was drunk and passed out, and she found my name on a letter. I sent him he tacked to his bulletin board. He said he doesn't know anything about it." Valerie replied. "I chose to believe him. What makes me the maddest is I gave him that comforter, and now it's going to smell like some slutty chick's cheap perfume."

"You're a better person than I am," said Caroline. "I'd come down here and kick the shit out of her."

"Like I said, he comes back to me, he does. If he chooses some skank, I'll come down here and kick the shit out of him. Then she can have him."

"If you need backup, let me know," said Caroline.

"I like his family very much." Valerie smiled at her.

"Yeah, we're fun to hang around. The Wilson family knows how to party," said Caroline. "Just one long rage, all summer long."

"Your family does like to party. I do wonder about Greg, though. It seems like he doesn't know when to stop. He just keeps drinking until he passes out," Valerie expressed. "Should I be concerned about that?"

"Typical college stuff. It seems pretty benign. He'll finally get sick of being hungover. I sure did."

Thanksgiving came, Greg's family went to watch him play football, and Valerie stayed home, spending time with her siblings. She was the last one. The oldest, her brother Jack, came with his crew in tow, his beautiful blond wife and adorable identical twins. They were a little older now and a lot more interesting.

They had conversations between themselves, nobody understood, and they liked to climb all over people like jungle gyms.

Her sister Rachel brought her fiancé, both in finance. There was a five-year gap between the two girls, but they were still close. Valerie told her family about Greg and his success on the football field. Her dad and brother were jocks from way back and very interested in his progress.

Unfortunately, Greg wasn't there. They had a game in the Midwest. She didn't hear from him in the evening. Things were all messed up with the holiday and time difference.

The ringing phone woke her early in the morning. She thought it was from Greg and answered, and tried to keep the sleep from her voice.

"Morning, babe. How was the game yesterday?"

It was Greg's mother. "Greg got hurt last night, Valerie. He blew out his knee."

Valerie sat straight up. "Is he okay? Is he going to have surgery to try to repair it? Do they think they can? Repair it? Oh, please call me when you have some news."

Imagine that, Valerie thought. A possible career-ending injury right when he was starting to do so well on the field. Lots of players got injured. Greg was going to be okay. He could work through it. He had the drive. If it took sheer determination and force of will, Greg would heal and be good as new.

Six

GREG AND VAL

GREG CAME BACK to campus to be evaluated by the team physician. He had an MRI and had to wait until the swelling went down before any decision was made. Valerie went through the rest of the semester, and once finished, she took the bus to Greg's campus. She was leaving for Italy in January and wanted to spend as much time with him as possible. He had his car, and if he needed to come home, she could drive him. His mother came down right after he got hurt. She went home after Val got there.

Greg was very depressed; he couldn't accept the fact he got hurt. Valerie being there helped him immensely; she propped him up and gave him hope. When they decided he needed surgery, she was there. She missed Christmas and stayed with Greg, waited on him, and took care of him. She listened while he expressed his fears, his grief, and the unknown he faced. Valerie wouldn't let him get down. She remained positive and hoped he couldn't see through her to her own fears.

He had the surgery right before Christmas. His knee was a real mess. All the ligaments were torn, his kneecap broken, and he had problems with tendons as well. Greg stayed in the hospital for a few days, and Valerie stayed with him. The doctors were cautiously optimistic, but Valerie clung to the hope he would be fine, and he clung to her. His internal well of self-confidence wasn't as deep as Valerie thought or as Greg projected. He was afraid.

Greg was terrified of life as he knew it was over. Valerie wouldn't let him sink into self-pity; she put her hope in the fact the best doctors operated on him and the best therapy was available to him. He was in a really good place to heal. He had the best people, the tops in their field, whose job was it was to get him better and back on the field. Soon, Valerie had to leave. She felt awful going away when Greg needed her the most.

"I don't want to go, Greg. I should be here, helping you."

"You have been so good to put your life on hold for me, but we have to get to work. You have to go do your semester abroad. I have to put my energy into my rehab. I would worry about you not doing what you need to do for yourself if you stayed. You don't have to worry about me chasing girls if that helps any," he joked.

That eased Valerie's mind. If he was able to laugh, he was getting better. His mom would be here for moral support, and the trainers and therapists would help him heal physically. She could leave knowing he had whatever he needed to get back to his old self.

Valerie went to Europe. It was everything she dreamed of and more. Italy was so old; there was layer upon layer of history. She toured everything she could, as touristy as it was. One guy, Drew, had the same goal as her: to see as much as possible. The girls wanted to go to Milan and check out the fashion houses. Valerie wanted to do that.

She wanted to go to Rome and look for the Pope, not that he'd be wandering the streets, but still.

Valerie wanted to go check out the sunlight in Tuscany. She wanted to stick her toes in the Mediterranean. Valerie mailed him letters often with strange-looking stamps affixed to the corner. Even though she was there, fulfilling a dream, she was worried about him. He didn't say anything that caused her concern, but she still had the nagging doubt in the back of her mind. Greg sent a few letters saying rehabilitation was slow going but moving forward nonetheless.

Greg said the doctors were still cautious but optimistic; he just had to do the work. He was glad Valerie was enjoying her trip. She said she'd bring him home in a coffee mug blessed by the pope. Her flight landed at JFK, and the first thing she did was call Greg. His mom answered.

"Mrs. Wilson, what are you doing there? Is Greg okay?" Valerie said the panic caused her voice to rise high in her chest.

"Val, nobody told you. Greg asked us not to, but he had to have another surgery. The doctors weren't happy with his progress. He had another operation earlier this week."

"Is he going to be all right, Mrs. Wilson? How is he taking this? Is he there? Can I talk to him?"

"Caio, Bella," he said. "Welcome home, Val."

"Where are you, Greg? Are you still in the hospital?"

"No, I'm in my room. My mom's just leaving."

"My flight boards in an hour. I'm going to drop my stuff off and get on the next bus. I'll be there as soon as I can."

"No, Valerie, don't. I don't want you to do that. See your family. Get over your jet lag. Come see me next week. I'll still be here."

"Look. I haven't seen you for two months. It sounds like a lot of shit went down, and nobody told me. I know you think you were protecting me so I could enjoy Italy, but you don't need to protect me anymore. What I need is to see you, and I'm coming whether you like it or not. I need to go now. I'll call you when I get home."

She could be there in a few hours. She went to the gate and explained she'd have her luggage picked up by her family, but she needed to rent a car due to a change of plans. Valerie headed to the rental car's kiosk and was on the road quickly. She was nervous driving out of the airport and the city. The car people got her a map and highlighted the route in magic markers.

Valerie got there in a few hours; renting a car was so smart. She'd pay her dad back; the card was supposed to be for emergencies only, but she considered this an emergency. She parked the car and ran into his dorm. Val hit the number, and the elevator took her to his floor. She practically flew down the hall to his room. His door was ajar, and she heard voices. Valerie stopped to catch her breath and heard a female voice say, "When do you figure she'll get here?" with a laugh.

Valerie pushed the door open and didn't like what she saw. A girl was sitting on

Greg's bed, too close for Valerie's liking. She stormed into his room. Valerie grabbed the girl by the collar and yanked her off the bed, where she tumbled to the floor. Valerie looked at the girl with fury in her eyes.

"She's here now. Who the fuck are you? What are you doing in bed with my boyfriend?" Valerie yelled down at her. The girl backed up, scrambling away like a crab going backward. Valerie followed her.

"I asked you a question!" Valerie yelled. "Who the FUCK are you?"

The girl got up. "Why don't you ask your 'boyfriend,'" she said as she ran out of the room.

Valerie looked at Greg, who sat there in total shock, his mouth hanging open.

"Well, Greg, who the hell is she?" she said, sat in a chair, and burst into tears.

"What the fuck's going on in here? Who's doing all the yelling?" his roommate said as he entered the room. He saw Valerie crying and looked at Greg. Greg shook his head in confusion.

"Val? Valerie?" Greg asked her gently. "Hey, come over here."

She looked at him. "Do you know what I did to get here? I was so worried, so scared, I would have crawled to get here. Looks like it was a huge waste of time. You didn't need me at all. No wonder you wanted me to come next week. I guess I should have called ahead and gotten a place in line. You asshole. Fuck you."

She stood up and grabbed her backpack. "I'll be in touch." She started to cry again, but didn't move. Greg motioned to his roommate to bring Valerie over to his bed. She allowed herself to be led to his bedside. Greg reached out and rubbed Valerie's arm as his roommate left.

"Hey, Val, come up here. Take your coat and shoes off and get in." She was too tired to fight. She was too tired to cry.

"I don't want to. I'll go sleep in the car," she said, but didn't move. "It's my fault for not calling. I shouldn't have come."

"I'm really glad you came, Val. I'm so happy to see you. Come get under the covers. Let me hold you. Come on. You'll feel better."

"You don't have room. Your leg. There's no room for me. I shouldn't have come. I should go," Valerie said as if in a daze. "I don't belong here. I should go."

"No, Valerie. Get in here. Now. I'm really happy you're here."

"I can't stay here. You don't have room. You don't need me," she started crying again. "You don't need me here. I shouldn't have come. I'm sorry, Greg. I'm so sorry." Valerie seemed to implode, to collapse within herself.

Greg reached out and pulled her by her arm. She fell onto his chest, and Val fell sound asleep. He felt so badly for her. Valerie raced here; she didn't even go home, and she walked in only to find Missy sitting on his bed.

The only reason Missy was here was because Greg couldn't physically throw her out. That was what he told himself. He liked her coming around. Greg missed the attention being on the team gave him. Greg was stuck in his bed, and Missy helped break up the monotony of his day. Since he couldn't avoid her, she kept coming around more and more. Greg doubted she'd be back since Val tossed her out on her ass. He looked at Valerie, asleep on his chest. God, how he loved her. With her away, he could pretend everything was all right.

With her home, things seemed all too real.

Early the next morning, Greg shook Valerie awake. The trainer was here to take him to his rehab session.

"Where am I?" she asked, blinking. She looked around and sat up. "Greg? What happened? How did I get here?"

"You rented a car and drove in from JFK last night."

She took a minute and sorted things out in her mind. Valerie asked for the bathroom. Val brushed her teeth and splashed cold water on her face. Valerie just wanted to go home. What a mess. She needed to leave.

"Sorry, Val. I have to go." He was standing up with crutches.

Val came out and smiled. "Well, look at you. Standing up and everything." She patted down her pockets and found the keys. Valerie looked at them like she had never seen them before. She picked up her backpack.

"I hope I remember what car I drove. Glad to see you up. Have a good session. Goodbye, Greg. I'll give you a call." She looked at the trainer. "Beat the crap out of him," she said and walked out the door.

"Valerie, wait," he called after her. She kept walking to the elevator and pushed the down button.

"Call me and let me know you made it home."

She didn't say anything. When the elevator came, she got on it and left. "Who was that?" the trainer asked.

"She was my girlfriend until she saw Missy in here. I'm not sure what she is now," Greg said. "I hope she forgives me."

"How'd she end up here?" the trainer asked.

"She rented a car from JFK to come make sure I was okay."

"Dude, if a girl is that worried about you and you're with another girl, no wonder she's pissed. You better hope she's the forgiving type. That kind of girl's a keeper," the trainer said and took him down for therapy.

***

Valerie drove home, a trip she thought would never end. She thought about Greg. She hoped he would gain back what he lost and be back on the field by fall. Valerie had a summer internship coming up and wasn't going to have much, if any, free time. That probably was the last time she'd see him for a while. It was for the best, considering the way she behaved last night. She was beyond exhausted. Valerie just wanted to get home.

When she pulled into the driveway, she grabbed her backpack and went inside. Her mom and dad were having a quiet, peaceful Saturday cup of coffee when she entered. After a brief rundown of yesterday, her mother insisted she go straight to bed; they would handle getting her luggage and returning the rental.

Valerie told her parents she wasn't taking calls and barely had enough energy to undress and get in bed. She slept for almost twenty-four hours straight. When she finally got out of bed, she felt semi-human and needed a cup of coffee immediately, if not sooner.

She made a cup of coffee and sat at the kitchen table. Her mom came out of her room and gave her a big hug.

"Welcome home, darlin'," her mom said. "I guess things didn't go so well at Greg's, did it? He's been trying to get a hold of you. He kept calling, so I finally answered. He'd like you to call him back when you wake up."

"Yeah, and I'd like to lose ten pounds, like that's ever going to happen."

"Oh, honey. Cut him a little slack. He can't move around, and that girl came into his room and wouldn't leave," her mom explained.

Valerie looked at her mom through tired eyes. "That's what he said? I guess now I know why you should call first. I panicked when I heard he had another surgery. I had a picture in my mind of him being all alone and bummed out, so I rented a car because it was the quickest way to get to him, but I was wrong. He's doing fine without me."

"Valerie, he's not okay. Greg feels awful about it. He wants you to call him."

"Mom, his job is to get better. My internship starts on Wednesday. That's the plan, anyway. I should have just come home. He can be friends with anybody he wants. That girl, another girl, who cares? I shouldn't have overreacted like I did. I went in there, guns blazing." The phone rang again. Her mother answered it. It was Greg. Her mom extended the receiver to her.

"I'll get it. I have to talk to him sooner or later," Valerie said. Her mother left the room to give her some privacy.

"Hi, Greg. How are you?" she asked him calmly.

"Valerie! My God, are you all right? I've been worried sick about you!"

"Well, that was a waste of your energy. I'm fine. Tired, but fine. I owe you an apology. I should have called first. I was so tired and worried I might not have used the best judgment."

"You just left like that. I was coming back from rehab in an hour or so; we could have talked then. I was so happy to see you, and you just left," he said.

"No, it was a mistake to come in the first place. I shouldn't have come. I thought you'd be sad and all alone, all I could think was you needed me, and I was wrong. You were fine."

"Look, that girl means nothing to me. I'm kind of stuck in one place, so I'm an easy target. You have to believe me. She doesn't mean a thing. Honest."

"Yeah, sure. It's none of my business what you do or don't do. If you see her, tell her I'm sorry. I overreacted," Val said, her voice still tired.

"Val, please. Don't be like this."

"Be like what?"

"So, so, unfeeling. So cold."

"I don't mean to be. You're at school. The deal was to explore the world and figure out who you're meant to be. You can hang out with whomever you want. You can do whatever you want. You can do whoever you want. If you don't do that, how will you know I'm the one you're supposed to be with? How can you say I'm unfeeling? I just took some chick and threw her out on her ass. I'm just tired, that's all."

"No, you're not. You're mad. I'll ask you how Italy was, and you'll say, 'Fine.' No matter what I ask you, you'll say, 'Fine.' Talk to me. I love you, Val. Please."

"I'm pretty embarrassed. I behaved like some crazy girlfriend, and that's just not me. I lost it, and I'm sorry. God, I embarrassed you among all those guys, all those football players," she remembered.

"Quit saying you're sorry. You did the whole team a favor, tossing Missy out of here. She left and hasn't returned, and all the guys said to say thank you for getting rid of her. As far as being crazy, well, that elevated me to rockstar status."

"How so?"

"I had a girl land at JFK, rent a car, and drive all this way to make sure I was okay because she worried about me. And when she got here, she tossed some bimbo out on her ass. No other guy ever had a girl ever come close to doing something like that for them. I had two girls fighting over me. Like I said, me, rockstar."

"There was no girl fight."

"I know you know that, but the way rumors fly around here, you did, and you won. I'll break my other leg if you'll do it again," Greg joked. He could tell Valerie was relaxing. The clipped, dispassionate tone of her voice was easing. "I wish you stayed. I was so happy to see you."

"I wish I didn't just drop everything and haul ass after that flight. I should have gone home and pulled myself together before I came down. I'm really sorry I didn't stay. I missed you so much. Everything I saw in Italy, I kept wishing you were there to see it. When I finally see you, I act like a lunatic and walk out," Valerie told him.

"I'll take you there for our honeymoon. You can show me everything. We won't need a tour guide," Greg said.

"Honeymoon? What are you talking about?"

"It's getting close. One year from now, we'll be done with school. I think we'll be on the same page, and if we're not, I'll rent a car, go where you are, take whatever guy you're seeing, toss him out on his ass, and take his place. I promise," he said with a laugh.

"So, no other girl has taken my place? Not in your bed? Not in your head? Not in your heart?" she asked. "We haven't talked about this in ages."

"Yeah. I know. We've both, for the most part, lived our college years the way you thought was best, and I think you were right. The future's coming up soon, Val."

"I have to get through this summer internship and then the next year," she replied.

"The future's coming up soon, Val," he repeated. "We played the college years by your rules. Fine. One more year, Valerie, and the next four years, we play by mine."

"I can't talk about this now, Greg. It hurts my head to think that far ahead. It hurts my head to think at all."

"That's fine, Valerie. You finish your business; you take care of yourself. I'm in no hurry. I have a lot of rehab coming up. Hopefully, that second surgery worked. I lost a lot of time after that first surgery. I'm scared, Valerie. I didn't want to say it out loud, but yeah. If this doesn't work, I've run out of options," Greg told her. "I'm glad you're home. I've had to plaster this smile on my face and be Mr. Positive. You're the only person I can be totally honest with."

"You'll be fine, Greg. You're young, healthy, and committed to getting better. You have the best people working on you. It may take a while longer than you think, but it will work out."

"Thanks, Val. You're my girl. You kick ass and take names."

"That's me. Maybe I'll join the Army. I hear they are looking for people like me."

"If I wasn't in love with you, I'd say, 'Kill 'em all and let God sort them out.' But no. You stay put. Don't go away without me ever again. Promise?"

"I love you, Greg. The worst part about leaving is coming home and learning everything has turned to dust. I don't want that, ever."

Val interned that summer with a major development company similar to Greg's family business. His family built it, and her company supplied tenants. They owned a number of large apartment and business complexes. Valerie shadowed leasing agents around and observed their responsibilities. By the end of the summer, she could lease a property as well as their top producer. More than one agent made a commission on leases she signed. Val studied for her real estate license so she would have it before she graduated.

Greg's father laughed and said he considered her a corporate spy working for his competition.

"Working for the competition?" she laughed back. "More like indentured servitude. I wish I was getting paid."

"Use them. Learn as much as you can, then come work for me," he told her.

"I'll learn as much as I can and start my own company. I'll hire you to work for me, Mr. Wilson."

"Atta girl, Valerie. Stay hungry," he advised her.

***

Greg came home in July. His leg still wasn't at 100%. In fact, the team doctor recommended he not play at all. If he got hit, he might lose the ability to walk. He was never going to have the speed he used to be known for, and he couldn't scramble behind the line of scrimmage when a play fell apart; he didn't have the footwork he needed to play. Everything that made him exciting to watch was gone. He would probably be left with a permanent limp. Greg spent the spring semester recovering instead of going to classes.

To add to his misery, he lost his scholarship. They gave it to a sophomore. Greg felt the ground beneath him crumble, and everything he thought he knew about himself was gone.

He plunged into a deep depression. Greg mourned what he lost, and he had no idea who he was without it. He plastered a smile on his face and was Mr. Positive when asked about his injury, saying he'd be back on the field in no time. Greg feared if one more person asked about his knee, the truth would come pouring from his mouth. The only person he couldn't hide the truth from was Valerie.

"Look, Greg, spill it," Val said one night when she took him out for ice cream. "I know you. Something's very wrong, and you're hiding it. You've distanced yourself from your parents and your friends, and you're trying to do that with me, but I know you, and I'm not going to let you."

"Well, Val, I'm not sure what you're talking about."

"Bullshit," Val said. "Let's talk about football."

"Football? Why bring that up?" he feigned ignorance.

"Greg. It's almost time to report for camp. I think you haven't mentioned it because you aren't going, correct?"

He just looked at her, blinking. Once they finished their ice cream, she started the car and drove to a nearby park. She pulled in, parked in a far corner, and got out of the car. Before she shut her door, she put her head down so he could see her.

"Come on, Greg. Let's sit out here and talk."

He got out and went with her to a picnic table. When he went to sit opposite her, she told him no.

"I want you to sit next to me. You've been holding it in all summer. Talk to me before you have a nervous breakdown. I can see you starting to crack, and I'm getting really concerned about you. It's football. Your career's over, isn't it?"

Greg sat there, silent. He could not say the words out loud. She put her arms around him and hugged him hard. She remained quiet and rubbed his back. Valerie put her hand on the back of his head and guided him so his face was in her neck and his head on her shoulder.

Valerie could feel his body start to shake, and his tears wet against her skin. Greg tried to pull away from her, embarrassed by his display of emotion, but she held him tighter. He trembled in her arms; he wept on her shoulder. She would not let him go.

"I've got you, Greg. I'm not letting go. I'm here, I'm here," she whispered. "It's okay. It's gonna be okay."

He pulled his head back and looked at her. He wiped the tears off his face and said to her in a voice she could only describe as broken. "It's not okay, Val. It will never be okay."

"Yes, it will. It will, I promise. I love you, and I'm not losing you to this. You lean on me if the load gets too heavy. You can get through this."

He cried even harder. "That's not your job, Valerie. You don't carry me. I'm supposed to carry you."

"Says who?" Valerie told him. "I can help you now. You can help me later. Take as long as you need to get better. I think you need to talk to a therapist. Learn to let go of what's not coming back."

"No way I'm talking to a shrink."

"Okay, okay. Have you talked to your parents yet?"

"No."

"After we get done here, we should. I bet they know a lot more than you give them credit for. I'll tell them if you can't. Don't worry. I've got you."

"Oh, Val," he said, his voice breaking. "What am I supposed to do?"

"We'll figure it out. We can, and we will. But first, we need to talk to your parents. People can't help you if they don't know you need it."

They sat in silence for a while, holding hands. He stood up, grabbed his crutches, and said, "Let's go. I can tell them as long as you're with me."

"Baby, I'm with you even when I'm not with you. Remember that you don't ever have to go it alone," Valerie told Greg. He smiled. "What's that smile for?"

"You called me baby," he said, his spirit a little lighter. Valerie squeezed him and left little kisses all over his face.

"Baby, baby, baby. Greg's my baby. I'll love him even if he never picks up a football again. Baby."

They went to his house, and his parents were on the deck enjoying a cocktail. His dad got up and got Greg a beer, Valerie a glass of wine.

"What can we do for you kids?" his mother asked. Greg looked at Valerie, so she started.

"Greg and I just had a heart-to-heart talk, but it involves more than just us. He really needs to have a heart-to-heart with you guys, too. His football injury is more severe than he let any of us know. It's a career-ending injury, and if he plays, he could lose the ability to walk. Football camp starts at the beginning of August, and he wasn't invited back."

"Greg! Is this true?" his father said, shocked.

"Tell them all of it, Val. Please," Greg said.

"He lost his scholarship. He didn't go to classes last semester; he focused on getting better. He hasn't done his internship by now, so he has to make those up before he can be considered a senior. He pretends everything is fine, but it's not.

"He's beyond devastated. I'm worried he can't see life beyond football, but there is one. A good one, but he's too depressed about where he is now to see it." Valerie asked him if she left anything out. He shook his head.

"Oh, no, honey." His mom got up and hugged her son. "Don't worry. We can help you take care of things. I know it seems like football is all you know, but it's not."

"It's all I know. It's all I've ever been good at," Greg said, the sadness in his voice threatened to overwhelm him.

"Greg. You'll be fine," his father said. Greg heard the part he didn't say, too. The part where he needed to man up.

"No," Valerie said. "He needs time. Time to heal and time to figure things out. He needs time to redefine who he is without football. Without the glory or the roar of the fans. He never thought life could be different than he imagined. Greg needs to grieve over his lost self. Once he gets a little more used to things, he can consider his options. Right now, he needs to be sad, with our help and understanding."

"Valerie, that sounds all well and good, but he's not a quitter. He'll rise up and meet whatever challenges come his way. He's a man, not a little boy. Greg doesn't need you and his mother to coddle him. He'll be fine. Don't underestimate his ability to come back from this."

"Mr. Wilson, I respectfully disagree. He needs time to figure out who he wants to be. He doesn't need more pressure to be somebody he's not. Greg is smart. You're right. He'll be fine. But on his terms. Not ours."

"Valerie," his father said, "thanks for helping him tell us what's going on, but we can handle it from here."

Greg looked lost at his father's remarks. Being good at football was 90% of his relationship with his dad. He couldn't remember the last conversation that wasn't about football. Putting it all out on the table didn't make him feel better. It made that pit in the bottom of his stomach feel dark, deep, and endless.

Valerie finished her internship and spent all her free time with Greg. They didn't do very much; they just hung around and goofed off. She made no expectations as far as Greg and his future went. She worked very hard, not even to mention football, the upcoming fall semester, or his plans.

Every once in a while, he would bring it up, but just to bounce things off her. He mentioned going back to school or working for his dad. The thought that came fall, he could work for his father and use the experience as his internship was something he considered; that way, he wasn't losing a semester. Valerie was very supportive and approved wholeheartedly. Secretly, she hated the idea. She thought his dad was going to pressure him to go too far too fast, but she didn't want to shut down Greg's optimism, so she said nothing.

***

Valerie went back to school, the final year ahead of her. She had enough credits to satisfy her major. Now, she had some leeway in her schedule. She took a couple of art classes and an art history class. Knowledge for the sake of knowledge is what Valerie enjoyed. She was a business major, like a lot of kids here.

At school, she still lived in the house she shared with Lauren and Tony. She was excited. Greg was coming to visit. He had never seen her place, so focused on being a student-athlete he never had time. He decided to go the corporate route and work at Conover Property Development.

Conover was his mother's maiden name. His dad bought the company when his father-in-law wanted to retire. Greg's dad had been running the company for a while. Mr. Wilson took it beyond what it was to a formidable business entity. The Conovers retired to Florida with a nice financial cushion.

Greg was going into the office every day, wearing suits and ties. He followed his father around as his protege; he sat in a lot of business meetings, and the most he was required to do was nod his head at the right moments. It was considered an internship, but he considered himself a well-dressed grunt. Greg didn't care. It was nice to have a purpose.

Greg was interested in Valerie's past four years of academia. He wanted to see the dorm she left her freshman year. He wanted to see everything about her college experience. Valerie took it as a good sign; he was interested in where she was and what she was doing. Greg was expanding his world little by little, a very good sign. He was moving away from something towards something else. Progress. He had come a long way from the summer.

The first thing she showed him was her house. Two computer geeks rented the other rooms after Lauren and Tony graduated. He tackled her onto the bed and started kissing her neck, right behind her earlobe. She giggled and squirmed out from under him and rolled off to the side. He was on his back. She held his head up with one hand and with the other, gave him a little tenderness. She gently stroked his cheek and outlined his eyebrows. Her index finger went from the center of his forehead, down his nose and lips to the very slight but visible cleft in his chin.

"Do you know a cleft chin is a dominant trait? If one parent has one, all their kids would have one, too."

"So, if we had a kid, and it didn't have one, that would mean it wasn't mine?"

"You would have to take me to paternity court. We could be on TV."

Greg looked at her. She was the left to his right, the yin to his yang. Valerie had grown a lot since high school. She was confident. She didn't walk into a room trying to stay below the radar anymore. Val still wore the clothes of an eighth-grade boy, but he knew there was a goddess underneath. She was his goddess. He knew better than to ask God why; it was purely his good fortune.

"If we ever have a baby, I hope it looks just like you," he told her. "With your big eyes and your beautiful soul."

"Really? That's so sweet. I've seen your baby pictures. Your hair was so blond it was almost white. I'd want a blonde-haired, blue-eyed baby with just the suggestion of a dimple in its chin." She laughed, it was so far away it was ridiculous to consider. Not so for Greg.

"You think about having a family with me?" Greg said.

"Yeah, of course. That's for the future, though. Things haven't changed. Maybe they got rearranged, but I haven't changed my mind about you. I've been here almost four years. If there was somebody better, I would have met him by now, don't you think?"

"Have you been looking?" Greg asked.

"Of course not. There's no point. Our spirits are fused." She pulled him closer. "You still have to get yourself straightened out. Like going back to school and stuff," she told him.

"What would you say if I didn't go back to school?"

"I'd say, why not?"

"It seems stupid to go through all that trouble only to end up where I am now," he replied.

"Don't you want to finish it? You're two semesters away from your degree. You don't want the paper? The diploma? It's so close. You've already invested so much in it."

"It's more like three semesters. Like I said, I don't need a degree. I'm learning how to run the business now rather than later."

"Don't you want the luxury of moving around and having some control over where you go? It seems now you're pretty locked into the family business. Maybe someday you'll want to do something else, but you can't because you don't have a degree."

"Maybe. I could take night classes. I don't want to go away to college. I'm too old to hang out with college kids. I've already had that experience."

"There's that. You start out slow, one class at a time. Maybe the longer you're away, the harder it will be to start back up." She tried not to tilt the issue one way or the other. She tried not to care; he was a young guy. Maybe it would take a few years to get his footing, but it would give him a more mature view of college.

Since he valued the experience more from work, he decided to stay at Conover Property Management, Inc. and be a management trainee. He was glad. Greg pondered which kid of his mother's family would show up and want a job or a cut, but it's been over twenty years since his dad legally bought out his in-laws. His brother had his third invested, Caroline, too. Greg would get the business. Valerie went back for her last year. She came back for winter break and never returned until graduation. She filled in at her summer internship over the break. They offered her a job. Val had enough credits. She went back to clear out her bedroom. She paid the remainder semester's rent; she didn't stiff them on the money, and they didn't have to find a roommate. Val moved back in with her parents, but used to the independence of four years away, she lasted only a week.

She brought Greg along apartment hunting. He wasn't his usually jokey self; he didn't ask her if she had a bedroom for him. She only looked at two bedrooms, knowing full well he'd be eventually living there. He'd have his own room for his own shit. Everything else was communal space, and nobody's shit was allowed there. That would be a rule. If he left stuff lying around, she'd collect it and put it on his bed. He's supposed to do the same to her, but he thought if he won't pick up after himself, why would he pick up after she crossed her mind.

Valerie found a place for June first, the week after she graduated. She was busy working, and Greg was out on job sites, they usually had dinner out. Greg could come to her parents, and she could go to his, but more than once a week seemed like they were back in high school.

She had most of her things packed from moving home. Valerie lived out of a suitcase until she moved in. She did need to buy a bed and a couch. She invited Greg to go shopping with her, and he said he would, but he didn't seem that thrilled. He drove his truck in case they had a big purchase. He pulled into the parking lot and parked his truck, but made no effort to move any further.

"Okay, Greg. Spit it out," she said.

"What are you talking about?"

"I know you, Greg and I'm pretty tuned in to you, and I know when you get in one of your moods. Please tell me; I want to help."

"You think you can fix everything, don't you?"

"That's kind of harsh, isn't it? I wouldn't ask if I didn't care. Suppose you'd rather keep it to yourself, fine. Why don't you take me home if you'd rather pass on the shopping? I'll order one and have it delivered." She looked directly at him, willing to wait him out until he felt like talking.

"It seems like you are graduating, and getting your own place means you're growing up, and I'm still in the same spot, doing the same thing."

Valerie wasn't sure how to answer him. Yes, his injury cost him a semester. Not going back lost him two. He could probably get his work experience to count as an internship, but he was still a year and a half behind. She didn't know what he expected her to say. Any words she chose would only make him angry, and maybe he wanted to be angry. Maybe he felt picking a fight might make him feel better and shift the blame to her for his discontent. Greg figured it wouldn't bother him as much as it did, not going back. But it did. A lot.

"I'm sorry, Val. I just feel left out and left behind. I look at you and what you've done, and I feel like a piece of shit," he confessed.

"Greg, baby," she touched his knee, "it's all right. There's plenty of time to do what you want. Yeah, you're behind. For a good reason, but you can't stay stuck here. Make a move. Go register for a class. One class, have a copy of your transcript sent, and then meet with admissions. Get an idea of the big picture."

"What if I changed my mind? What if I want to do something else, not engineering? What happens then?"

"Greg, you could get a degree in poetry if you wanted. You'll still be going to work for the family business. But I don't get why. You love to build things. You're out to dinner, and you try to make something out of the sugar packets. If you go someplace where there's going to be kids, you're on the floor building with blocks or Lego. You love that stuff."

"I don't know what happened. Somewhere along the line, I lost my, I don't know, passion or maybe desire to do that. I wish I knew."

"Get ready to get mad at me," Valerie said. "I'm going to say what I always say. You think your injury meant your life was over. I'm not going to argue that you can't help the way you feel. I still think you believe that one event and its subsequent impact defined you. It doesn't. Not to me, anyway. I could give a shit about football—"

"See, that's it right there. You don't care about it. You never did. It didn't matter to you. But it mattered a whole lot to me. I can't expect you to care about something you think is stupid."

"What does it matter what I think? How come I care about you? How come I love you, injury and all? If I didn't feel that way, I would have been out of here months ago. I'm here because you're more than football to me. Way more. You need to talk to a professional about it. You can't get past it on your own."

"That's what you always say. I need a shrink. It's not that easy for me to talk about my feelings. I don't even like talking to you about them. Why would I talk to a stranger about them? They can't cure me."

"You know, it's not about a cure. It's about acceptance. That's how you move forward." She looked at him. "I don't want to talk about your feelings anymore, either. We don't need to. It's not like some new revelation is going to come about. The only thing I want to talk about is a new mattress. Do you want to go in and roll around on a few? Your input matters since you'll probably be spending a lot of time on it. Or take me home, and I'll get my car."

"My input matters?" he asked, sounding surprised.

"No shit, Sherlock. You know, if you were in Iraq and had both your legs blown off, you'd still be sitting there. I don't understand why you don't know that. So, if you want your input to matter, come inside. If you don't, bring me home, but realize you can't complain about the mattress being too hard or soft. You forfeit that right."

Greg smiled at her. A smile that was genuinely happy, one that used to be so quick to appear but was rarely used nowadays.

"Oh, Valerie," he told her, "I don't know why you're here, but you are, and I'm so lucky to have you. I believe you when you say you love me."

"Why would I lie about loving you? Now shut up. You're starting to annoy me. Get out, or I'll roll around on the beds with the sales guy. Or girl."

"Oooh," he said, his good mood back. "The salesgirl? Can I watch?"

"Play your cards right and you could end up the filling of a Greg sandwich," she replied.

"You do love me."

"Again, that's what I don't get. Why do you doubt it? I've never given you any reason to think otherwise. Come on," she said as she opened the door to head into the store.

He got out and took her hand. "You're the best, Val," he said as he walked into the store with her.

"I know, so quit pissing me off."

The delivery was scheduled for Thursday, so she needed something to sleep on for the next couple of days. They stopped at a sporting goods store, got a blow-up air mattress, and ordered Chinese to pick it up on the way to her new place. Valerie had a couple of lawn chairs, some plastic silverware, two pillows, and a comforter. She could pick up everything else as she went along. Work gave her the week off to get settled. They took the items back to her new place. It was in a two-family house. She had the bottom flat. Two bedrooms, a living room with a fireplace, a dining room, and a small kitchen. There was off-street parking for two cars. It was old but bright and cheery. Most of it had been updated, but the original molding and doors with their heavy crystal doorknobs spoke to her. Greg approached from a contractor's viewpoint; he would gut the place and start over, but when he mentioned it to Valerie, she didn't want to hear it.

"You want to get rid of the charm? The authenticity? How dare you! Have you no appreciation for history?" she told him.

"Tell me that when you have no water pressure, and the windows leak cold air in winter," he pointed out.

"I'll ask you to fix the water pressure and caulk the windows," Valerie replied.

"Why should I?"

"Because when you're here, that stuff will bug you as much as it will me," she said.

"How much will I be here, anyway?" he asked. "As much as you want. You have your own room."

"What if I don't want my own room? What if I want to stay in yours?"

"Then you stay in mine, but don't think you're getting out of paying your half of the rent, mister."

He grabbed her in a bear hug. "I wouldn't think of it. Are you asking me to move in with you?"

"I guess I just did."

***

Seven

VAL AND GREG

VALERIE AND GREG moved into their new place. Since he lived there, it was no longer her place. It was their place. Over time, they accumulated enough furniture they no longer needed to use the lawn chairs indoors; those now were out on the porch where they belonged. They got in the habit of having a drink after work, sitting in the chairs, watching small-town life pass them by. They lived there a few summers, happy to be together. Greg thought about how content Valerie was, not in any hurry to advance any further into adulthood.

They got into the routine of cooking dinner on Saturday and Sunday, enough for two days of leftovers during the work week. They ordered out the other couple of days since neither had the desire to cook after a long day at work. As soon as Greg walked in and changed, he opened a beer.

He drank it while waiting for Valerie and getting dinner together. His day started at seven, and he was usually home by four; Valerie, eight to five. She would change out her work clothes and eat what Greg had ready; she would do the dishes. He had a glass of wine ready for her when she was done with the cleanup; they sat on the porch and enjoyed the warm summer nights.

There was nothing like being in Greg's arms after a long day of dealing with people and their problems. Valerie loved this part of the day. He was strong and not always into talking, but the strength of his physical presence made her feel safe and secure.

They passed the summers like that; they entertained a couple of times. They had a "housewarming party," for lack of a better phrase.

It was a hot weekend in early August. Greg bought a new grill, especially for the party, he told her. She knew he wanted one anyway. The party was a good excuse to pull the trigger and make the purchase. They invited family and friends for burgers and dogs. Everyone brought a side dish.

Valerie loved a good salad, so that's what she made: fresh ingredients from the farmer's market. It started at three. By seven, the older adults cleared out, and just the young people were left. Evan and Emily were there, living at home after college, trying to figure out their next career moves. They enjoyed a "fling" when they both happened to be in the same town at the same time. Kayla was down south, still at school; she was going on to get her master's. A number of Greg's high school buddies came, too.

Valerie, since she was hosting the party, kept her drinking in check; she only had one glass of wine. She didn't mean to, but she noticed the way Greg seemed to be pounding down the beers. Once these guys got together, it was all stories from their glory days, high school, back when Greg was the top dog.

Instead of being upset or depressed, he was almost manic, keeping up the flow of memories. He was laughing and joking around like his biggest problem was he burnt the hot dogs. Valerie hoped seeing his old friends would make him feel better about his situation. His bad knee didn't matter to them; all their stories were of Greg in his prime. They didn't know him any other way. The party broke up at about midnight. Emily and Evan were left and helped clean up. Once they finished, they went to find Greg to say goodbye.

He was passed out couch. They shook him and told him they were leaving. He mumbled, "Thanks for coming," and passed back out. Valerie walked them to the door and locked them. She turned around and looked at Greg. He didn't look like he was moving anytime soon; she took his sneakers off and tossed a light blanket over him. She told him goodnight as she turned off the lights. He didn't say anything, and she went to bed by herself.

When she awoke the next morning, she was still alone. Val got up and looked at him, still on the couch. She shook her head and went and made a pot of coffee. She checked her junk mail and played solitaire and won. It was almost noon when she heard groaning from the living room. He got up to use the bathroom. Greg took the longest leak she had ever heard, ran the water, and splashed his face. He came out, drying his face, and looked at Valerie.

"Morning, sunshine. How's your head?" Valerie asked him.

"Not good. I won't be doing that again any time soon," he moaned. "It's all your fault."

"How so?"

"You really know how to throw a party. Do we have any aspirin?"

"No, you really know to enjoy a party. Aspirin's in the cupboard over the sink," Valerie answered. "Would you like some coffee?"

"Not right now. I gotta go lassy down," he told her. "Did I sleep on the couch last night?"

"Yes, you did. That's where you passed out, so that's where I left you."

"I'll be in bed," he said. He didn't get up until late afternoon.

***

Summer ended, and fall came in on a gusty wind. It seemed to arrive almost overnight; the mornings grew dark as the days shortened. Coats came out of the closets, and summer clothes were stored away for next year.

The wind blew the fallen leaves everywhere, and occasionally, it blew in through the leaky windows. Greg was right; they might be charming, but not very efficient. He spent a Saturday afternoon caulking.

"You know, Val," he said, "there's a ton of other things I could be doing besides working on somebody else's house. I'm not sure I did any good; these really should be replaced."

"Well, I feel better," she said.

"That's why I did it. For you," he told her.

"Thank you, sweetie," she replied and hugged him.

"Sweetie needs some sugar," he said as he pulled her into their room. He grabbed her and kissed her. Greg kissed her again until she was flat on her back in bed. She started removing her clothes. He unbuttoned her shirt. She wore bras with a front closure at his request. He said the other kind reminded him of his mother or old ladies. Greg undid the front clasp and released her breasts. He put his face between them and looked up at her.

"What?" she asked.

"You didn't think I fixed those for free, did you?"

Towards the end of October, the neighborhood lay quiet. The trees waved their bare limbs instead of colorful leaves. Valerie liked the monochromatic palette of this time of year; she enjoyed the brisk pace you had to walk because it was too chilly to stand around. The families with their dogs and kids on bicycles no longer passed by. Only joggers went by the house, warm from their efforts. The lawn chairs were brought around back and stored in the garage, waiting for summer to return.

Halloween was near, and Valerie loved Halloween. She hung a paper skeleton on the front door and changed the porch light to orange. She always had jack lanterns placed on the steps leading to the door. Then she switched them to the porch. Valerie switched them back and forth. She did every year.

Greg laughed at how obsessed she got with the pumpkins. Valerie was able to convince Greg to go to a pumpkin farm without too much difficulty. He even carved the pumpkins for her. She helped by doing the worst part: removing the seeds and guts.

Valerie realized a melon baller could scrape the insides once most of the guts were out. She did three; it took most of her Sunday. Greg felt sorry for her, so he did the fourth one for her. Once they were done, she put them on the steps. After a few days, she decided she wanted them spaced out along the porch railing, looking out.

"Greg," she said in her sexiest voice, "would you please help me with the pumpkins?"

"I already helped. I helped enough," he called over his shoulder. "I'm watching the game."

"Please, Greg, please. At halftime or whatever, please?" She shifted from sexy to whiny. "Please."

"Yeah, sure. But you have to come in here and watch the end with me." She sat next to him and watched the game. She even argued some debatable calls.

"That's bullshit," she said. "That was a touchdown. He broke the plane." Greg looked at her with newfound respect.

"Plane?" He looked at her. "What do you know about the plane?" Sometimes, Valerie seemed to accumulate knowledge out of thin air. It bothered him, it seemed like life took no effort for her, where he had to bust his hump just to get out of bed.

"I know enough to know he broke it," she told him. He answered by playfully putting her in a headlock.

"What do you call this?" he asked her.

"A half-Nelson. Now let me go." He did. Greg picked up the remote and turned the TV off.

"Let's go fix your pumpkins, you pumpkin head," he said as he got up.

"I'd get mad and start a fight because you called me that if I didn't need your help. Your head is bigger than mine. I bet when you played football, they had to special order an extra-large helmet."

Greg took the pumpkins from the steps and put them on the rail.

Valerie went down the stairs and stood on the lawn. He watched her look at each pumpkin. He placed them where she wanted them, only to have her change her mind. She considered her options again. He laughed at her.

"What's so funny?" she asked him.

"You're studying them like you're curating an exhibit or something. You do this every year. They're just pumpkins."

She had him move them around a bit more until she was satisfied. "Last chance," he called down. "I'm cold. I'm going inside, Val."

He went in the front door, looked back, and smiled. She was still on the lawn, squinting. 'Ain't that my girl,' he thought to himself. Valerie came inside a few minutes later.

"You happy now?" he asked her from the couch.

"Very. Thank you. You're right about the cold." She jumped on the couch.

"I we don't get any trick-or-treaters, our driveway's too long. Your display will be wasted."

"Not on me," Valerie said. "I'm going to walk down the driveway and appreciate it. Now warm me up." She crawled on his lap and snuggled into him.

"Cut that out," he told her, snuggling back. "That tickles."

Valerie bought candy anyway in the hope of a few trick-or-treaters. The candy she purchased was something she didn't like, in case there was a lot left over. She didn't want to binge on what they didn't give out. Greg liked what she got to hand out, he could eat the leftovers.

Halloween came. She had a few errands to run and didn't arrive before dark. She pulled into her driveway, and Greg lit the pumpkins so she could enjoy them when she got home. The three lit faces greeted her as she got home. That made her smile. Greg did a good job carving; the faces were generic but well done. She noticed the last one had gone out, so she needed to re-light it.

"Greg," she called out. "I'm home." He came into the kitchen.

"Hi, babe." He smiled. "So, what do you think? Did it come close to your vision?"

"It's perfect!" She put her bag on the counter, went into his arms, and kissed him. "That's exactly what I wanted. The last one went out, though."

"Yeah. I couldn't find where you keep those fake candles," he said, referring to her flameless tea lights.

"I'll get it," she replied. "They're in here." She pulled open a drawer.

"Can you do it?" he asked her. "You still have your coat on."

"Sure," she said and went outside. She took the top off the dark pumpkin. She clicked the light on and stuck her hand in to place the light, but her fingers touched an object. She figured he left the old one in there. She removed it and replaced it with a working one. She looked in her hand. It held a small velvet box. She opened it, and her mouth fell open, almost to the floor. It was a ring box containing a diamond ring, so beautiful it even sparkled in the dark. Valerie stood there, stunned.

"Well." Greg stood in the open door. He got up to watch her. "What do you say? Will you marry me?"

She walked over and said yes, and threw her arms around him. "Yes, Yes, YES!" she shouted. She let him go and turned to face the road. "He asked me to marry him, and I said YES!" she yelled into the night.

"Congratulations!" a voice somewhere in the dark shouted back.

He took the box from her hand. "Come inside and let me do this properly." He sat her down on the couch and sat next to her.

"Forgive me if I don't get down on one knee, but I'm not sure I could get back up. Valerie Anne Reynolds, will you do me the honor of marrying me?" She started crying.

She nodded through her tears. "Yes. I would love to be Mrs. Gregory Joseph Wilson."

He took her hand and slid the ring on her finger. "There. We are officially a 'we.' I love you, Valerie. Be mine forever."

She couldn't answer him because she was still crying.

"I'm sorry it's not bigger. I wish I could give you one you could brag about to all your friends, but on my salary, well, that's the best I could do."

"Oh, shut up. It's perfect," she said as she admired the ring on her outstretched hand.

Greg felt something inside flare up. Why didn't Valerie ever want more? She was always so happy with whatever he gave her. He wondered why she didn't want something more out of him, content with some old, washed-up football has-been.

Why is she so willing to settle for me? My injury cost her as much as it did me, only in different ways. Why didn't it hurt her as much as me? She's never cursed fate for sticking her with a useless, damaged man.

Greg felt diminished in her presence. Valerie was growing and evolving as he shrunk and became less than. He wished she'd get mad he wasn't the same guy she fell in love with, but she didn't. Greg felt his injury cost her as much as him, and she should be plenty pissed off, but Valerie just smiled and kept moving forward. Greg felt his injury should hold her back, too. She loved him anyway, and that made him feel like a piece of shit.

Once she regained her composure, she asked him to handle the trick-or-treaters. "I have a few people to call," she told him.

She dialed her mother first. She couldn't wait to share the news.

Her mom picked up the phone after a couple of rings. "Trick or Treat?" her mom answered.

"A treat, Mom, a treat! You won't believe it!" Valerie spoke the words so fast they tumbled out of her mouth.

"Better than dark chocolate?" her mom said.

"Greg! He asked me to marry him! He gave me a ring! He hid it inside a pumpkin!"

"Do you love it?" Mrs. Reynolds asked her.

"It's so beautiful, Mom. He got the right size, too!"

"I knew you would love it. Greg came over and showed us. Your father is such a poop. Greg wanted to be traditional and talk to your father, but your dad had to be a joker and said he you were a smart girl with a good credit rating, and if he ruined either, that's when they would need to talk, but otherwise, you made your own decisions."

"You knew?" Valerie sounded surprised.

"Greg called me to find out your ring size. I saw it when he came to talk to your father."

"How do you know my ring size?"

"Why is that so important right now? Your class ring. I ordered it. Now, you were saying."

She went over the whole proposal, talking so fast it was amazing her mom caught it all.

Greg had ordered a pizza for dinner. She was starving and grabbed a slice and ate it while she called her friends. After she finished her calls, she grabbed another slice. She went into the living room and sat next to Greg, putting her head on his shoulder and her arm through his. He leaned his head on hers.

"Happy?" he asked her.

"Yes. Very," she said with a sigh. "Surprised?"

"Absolutely. Shocked. Overwhelmed. I know we've talked about it before, but whatever made you do this?"

"I thought about Christmas, but everyone does that. Thanksgiving? If I did that, where would I put it? Somebody would probably eat it. I wanted it to be just us, and the way you obsessed over the pumpkins being perfect, I thought Halloween. Why not? I knew you'd go right out there and fix it. You got it fixed, all right, and then some. You'll be fixed right here next to me, for good."

"I can't think of anywhere else I'd rather be."

They decided on a smallish spring wedding. She wore a white calf-length dress with a satin top and a full tulle skirt. Her sister was her maid of honor, Kayla and Emily as bridesmaids. Valerie couldn't help it; she wanted her twin nieces to be flower girls. They looked like angels with a ring of flowers in their hair instead of halos.

Greg's brother Jason was his best man, and Evan and Brandon, friends from high school, were groomsmen. It was a beautiful day, and everyone had a great time. He was taking her to Italy for their honeymoon.

That night, they had a room reserved at the hotel downtown. In the limo afterward, on the way to the hotel, he said, "I've been dying to do this all day," and dove under the layers of tulle. She had her first orgasm as a married woman before they even checked in.

Married life agreed with them. It wasn't that much different than living together. The first few years passed uneventfully. They lived in her flat. She still worked for the same company and had been promoted twice. Greg didn't return to finish school. He switched from button-down suits to jeans and a hard hat and worked as an on-site supervisor.

***

Eight

VAL AND GREG

AFTER THEY HAD BEEN MARRIED a few years, it was time for them to move out of her flat and into a house. Greg was out there, in different locations, and waited for the deal of the century, the worst house in the best neighborhood. He found one, a home where the older man had lived there for over sixty years.

His worsening health required him to relocate to an assisted living facility. His kids from out of town decided to sell the house.

Greg was working at a job site a few houses away. The eldest son approached Greg; he wanted an idea of what they needed to fix to put it on the market. Greg said there were a number of things necessary to bring it up to code. Since they were preparing to sell, Greg offered to buy it as is. His father gave him the money to make it a quick and clean cash offer. He had already decided to buy it; he just needed to convince Valerie they could manage a fixer-upper.

Valerie wasn't quite as excited as Greg was about the property, even when the electrical and other improvements were made to bring it up to code. He told her when it was done, if she hated it, they could flip it and use the profit to get her the house of her dreams. Greg kept talking about how it had "good bones."

Valerie could see it, three bedrooms downstairs, two full baths, one bedroom upstairs with its own bathroom. A larger kitchen, and if they knocked down a few walls, it would be a great open living/dining room. A finished but dated basement. What used to be known as a rec room now to be made into a man cave. Valerie gave him the okay. He was so excited and had such fine plans for the place, she didn't want to be a buzzkill. Greg was in the industry, and she trusted his judgment, so they bought the place. She said after they painted the inside, brought everything up to code, and had adequate water pressure, she'd move in.

Greg figured about two months of working weekends would be enough time to get the place ready.

They gave two months' notice to the landlord and started preparing to move. Val did most of the packing while Greg worked on the house. She did stop in once in a while and check his progress. He was smart to paint it first; it was kind of like an old lady in a new dress, but it made it more visually appealing.

Moving day came, and Greg had a crew together that finished in no time. Valerie felt sad about leaving the flat, it was the place of so many firsts for her, but the house would give her the opportunity for more firsts.

She did a thorough walkthrough once Greg and the movers left. He was right. It was a house of endless possibilities, and possibilities cost money. But Greg said he would invest in sweat equity. They could upgrade anything because he could do the work.

She wondered if he honestly could do the work after working all week. Won't he be too tired to spend time with me? Or am I going to spend all weekend fetching wrenches and screwdrivers? I should be grateful he wants to create a home for us.

The first thing he did was gut the kitchen. She moved the coffee maker and her old dorm-room-sized fridge and put them in the dining room. She lived for a while like this. She heard Greg and the workers working on weekends. They'd have a few beers while they worked. She permitted him to do whatever he thought would bring the most value to the place. She really just wanted functionality. She was by no means a "foodie"; she just wanted it quick cook to clean up. The Subzero refrigerator she thought was a bit much, but he assured her it was for the best.

"Kitchens sell houses, babe. Trust me," he said, so she did.

It was a rare Sunday morning when she let Greg sleep in. She got up ahead of him and made herself a cup of coffee. She only drank half a cup, and it tasted strangely like metal. It tasted so bad she threw it up in the bathroom sink. She opened the medicine cabinet to grab her toothbrush when she noticed on the top shelf a box she had purchased a while ago when her period was late, but she got her period before she needed the test. She opened the box, read the directions, and peed on the stick. She waited the allotted time and looked at the result. She went into the bedroom and sat on the bed, and woke Greg up. "Hey, shove over," she said, crawling in next to him.

"What? What?" he mumbled. "What's wrong?"

"Define what you mean by wrong, Dad." She passed him the positive pregnancy test.

He looked at the stick and suddenly woke up. Greg had a big, stupid smile on his face. "Hey. Is this real?"

"No. It's fake. I found it in a cereal box. Of course, it's real. Now hush. I feel nauseous." Valerie pulled the blankets around her and closed her eyes.

Valerie was shocked; she had been on birth control, but she wasn't necessarily unhappy. She figured she'd have a baby sooner or later, so this answered that. Everyone was excited for them: a new baby, a new house, a new family.

The first trimester wasn't as bad as everyone said it was. She had bouts of nausea and vomiting, but nothing too distressing. Greg was very conscientious of Valerie. If she needed him or anything, he came running. The only thing she wanted was for the kitchen to be finished by the time the baby came. There was progress, but not enough to see the end. She was afraid of the baby being too big a distraction once it came. Val needed to express her concern to her husband.

"Look, Greg, I understand you want the kitchen to be the focal point of this house, and I agree. We need to outline the project and make sure we have certain things done on time, or I'm afraid if there's no end in sight, I might have to move home with my mom. The baby can't breathe in construction dust."

That got Greg's attention. "Move out? No way. I'll see if the guys can do a couple of hours after work. I see your point. That wouldn't be healthy for a newborn. I'll increase the work hours. We'll do some overtime and get back on track."

When Valerie got home from work, there were two men in the kitchen, but no Greg. She decided to take a nap while she waited for Greg. Growing a baby is hard work, Val thought. I've never been so tired in my whole life. She could even sleep through the pounding and hammering going on in the kitchen. Greg woke her an hour later.

"Hey there, little momma," he said as he kissed her. "Are you hungry? I've got the guys staying until seven. Do you want something now, or do you want to wait until they leave? I can pick up something then."

"I'm afraid I'll be up all night if I eat too late. I'll just take some crackers and ginger ale," Val said.

"Coming right up. We are really starting to make some headway now," he said, referring to the kitchen.

Greg had arranged to have dinner ready for her when she got home. He knew to avoid red sauces; they upset her stomach. Too much cheese disagreed with her. He had plenty of salads with grilled chicken or steak ready for her when she walked in the door from work.

The odd thing she craved was sausage. All the pizzas had to have sausage on them. If he cooked breakfast, she'd have toast and sausage. As she entered the second trimester, she started feeling better. Right about then, she started to show, happy to have a belly to compensate for her humongous boobs.

Greg was fascinated by her changing body. He was in awe of her breasts. They were very tender and huge. He touched them gently, almost reverently. When her belly started to show, he became enthralled with the smoothness of her skin. He could rub his hand over it for hours. The first time the baby kicked, his hand was touching her.

"What was that? Was that the baby?" he asked, excited. "Did you feel that? I think it just kicked."

"Baby," Greg spoke to her stomach, "do it again." As if in response, the baby kicked. "He did it! The baby kicked!"

"He?" Valerie questioned him. "How about her?"

"As long as we name it Greg, I don't care what it is!"

"We'll have to table this discussion for a later date. I'm not sure I'm down with a junior. Deuce, maybe, but not junior. But that's slang for taking a dump. Number Two? The same thing," she said.

He kissed her belly and got up. "Duty calls. I've got to go to work."

"See? Right there. 'Duty.' Doodie. Poop."

"You're crazy. I'll see you later."

Later in the pregnancy, she was more active. The kitchen was on schedule. She gathered up some trash and brought it to the can in the garage, passing by a rather large collection of empty beer bottles and cans that were in the way. Man, they drink a lot of beer, she thought and kicked a path to the garbage can.

They had everything finished before the due date. Greg painted the bedroom a pretty yellow. They chose not to know the sex in advance. It was killing everybody around them, not knowing. "Surprise me," she said to her obstetrician.

Since most of the work in the kitchen was completed, Greg demoed the bathroom. He said it would be good to get that out of the way before the baby came to keep the noise down. Valerie didn't care about any construction; she was in the last trimester, and her only concern was her due date. She was so big she wouldn't be surprised if she gave birth to a Saint Bernard.

Greg went with her to the doctor. He rubbed coconut butter on Valerie's mountain of a belly whenever she asked. She read it helped with stretch marks. Her due date was one week away, and the doctor told her she was seeing changes that meant any day now. Valerie was in a bad mood after the visit.

"I can't take this anymore," she grumbled.

"What? Did you expect to walk out of there with the baby?" Greg teased.

"Well, it would have been nice. I'm getting sick of being pregnant."

"It will be here before you know it, and then shit's going to get real."

She didn't make the next appointment; the next time she saw the doctor, it was at the hospital. Valerie woke up around five a.m. Sunday morning felt odd. She couldn't eat anything, and there was pressure down low. She went into the bathroom. She thought she needed to take a massive dump. She didn't, but she felt her abdomen suddenly turn rock hard, and the plop into the toilet was not poop. It was the mucous plug. She went to tell Greg.

"Something's going on," she told him. She took his hand and placed it on her belly. "Feel this."

"I don't feel anything."

"Just wait," she said and held his hand in place. A few seconds later, he felt her uterus suddenly grow hard as a cinder block.

"Whoa. What's that? Is that a contraction?"

"Beats me. Check your watch. Start timing to see the time between. If it's regular, it's probably early labor."

"How do you feel? Do you feel like you're in labor?"

"I can't say. I just know it feels weird." She stood up. "Oof. I'm getting so big I can barely stand up."

He looked up at her. "When are you supposed to call the doctor?"

She felt her belly go hard again and fluid run down her leg. They both looked at it. "Probably now. What time was that last one? Seven minutes? I'll go call now."

He jumped out of bed. "I'd better take a shower. I don't want to go to the hospital all greasy." He headed off to the bathroom. He was toweling off his hair when he came back into the bedroom and noticed Valerie standing there.

"Time to go?" he asked.

"Yeah, no hurry, though. It's a first baby, so it's probably going to take a while, but since my water broke, she wants me to go."

"We can do that. Let me get dressed and grab the bag, and we'll be off."

Things did not go as planned. As soon as they got to the Birthing Center, the baby kicked things into high gear. She was already at five centimeters, and the contractions were coming hard and fast.

Valerie, who never said much about childbirth beforehand, surprised Greg when she panicked.

"Greg," she said between contractions, "I thought I could do this, but I was wrong. I can't. I can't." She stopped talking as another contraction wracked her body. Greg spoke to her after it eased.

"Val, you can. Just focus on me. We'll do the breathing together." He looked at the monitor and said, "Okay, Val. It's gonna start. Look at me. Now breathe. You're doing great, Val, breathe. Don't lose it now. Breathe. Okay, there you go. We just keep doing it like that."

They labored on like that until it was time to push. Valerie caught a second wind. She was going to push this baby out, whether she was ready for it or not. She pushed so hard she was surprised it didn't come flying out of her and hit the wall on the other side of the room.

Greg was in awe of her determination. He watched her turn inward and channel everything she had to get this baby out. Anybody else would have collapsed under the weight of the task at hand, but Valerie seemed to grow stronger. Greg watched until the baby was crowned. At that point, he turned back to help Valerie. Another push later, the doctor had Greg push Valerie forward.

"Now, Valerie, I want you to push as hard as you can. You're almost done."

"What? Are you telling me I haven't been pushing hard enough? I'm going to push my tonsils out if I push any harder. Ow, ow, OW! Here comes another one."

"This is it, Val. Bear down as hard as you can. Now PUSH! That's it! PUSH! PUSH! Atta girl!"

He cut the umbilical cord, and they placed the baby on her bare breast. Val started to cry, because they did it. They were a family. Welcome to Earth, Baby Girl

Wilson, she thought. They took the baby away, cleaned her up, and returned her all cleaned up and swaddled.

"Look! Greg! She's just like a football."

He cradled the baby in the crook of his arm. He had tears in his eyes as well. "You did it, Val!"

"No, Greg. We did it."

She was born with a full head of curly white hair, just like Greg's. They named her Astrid, after his Swedish grandmother.

They were done by dinnertime, and she was starving. She wanted to eat and then pass out; she was that tired. Baby Girl Wilson had other plans, so she spent the night in a semi-delusional state with her milk yet to come in, trying to satisfy her hunger with colostrum, and the baby just wasn't having it. Then it came in, and that's all she did. Her company generously gave her three months' leave, all of which she nursed and stopped when she returned to work. She was so glad not to nurse anymore. She didn't tell anybody, but finally reclaimed the last sense of herself, her body. Only her body didn't look the same. Would it ever?

The baby was the blondest baby she ever saw. She looked so much like Greg and his side; this white-haired child looked like if she floated by on a chunk of ice with a polar bear, she wouldn't be out of place.

She had her father enchanted by her very existence. After witnessing the act of childbirth, Greg feared Valerie for the longest time. If the female body can produce a living, breathing human, it is capable of anything. His wife and his daughter were his whole world.

Valerie's company loved her, and she was so valuable to them that they made any accommodation she needed. Since she left after Greg, it was her job to get the baby to the sitter, her mother. His mother was kind enough to watch Astrid. She was willing to watch her as a baby, but other arrangements were needed once the baby started walking; her mom's bad back made caring for a toddler impossible. Fair enough, Valerie thought. Greg would pick her up, and they would meet at home.

It didn't hurt that she was such a good baby. She liked to watch. If you were cooking, put her in her car seat on the counter and she quietly observed, and when you looked at her, she gave a wide, toothless smile in acknowledgment. If you folded clothes, she was fascinated.

Her mother had a little mutt named Chica, who amused Astrid for hours. If Astrid threw something on the floor, and the little dog would pick it up and drop it in her car seat or as close to her as she could. She took a nap in the morning and in the afternoon. Greg picked her up and met Valerie at home. He was supposed to get dinner started, but usually, he was busy with the baby and never did.

She walked in through the kitchen door like any other workday. She put her tote of work she brought home every night but never looked at on a chair, hung up her coat and called out, "Hello? Anybody home?"

"Shh. She's sleeping. Come on. Let's do it while she's asleep," Greg said as he slid into the room in just a t-shirt and his socks. He grabbed her and kissed her breathlessly. "But—" she started.

"No. Now," he said, his lips up against hers, "don't you miss me?" He walked her backward into the bedroom. "I miss you. So much. Come on, Val. Let's!"

He unbuttoned her shirt and undid her pants. He pushed her on the bed. "I want you, Val. I need you."

"But I'm not—" she tried to say, but it felt good to be the object of his affection. He touched her like he used to, with reverence and awe.

Greg said, "The baby doesn't need you as much as I do."

Valerie came alive and said, "Oh, Greg, I've missed you, too." Instead of arms, she had tentacles; she reached around him and touched him everywhere. Greg responded with equal enthusiasm. It meant they reconnected back at the spot that temporarily pulled them apart.

They even had fifteen minutes of post-all-alone-in-your-arms time before they heard Astrid. She was awake and talking, what about was yet to be determined. They got dressed. "I'll grab her, you order the pizza." He told her and went towards the baby's room.

Something nagged at Valerie weeks after she and Greg had their romantic interlude. Nothing had changed between them, that wasn't it. It was nice to know when they were able to get back those moments. They were still the same two people. Parenthood may have changed them as a family, but it hadn't changed them as a couple. At least, that's what she told herself. The thing that nagged at her was the fact she hadn't started taking her birth control pills, and her theory about them as a couple would be tested soon.

"Greg. We have to talk. I have some news," she said on Saturday morning while they enjoyed coffee.

"From the tone of your voice, I can tell it's not that we won the lottery."

"Depends on your point of view," she said. "I'm pregnant."

✱✱✱

Nine

GREG AND VAL

GREG LOOKED AT HER, stunned. "What? How did that happen?"

"You know, you were there." Her voice was starting to waver, trying to hold onto her optimism and not dissolve in tears. "Greg, I'm scared. How do we do this? Astrid's just six months old. The baby will come, and they'll be less than two years apart. Less than a year and a half apart. That's too close, isn't it?"

Greg reached for her hand. "Baby, it's too late to worry about it now. It may be rough, but at least it will be over with, and they'll be close in age," he told her, and then to himself, "I have to finish that bathroom."

"Yes, you do. There's no reason it's not done. You started it months ago. And the kitchen. Finish that, too. You still need to finish that."

The kitchen was, for the most part, finished; it was usable. It lacked the finishing touches like trim, outlet covers, and paint. Greg was a big-picture kind of guy. He had a grand vision for a project. However, he had some trouble with the execution. He would pull guys to start on something new when there was still work to be done on the existing project.

"I don't know, Greg. Maybe I should quit my job."

"Don't be in such a hurry," Greg said, alarmed. Having the success or failure of his family rest solely on his shoulders scared him. All the responsibility. He was filled with doubt. "We have nine months to figure it out."

Greg was on edge all the time. He was so lucky Valerie wanted to go back to work. What would they do without her income? Greg didn't know how he could manage two kids. Valerie's boss was so afraid she'd quit, he gave her six months of nanny service.

Valerie sailed through her second pregnancy. All the strange things her body did with Astrid didn't faze her. She certainly didn't have time to obsess over every little thing; she was a woman on a mission. Two days before her due date, they added another girl to their family. Another white-haired, blue-eyed girl with a hint of a cleft in her chin. She looked like Astrid, who looked just like Greg and Greg's mom. She needed a name, a Swedish name to match. All Mrs. Wilson remembered was Astrid had a sister named Ingrid.

"Done. Ingrid Reynolds Wilson," Valerie chose.

"We can do a little more research, find another name," his mother offered. "Ingrid? For a little girl? Are you sure, Valerie?"

"Too late. Ingrid, it is."

Greg could not believe he had these two white-haired little girls as his daughters. People commented on them wherever they went. People confused them as twins despite the size difference. Astrid grew up as quite a charmer, and Ingrid did whatever her sister did, so they were two charming little girls. When Greg looked at them, he sometimes was struck with the immense responsibility of it all. How would he protect them and keep them from harm? When he expressed his doubts to Valerie, she laughed.

"You're a great dad, Greg. They light up when they see you. You don't have to do anything but love them. Just make sure you pay close attention to them. They're going to grow and change, and if you're not looking, you'll miss it."

"You think I won't pay attention?"

"What are you talking about? Who cares what I think? I'm saying it as much to myself as you. I need to pay attention. I don't want to miss anything either because time passes so quickly. That's all I mean. Was it John Lennon who said, 'Life happens while you're busy making plans'?"

Valerie's work never hassled her. She set her own schedule. As long as she hit their projections, she came and went as she pleased. The girls were in the afternoon preschool. She worked from home in the mornings. Her parents came around eleven, got them lunch, and dropped them off. Greg picked them up at four-thirty, and she tried to be home by six. She picked up a couple of West Coast clients to give her something to do after five. If she needed to come in later, she needed to work later. She gave herself the afternoon off and went home after the dentist. When she pulled in, she thought it odd Greg's truck was home. She pulled in and went inside.

"Greg, hon, you home? You feeling okay?" she called out. She found him at the kitchen table, having a beer.

"Hi. How come you're home?" she asked, glancing at the beer.

"I could say the same to you. Why are you home?"

"I went to the dentist and came home to get something to eat. Want a sandwich? I'm going to make myself one."

"No," he said. She made a sandwich and sat down.

"Come on, Greg. Let's talk it out."

"Talk what out?"

"You. You have these episodes of anger. Harshness. Depression. What's got you so down?" She reached for his hand. He pulled it back. "This hostility, Greg, where's it coming from? How can I help?"

"Well, it's nice of you to notice. Me, I mean. You haven't paid much attention to me lately," he pouted.

"Is that it? Really? It's hard right now, with the kids and a job and everything else. I'm sorry if I've been ignoring you. Speak up and say, 'My turn now.'"

"I shouldn't have to. I'm not going to beg my wife to pay attention to me."

She stood up and took his hand. "I think I know what you need. We have all afternoon without interruption. Would you like to get naked and roll around in bed? Because I miss you, too."

He smiled at her, and she saw in his eyes the old Greg. "That's exactly what I need."

"Come on. You have to gargle, though. It's too early for stale beer." It was one of those afternoons that saved a marriage. Greg got her sole undivided attention at the crossroads in a marriage where people choose. Life got pretty demanding. He could have decided to go somewhere else where the encounter was a new, illicit, unfamiliar rush, or he could have stayed here and wrapped himself in the warmth and security of his wife. This time, he chose his wife.

Somewhere deep down, he knew his wife would always choose him. He felt she deserved much better than he offered. Greg felt terribly guilty that he wasn't that guy she fell in love with, that he hadn't fulfilled his promise to her. He was as far away from his injury as he would ever be, but he was left damaged. He couldn't help but damage those around him. At least, in her arms, he felt like his old self. He didn't have to be anything other than what his heart told him. He didn't have to be a boss, employee, dad, son, or a used-up, has-been football star. He just had to be Greg, the man she loved.

Valerie wanted him. She felt her own loss of sense of self. All the labels hung on her, too. Wife. Mother. Star employee. She felt a lot of pressure. When they had kids, they never talked about her staying home with them. It was always assumed she would continue to work, bring in money, and carry the benefits. If she didn't have such an accommodating employer, things might have worked out differently. As it was, she parceled out chunks of herself for each role she needed to play. There wasn't much left at the end of the day. She needed to save more for Greg. Valerie needed to save more for them. They were growing away from each other, and it was one more thing she took on her shoulders because she didn't think Greg would notice until it was too late.

There was a certain fury to their lovemaking that afternoon. Usually, it was one more thing on the to-do list. She came to Greg with a passion he hadn't seen since before the kids were born. Valerie came at him from all angles. She approached him like she wanted to devour him and leave nothing but his bones in their bed. Greg remembered this side of her; it both scared and excited him. He decided he was going to give as good as he got. If Valerie wanted to take him down, he'd gladly go, but she was going down with him.

When they were finished, their sweat and the smell of sex were all that was left. Greg grabbed her and held her naked body against his so tightly it was like he wanted to fuse her to him. He wanted to eliminate any space where things that didn't belong could get a foothold and wedge them apart.

"Feeling better, Greg?"

"I've never felt better, Valerie. I thought that part of our lives was long gone, but I guess there's still some gas left in the tank."

"Do you mind telling me what was wrong earlier? If you don't because it'll ruin the mood, that's okay. I just worry about you. If it's something about me, tell me. I'll try not to do it."

"Valerie, it's not you. I start feeling down, and I can't stop it. The hole gets a little deeper each time and a little harder to climb out of. I'm just not where I thought I'd be at this point in my life. I thought there'd be more. I'd be more. I look at you, and I'm awed by all you've done and all you keep doing. I feel like a piece of shit. Then I'm mean to you, I don't know, to take you down so I don't feel so low. I feel terrible about that; you should be celebrated and get breakfast in bed every day instead of being bitched at because we ran out of paper towels. You deserve the very best, and I'm not the guy who can give it to you."

"I know this side of you, and I know now's not the time to get into it. I want to ask you one thing: when you sit on the couch, and you have those two little girls climbing all over you, arguing over which one loves you more, that's not enough. That's love in its purest form. Everything you want or need to be happy is right here, and that's not enough. That makes me sad, Greg. To admit I'm not enough, the girls aren't enough? I don't know what else there is," Valerie said with a catch in her voice.

He held her tighter. "Don't let me go. Please. I know I can be moody, but it's not you. I adore you. I love our family. You guys are enough. You're more than I deserve. I feel like I haven't earned it, and I don't know what to do about it. I'll figure it out."

Valerie decided that the conversation needed to stop, or they'd be at the edge of the well soon. "The girls are wrong. I love you most," she said and snuggled deeper in his arms.

***

Ten

VAL AND GREG

THEY SPENT the rest of the afternoon in bed, not talking. Greg was relaxed and happy, and Valerie didn't want to ruin his mood. It felt like it used to when they were young and consumed with each other. The afternoon passed way too quickly. Greg went to pick up the girls, and she started dinner. He was on his way out the door when he turned back and walked over to her. He grabbed her and kissed her like he did earlier that afternoon.

"I love you, always. You bring out the best in me."

Life continued the way it always had. Everybody knew their roles and played them as best they could. Valerie started to notice a disturbing pattern. Yes, Greg always had a beer when he got home from work and one with dinner. When Valerie got home, more often than not, there were already two empties, and Greg had one in his hand. Plus one with dinner. Four beers seemed excessive on weeknights to her.

Every once in a while, he'd get trashed, like once a year, with his old buddies. She let him sleep it off in the car. She parked the car in the garage with the door down and left the door to the house open, so the only place he could go would be the door open to the kitchen. He'd make it as far as the bathroom and then the couch. All his high school friends seemed to be big boozers; there were a couple of rehab graduates trying to tie life together with gum and black coffee.

But this increase in bottles per day was a lot over a week, Valerie thought. She wondered what he thought. She sorted the recyclables, so her discovery of them wasn't odd. She was out there when he came home, and she brought the bottles to his attention. He walked over and said, "Hey, babe, need any help?"

"I was sorting the bottles, and there were a lot of beer bottles. Did you realize you drank that much? During the week?"

"No. That much? Really? That can't be good for me."

"Can you take a look at it? You might want to cut back. All those calories."

Yeah, he thought. That is a lot of calories.

You have to know what would motivate the customer, she thought. If I came right out and said, "I think you drink too much," a huge fight would follow.

Greg was unhappy at work. He started in the office and was sent out to work with crews on on-site projects. He was supposed to act in a supervisory capacity, facilitating the crews' needs to get the job finished on time. It was supposed to give him exposure and management skills, but he felt like a glorified flunky.

He didn't want to go back to the office and wear a suit and tie. He felt qualified to give estimates and proposals, to bid on jobs, but his dad said he needed more time in the field. Being with the crews was fun, but he wasn't sure he had any more to learn out there. He liked the guys; the camaraderie reminded him of his football days.

It was a reminder of when he was whole and his options were limitless. That would mark the onset of his descent into a continuous loop of depression and self-doubt; the only thing that blunted his feelings was a couple of beers. Valerie might have thought he drank too much, but he didn't think so. He only drank to take the edge off.

She overreacted like usual. Like the time she commented about the number of empty beer bottles in the recycling bin. There were so many they overflowed the bin into a large garbage bag, so judging from the sheer amount, Val had a point. Greg justified it by telling himself it was more like a month, not a week. The voice in his head asked him if he didn't have a problem, why did he hide the empties in his truck before Valerie came home? He ignored the answer.

During this time, something happened that took Greg off the front page and focused her attention elsewhere. Valerie got a phone call in the middle of the night from Mr. Dempsey, her mother's next-door neighbor. An ambulance had just left her parents' house. Her dad was on the stretcher. He was smart enough to ask the driver which hospital, so Valerie didn't have to call around to find him; he went to Johnson Valley Memorial. She woke Greg.

"Greg, it's my dad. He's in the hospital. I need to go. Now."

"What happened, Val?"

"I don't know anything more than an ambulance took him to Valley. I have to go."

"Let me come with you. You shouldn't be alone."

"No. You have to stay with the kids. I'll call you once I know more."

She grabbed a coat and her keys and opened the garage door. She noticed Greg's truck blocked her car in the garage. "Fuck." She ran back inside to grab his keys and ran right into Greg; he followed her into the kitchen. "I need your keys." He grabbed them, and she took them out of his hands.

"Here. Let me move the truck," he said.

"No. I'm dressed. I'll just move it and leave the keys in it," she replied, already halfway out the door.

Valerie jumped in his truck and started it. She wasn't used to it, and when she parked it, she came down hard on the brakes. She heard a clinking noise from the passenger side floor. Valerie looked down and noticed a couple of beer bottles rolled out from a garbage bag full of empties. She knew she should think about the significance of it, but her mind was on her parents and getting to them as quickly as possible. Valerie left the keys in the ignition and got in her car. She took off and got to the ER in record time. She ran to the desk, and the clerk called a nurse over to bring Valerie to her mother.

Her mom was seated behind a curtain next to an empty gurney.

Her eyes were wet, and a pile of used tissues was on the bed. The nurse brought her and left. Val sat down next to her mother and grabbed her in a hug.

"Momma! It's me! Where's Daddy?" Her mother looked blankly at her. If Valerie had to guess, her mother was in shock. "Mom! Mom!" she said and shook her mother. Her mom snapped out of it. She clung to Valerie.

"Val. Your father. He had a heart attack." Her mother started to sob. "He died right in front of me. He was looking in the refrigerator, complaining we never had anything to eat in the house, and he just collapsed and died. Daddy died, Valerie. He died." Her mother leaned into Valerie and sobbed.

"Are you sure?" Valerie asked. "He's not here. Maybe they took him to surgery. Who did you talk to? How do you know for sure?" Her mother just sobbed in response.

Valerie hit the call button repeatedly. She wanted to talk to somebody, but didn't want to leave her mom. She hit that button again and again until somebody came. A different nurse entered the space. Since it was Valerie's job to read people for a living, she knew this young girl was probably a student and had yet to develop the skills needed to counsel a family at times like these.

"Yes?" she said hesitantly. "Can I help you?"

"Yes, please," Valerie said kindly. She didn't want to rage on this poor girl, who really should be shadowing someone senior at this moment. "My dad. He came in by ambulance, and I needed to talk to his doctor. Please."

"Oh yes," the girl said, relieved that someone higher up the food chain needed to talk to the family. "I'll have him paged and come talk with you." She left and returned a bit later.

"I just heard from the doctor. He's up in the ICU and will be down to talk to you when he's finished up there."

"Thank you," Valerie told her as she hurried away.

Valerie waited impatiently with her mother for the doctor. She could feel herself getting agitated as time went on. Valerie was tempted to lay on that call button until he came, but knew it would just aggravate the people at the front desk, who had no more pull than she did getting the doctor to hurry up.

A young man finally came in. His name was Ryan, but all other info was hidden. He had conveniently tucked the rest of his ID badge in the pocket of his scrubs... He said he was very sorry your father/spouse died, and yes, he would be happy to answer any questions. He looked so, so earnest. He had his elbows on his knees, and he leaned so far into them but never moved his seat. Valerie worried he would run out of the chair and end up on the floor, but that didn't happen.

He said, "Mr. Reynolds, from the initial findings, suffered from a ruptured aorta. It was swift, and he was probably dead by the time he hit the floor."

"So that's it? Goodbye, Dad, behave yourself in the afterlife?"

"Yes, ma'am. Pretty much."

"I can't believe it," Valerie said. "Go check again."

"Sorry, ma'am, but we are sure."

"So, what are we supposed to do now?" Valerie asked.

"Follow through on any final requests he may have decided and guess the rest. If it was important to him, he should have written it down. It would help if you made those decisions now. Again, I'm very sorry for your loss." He stood up from his squat with unnatural ease. They watched him leave. Her mother still looked shell-shocked. Valerie followed him out.

"Hey, Doctor. Look at my mother. When she finally comes around, I need a few Valium for a couple of days, at least until my siblings arrive. It happened right in front of her," Val said.

"This should be a matter for her family doctor."

"It's until she gets in to see him. Maybe she won't even use it. It's only to have in exchange for her cooperation. I also have two little ones at home, and if you don't help me manage her, I'm going to be the one coming in here looking to score." She left with a prescription for three days' worth of anti-anxiety meds and her word that she would stay out of his ER.

Valerie called her sister, Rachael, for help. She ran the show. Her brother and his family came. The services were private, but they hosted a luncheon afterward. Greg's mom helped with the girls. They got through it somehow. Greg was a huge support for her. The spontaneous nature of it all had her family reeling. The motion allowed them to avoid grief. Valerie knew once the commotion died down, there would be a dark void where he used to be, and the idea that he wasn't anywhere struck her as odd. Her mom still came down to the kitchen in the morning, expecting to see him at the table having coffee.

She asked her mom to come stay, but her mother passed. She wanted to remain independent. She went south for the winter with her lady friends, many of them solo from losing partners, so not having a date for anything wasn't a big deal.

The kids went to full-time preschool and occasionally would need to be picked up at an odd time; Greg's parents helped out. Valerie's work gave her an extended leave, but she went back early. She leaned on Greg quite a bit, which he was happy about, to be there with a purpose.

It was another day of trash. After her father passed, there was a steady stream of people in and out, and they brought stuff. Food, mostly. There was so much garbage. Valerie decided to tackle it, and Greg came out to help.

"Please. When I go, I want none of this shit. Let me rest in peace."

"Deal," he agreed. They worked next to each other for a bit, consolidating the garbage when Valerie pulled a garbage bag full of empty beer bottles out from the pile.

"Oh. Good. I wanted to ask you about this bag of beer bottles in the front seat of your truck. Where did you get all those?" Valerie asked Greg directly.

"Bottles? What bottles? When were you in my truck?" His guard went up.

"When I had to move your truck. I needed to get my car out to go to the hospital."

"Oh, those. It came from a house we were working on. Another crew left them. Painters, I think. We always clean the job site before we go."

"I was curious, is all. I was worried about how many beers you were drinking. I wanted to catch you before you started feeling that was the best way to cope. My dad dying really threw us all for a loop. I get concerned when I see little problems, I could fix it before they get too big."

"No, Miss Valerie, your excellent skills in the problem-solving area are not required for this project."

"We could do this," he said, pointing to the bottles, "or we can do that." Pointing at the house.

"I feel really gross handling this shit. You want to take a shower and wash my back?"

"Oh, yes," he said, stumbling over the bags in his hurry.

They raced into the house, shedding clothes as they went. Greg got the water running, and they stepped in. He offered to wash her hair, and Val gave herself over to him. He lathered her up and took great care to make sure everything was covered. Greg rinsed her clean and had his leg between hers. He began kissing her like they didn't need to leave the room, and she responded. He picked her up and held her against the wall. She opened herself to him, and he entered her slowly. "Oh, Valerie," he mumbled near her ear.

"Oh, Greg," she said louder. "Give it to me. Give it to me good." Greg was as strong as ever; he could hold her up with one hand, raising her hips to match his and using his other hand to keep the water and her hair out of her face. Val closed her eyes and let the sensory overload roll over her. The warmth of the water, Greg's strong, solid back under her hands, the sensations piling on top of each other until there was nowhere else for them to go except to spill over onto Greg, which delighted him to no end. When he came, he tried to impale Valerie to the tiled shower wall with his orgasm. She wrapped her legs around him and tried to help get him as deep as he wanted to go. Valerie pulled him inside her and held him there. She laughed deep in her throat, and he laughed in answer, his deep in his throat as well.

Greg turned the water off and helped her into some dry towels.

After he took care of her body, he dried her hair using the blow dryer. She didn't have to open her eyes for half an hour. Val leaned into his hip and had her arms around him. After he finished, she felt warmth and security replace the nameless anxiety that had been plaguing her.

"There you go," he said. "The horny housewife has been satisfied."

"And then some," she answered. It felt so good when she sat on the toilet seat lid while he dried her hair. She hugged him around the middle and leaned into his bulk. He was so solid and strong it was easy to fall into him and let go of it all. She decided now was not the time to bring up the layer of fat around his stomach that one might perceive as a beer gut.

Greg had always prided himself on his physique. He used to spend hours in the gym. Maybe she should ask about him getting back into it, hiring a trainer, and working around his knee. She thought he might be drinking beer as a substitute for working out. Not going to the gym left him with a lot of free time, and the easiest way to fill it up was with a six-pack.

They dressed and sat next to each other on the couch and watched TV. His parents took the girls to the zoo for the afternoon. While they waited, they snuggled and talked about things and made stupid inside jokes, only the other understood. Valerie felt secure in her relationship with her husband. After all this time, they still had moments that brought them back to each other the way they used to be before adulthood exerted the invisible forces that required them to grow up.

The door opened, and the house was filled with the excited clamor of two little girls squealing and making animal noises. They ran in and climbed on their dad, pretty much ignoring Valerie. Greg would grab one and toss her on Valerie's lap, and she'd yell, "Daddy!" and climb over Valerie to get back to Greg. Valerie took a deep breath and felt hot tears prick her eyelashes. The thought, why isn't this enough? Shouldn't it be enough? Ran through her head. There was a pull on her heart as she considered the answer.

Ellin and Dave, Greg's parents, entered, laughing at the two little white-haired girls. They were getting older. Astrid would be five on her next birthday, and Ingrid, four. Soon, they'd start elementary school.

"Well, isn't that a happy family," his mom said. "I hope you don't mind, but we fed them dinner. The zoo made them very hungry; they even had room for ice cream."

"Ice cream?" Greg asked. "Did you bring any home for Daddy?"

"No, Daddy, No!" they screamed. Greg stood, and the girls tumbled to the floor; they giggled and laughed on their way down. He made his way to the fridge, offering everyone something to drink. He was the only taker and grabbed a beer. Greg proceeded to consume four more the rest of the day. Valerie couldn't help but keep count.

She could see it was going to be a significant issue for them, her keeping track of his consumption and him resenting her for it. Valerie decided to bring it up after the girls went down for the night. Being tired from the zoo meant they were too tired to argue about bath time or bed. Once they were in bed, the quiet returned to the house. Valerie knew if she said something, she would ruin the peace, but she couldn't love him and allow him to self-destruct.

They were in bed. He was watching TV, and she was reading a book. There was still some afterglow left from their earlier time in the shower. She put her book down. "Greg, I need to talk to you. I'm only saying something out of fear. I'm afraid. I fear the impact of your drinking and what it's going to do to you. Our family. Us."

He imperceptibly moved away from her. "What? Do you have something to say? Just say it."

"Okay, I'll just say it. I think you drink too much."

"Beer? What's the big deal about me having a few?"

"It's not a few. You had five today. You can't tell me it doesn't affect you."

"Oh, so now you keep track? Thanks a lot for the vote of confidence. You've had a bug up your ass about this for a while now. I shouldn't be surprised at your lack of support."

"That's not fair, and you know it. I know you hide the empties from me. You wouldn't do that if you felt it was no big deal. It's not about any of that. I'm worried about you: your health, your relationship with the kids, your relationship with me. You self-medicate with beer. You need to figure out why you need to put something between us. It's not fair. I love you. All of you, so fuck me for caring. I want you to be fully present when you're here. How do you think I feel? You used to come home, and the first thing you'd do was kiss me. Now, the first thing you do is grab a beer."

"That's not true."

"It's not?" Valerie challenged.

"I don't want to talk about this. You want me to stop. Fine. I'll stop. End of discussion."

"That's it?"

"That's all you had to do, you know, was ask me."

He did all right the first week. He tried to be pleasant. To illustrate, he was fine. Greg didn't need to drink. He was able to just have two, one when he got home and one with dinner. Valerie didn't want to admit it, but it didn't make him any more pleasant. He was nervous and on edge. Once he had his second, he relaxed.

The girls now were equal in height for the most part; people still thought they were twins. Five and four they were in regular school, pre-kindergarten and took the bus. They were too young to understand the tension that floated over their heads between their parents.

Valerie wanted desperately for things to be okay. She just wanted him not to drink so much. If it was this hard to cut back, he probably would never be able to quit. At least the girls were unaware; they never saw him passed out on the floor or vomit in the bushes.

She came to him early one day and went to the bathroom, sat on the toilet, and cried. Greg stopped at home mid-afternoon and heard her crying. He went into the bathroom and got on his hands and knees. He brought his face next to hers and gently touched her cheek.

"Baby, what's wrong? I know things haven't been great between us, but it'll get better. I'll try harder. Honest. Baby, please don't cry. Please don't cry, Val. I love you."

She grabbed a tissue and blew her nose. He was still leaning into her. "Tell me. What can be so bad?"

"Remember a few weeks ago when we were fooling around in the shower?" He nodded, smiling at the memory.

"And I was talking dirty, and I told you to fuck me?" He nodded, still smiling.

She let out a huge sob. "I'm fucked. I'm fucked all right." She passed the test. "I'm preg…preg…pregnant."

Greg sat back on his heels. How was he ever supposed to get his shit together when she kept doing shit like this? He heard her crying and realized it was probably because he pulled away, and she probably felt him withdraw from her.

Greg reached for her and held her. It didn't sound like she was all that happy about it, either. He stood and grabbed her hand, brought her into their room, and sat her on the bed. He took her coat and shoes off, finished undressing her, and tucked her in. Greg went out and took off his boots and jacket, called his mom and asked her to get the kids from school. He called the school and told them his mom would be getting the girls. Greg went back into the bedroom and got undressed.

"Here," he said. "I haven't showered, so I probably smell, but I think you need me now. Do you want me to jump in quick? Or do you want me to hold you and tell you everything will be okay?"

"I think I want you. I need you. Come here and sweat all over me. Tell me we'll be okay. Tell me we can do it," Val begged.

He pulled her over and enclosed her in the safety of his strong arms. Greg held her tight. He didn't know what to say. He felt their foundation cracking and had no clue if he should lie to her. Val felt so slight like she could be gone, taken away by a strong gust of wind. Greg truly felt awful. He had no answers. He wished he was as strong as she thought he was.

"Val, baby. Remember when we found out about Ingrid? We were scared to death. We had no idea what to do. But we survived and looked at them. Great kids. We may be a little older, but we'll be better at it. Just add one more kid to the mix. We'll be okay."

"But my dad. He helped us with Astrid. How am I supposed to do it without him? He was always there, in the background. I could always count on him answering the phone. And he's gone. I can't ask my mom; she can't do it all by herself. I need you, Greg. You have to be there."

"Baby, you don't have to worry about that. I'll be right next to you. The girls are older. It'll just be one baby. We can do it. I promise. We'll do it together," he whispered in her ear. He sounded so sure and sincere that he almost convinced himself.

Things went along as usual. Like all her other pregnancies, it proceeded uneventfully. She, however, was a little older, a bit more tired, and a bit more emotional. Greg was on edge. The two beers at the end of the day meant more to him than they should. Valerie must be psychic. She was right about why. It took the edge off. What edge? What exactly was he on edge about? Greg tried hard at the beginning and was able to limit himself. Once she began to show the reality of the responsibility of another child began to eat at him.

"How come your belly is so big?" Astrid asked.

"Yeah," Ingrid echoed. "How come?"

"You know how I told you if you eat a watermelon seed, it'll grow into watermelon in your stomach? I must have swallowed one. I think it's a watermelon. Or maybe a cantaloupe."

Both girls looked at her. They really were the cutest little things, with white-blond hair and arctic blue eyes. Astrid, being a year older, didn't fall for it. Where Ingrid thought of things like a child, still believing in Santa Claus and fairies, Astrid had a little more real-life experience and wasn't so quick to believe outlandish things anymore. She looked at her mother's face and back at her stomach. She squinted her eyes and said, "I don't think so."

"What do you think it is?" Valerie asked her.

"Well, Maddy's mom had a big tummy like that, and she had a baby brother in there."

"A brother?" Valerie answered.

"Ew," said Ingrid.

"Maybe Daddy might like a boy."

"Why?" asked Astrid. "What's so great about a boy?"

"You'll have to ask him when he gets home."

Astrid waited for Greg to ask him. She waited patiently, coloring in her zoo animals coloring book at the kitchen table. She pounced on him as soon as he came home. As he came through the door, she ran to him and grabbed his hand.

"Daddy, we need to talk to you," Astrid said and pulled at his hand.

"Sounds important. Can I take my coat and shoes off?"

"Okay, but hurry up. Ingrid, Daddy's home. Get Mommy."

They came out and sat at the table. Greg looked around and sat down.

"Am I in trouble? Did I forget to put the seat down?" he asked. Valerie smiled at him but only with her eyes.

"Okay, girls," Greg said. "Astro, what's up?"

"Why are boys better than girls?"

"They aren't. Who said they are?"

"Mommy said there might be a baby boy in her belly. She said maybe you might want a boy. Why would you want a boy?"

Greg looked at Valerie. She shrugged. "I thought I swallowed a watermelon seed, and a watermelon was growing in there, but they didn't believe it."

"Why do you want a boy?" Astrid asked him.

"A boy? Who said I wanted a boy?"

"Mommy did," Astrid answered.

"Yeah. Mommy," added Ingrid.

"Mommy?" Greg said. "Why would I want a boy?"

"Only because we don't have one. I thought a boy would keep you company and help you when you do smelly things."

"A boy," he said out loud, as if considering it for the first time. "No, I don't think so. Boys eat too much. They cause too much trouble in school. No, I'd rather have another girl. That's what I think." He stood up. "Boys get smelly. I need to take a shower after work, or I'll stink up the dinner table. Any other questions, girls? May I go shower now?"

"Yes, go shower. You smell," said Astrid. "Yeah, you smell," repeated Ingrid.

"Mommy doesn't care if I smell, do you?" He grabbed Valerie and kissed her.

"Yes," she said, laughing. "Go clean up. Dinner's in an hour."

Greg ran the water and stepped into the shower. He let the water wash over him. He started to cry. Him. A son. What kind of dad would he be? How would a broken man like himself raise a healthy boy? He remembered growing up with his own father and playing catch. Football. Soccer. Running. Things he can't do with a boy.

He cried because he ached inside. He never thought about having a son and what that would mean, and not having a son—never having a son—was a hurt he never imagined. He looked down at his scarred and wonky knee. He turned the water up to scalding and tried to compose himself. He put his face up in the spray, hoping the hot water would wash away his grief.

Valerie saw his red eyes and went and gave him a hug. "Soap got in your eyes?"

"No. I'm good." He opened the fridge and grabbed a beer. "You want anything?" he said. She shook her head. Valerie reached for the potholders, and he took them from her, nodding for her to open the oven door. He placed the casserole on a hot pad in the middle of the table. They silently put together the table.

When ready, he called the girls to wash up for dinner. They sat and looked across the table and pushed junk mail at each other. Greg looked at her, and she smiled at him. He smiled at her. Val smiled back. The kids came running in, and the moment they sat, the noise level went up quite a bit. Conversation couldn't compete with the chatter of two little girls forced to be quiet all day.

Her expression read, "This is good, right?" He answered her with a firm nod. Valerie exhaled a sigh of relief.

She grew larger by the day. He rubbed oil into her skin to keep it supple and massaged her feet. Brought her ice cream in bed and did the dishes. Greg told the girls the doctor said she had to rest all weekend. They could see her if they were quiet.

The girls spent their time running back and forth all weekend, wearing bathrobes and slippers, reading books, and leaving when they were bored.

Her due date was approaching. The doctor said any day now. Valerie felt familiar with the hurry up and wait, and she delayed her trip until the very last minute. Ellin and Dave stayed with the kids. As soon as she was assigned a room, she needed to push.

Greg told her, "You have to stop doing this. You have to give people a heads up."

They placed the baby all sloppy on Valerie's bare breast. Maybe because this was probably her last baby, she looked and marveled at every bare inch. Welcome to Earth, Baby Girl Wilson #3, she thought.

***

Eleven

VAL AND GREG

"**MOMMY! MOMMY!** WHERE ARE YOU?"

She could hear them before she could see them. They would look in all the rooms and say, "Not this one! Not this one!"

"This one, Dad! This one! Hi, Mommy!" They tried to climb up on the bed and started to fight.

"Hey," said Valerie. "Lots of tired moms and babies in here. If you're not quiet, they'll kick you out!"

"Okay, Mommy," Astrid loudly whispered. "Okay," said Ingrid in the same whisper.

"Don't you want to meet your sister?"

"Yes!" they both whispered, their voices a little louder with excitement.

"Pull that chair over here and climb up. Don't let the nurses catch us. Quick!" The girls were on the bed.

"Where? I don't see a baby."

"Shush. She's right here." Valerie extended the football-shaped object. "She's right here." Both girls had wide eyes and their mouths open in an O. Valerie leaned in and showed them the baby. Greg took a picture right at that moment. "My girls," he said.

"She's so little. Look at her little fingers!" Astrid said. "Are you sure it's a girl?" They laughed at that.

"So, you girls are meeting your new sister?" said a nurse with a bright smile as entered she entered the room.

"Are you sure?" asked Astrid. "It's not a boy, is it? Because if it is, we don't want it."

"No boys?" said the nurse.

"NO!" both girls said together.

"What's your sister's name?"

"Princess Fiona!" they yelled.

"Fiona's a pretty name," the nurse said.

"Princess Fiona!" they yelled again.

"Girls. We need to be quiet. All the other babies are sleeping," Greg told them.

"When are you coming home, Mommy?"

"I think tomorrow morning, after you go to school."

"Want to know a secret?" Astrid said, still loud.

"What's that?" Valerie asked.

"When we leave here, Daddy's taking us for hamburgers! We're getting French fries, too! And we can eat in the car!"

"Really? You're so lucky! Daddy never buys me hamburgers. He only gets me peanut butter sandwiches."

"No, he doesn't!" Astrid said. "He buys you diamonds!"

"I can't eat diamonds, Astrid."

"Yes, but they look so pretty on you!"

"No diamonds for you," Greg said. "You have to eat oatmeal and Jell-O like all the other patients. I'm taking my girls out for dinner! Come on, girls, let's let Mommy rest and go get burgers! Kiss her goodbye and say, 'See you tomorrow.'"

"Bye, Mommy, bye Fiona!" they yelled as they slipped off the bed and each grabbed a hand. "Come on, Daddy."

Greg kissed the top of Valerie's head. "See you tomorrow, Val. Enjoy your Jell-O." They left, and she could hear them chatter all the way to the elevators.

Greg came back the next day and took her home. They were going to fill out the birth certificate when he got there. She asked him to do it while she went to the bathroom. When she came out of the bathroom, it was just Greg and the baby.

"Where'd they go?"

"All done. Ready to roll?"

"But wait. Her name. What did we decide? What did you put down?"

"Fiona. Why?"

"That's not her name. Fiona is a cartoon character. Princess Fiona is no Cinderella or Sleeping Beauty. She's an ogre."

"Oh," Greg said and looked at the baby. "Let's hope it's not a self-fulfilling prophecy. What was it supposed to be?"

"I don't remember if we decided. I don't recall picking one out. What's her middle name?"

"Conover. She's Fiona Conover Wilson."

"Well, I'm not calling her Connie," Valerie said.

"Fiona, it is," Greg told her and picked up the car seat. The nurse came with the wheelchair. She told Greg to bring the car around the front and meet them there. Valerie carried the car seat in her lap, and he took the flowers. Greg took her home and got her and the baby settled.

"Do you care if I stop and check out a job site? I should be right back," he said on his way out the door. She dozed a little and fed the baby. Val happened to look at the clock. He had been gone over four hours. The school bus would be there in fifteen minutes, and she needed Greg to help with the kids. She called his cell and went straight to voicemail. Panic rose in her throat. Valerie called his mother, not knowing who else to call.

"Hi, Ellin, it's me. I can't find Greg anywhere; he's been gone for hours, and he's not answering his phone. He was supposed to help when the kids got home." Her voice wavered. "I can't move around too much. He was supposed to be right back."

"Valerie, don't panic. I'll call Dave to track him down, and I'll come right over. I'll be there to meet the bus."

Mr. Wilson drove to the job site where Greg was supposed to be, but it was deserted. He checked another, but Greg hadn't shown up there. He looked at the next obvious spot, and he was right. Parked behind O'Malley's pub, he found Greg's truck. He parked his car and went inside to get his son. He walked in, blinking his eyes to acclimate them to the dark bar. Dave Wilson saw his son at the opposite end of the bar.

"Greg. A minute, please."

"Yeah, Dad? What's up?"

"Aren't you supposed to be someplace now? Hours ago now?"

Greg looked at his father blankly. Suddenly, his face registered a lightbulb moment. He stood. "Aw, shit, the kids. I gotta go, Dad." He grabbed a handful of bills from his pocket and threw some money on the bar. His father followed him but beat him to his truck.

"Not just the kids, Greg. Your wife? The new baby?"

He tried to wedge his way to his door, but his father held fast. "No, Greg, get in my car. I'm driving."

He got in his father's car and looked at him, his father staring back. "Yeah?"

"How many did you have?"

"One more than I should have, obviously."

"Quit being a jerk. You dump your wife after she gets home from the hospital with a newborn and go out drinking. Valerie expected you hours ago, and your phone goes right to voicemail. I don't know if you see it, but something's not right."

"You're overreacting. I ran into Billy Reade, and he wanted to buy me a beer to celebrate the baby. I lost track of time. It's no big deal, Dad."

"Poor Valerie," his father said. "She can't get a hold of you. She's helpless right now. It's very disrespectful."

"Valerie's anything but helpless."

"She's a lot of things, and one of them is married to you. You better grovel. Big time. You fucked up. Big time."

"I get it, Dad." His father parked his car and went into the house.

Greg followed. His father ran interference. "Valerie! How's the littlest Wilson doing?" The girls hung off their father.

"You're late," Astrid scolded him.

"Late," seconded Ingrid.

"I know! Is Mommy mad, too?"

"Mommy's sad. She's been crying. I guess she really wanted a boy," Astrid said.

He brought the girls into the bedroom. "Mommy, I ran into some friends, and now I'm late. I'm very sorry. Now, what do you want to do for dinner?"

"Dinner?" They laughed at him. "It's bath time. Silly Daddy." After their bath, they each came in and "read" a book to baby Fiona.

The girls were mad it wasn't Princess Fiona. "Daddy forgot it." Is it so bad to let him take the heat for once? Valerie thought.

"Okay, kiss Mommy goodnight. It's bedtime. School tomorrow," he said and ushered them to their bedroom.

After Greg tucked them in, he came back into their room. He sat at Valerie's bedside.

"I know, let me have it. I know I have it coming."

"I'm too tired to fight it out with you. Just because I'm not arguing doesn't mean I'm not keeping track. But you were gone eight hours. You left me alone with no way to contact you for eight hours. The first day. I wish I could say I'm surprised."

He took the baby. "I'll take care of her and bring her back to the cradle thing, and then I'm taking a shower," he said, but Valerie was already asleep. He kissed her and apologized again, but she was already out.

She had her three-month leave and then went back to work. She wasn't sure about going back, but she was so popular it was hard to say no. Her mom came and watched the baby in the morning until one, and Greg's mom from one until four thirty-ish to meet the school bus. Greg would relieve his mom. Valerie would meet them, and hopefully, Greg would have a handle on dinner.

On the day she relieved Ellin, Greg had yet to show up. They had macaroni and cheese, baths, one story apiece, and a bed. Fiona couldn't be a better baby if you custom-ordered her from Gerber's. She went down like a dream. Valerie locked up and took a shower. She dried her hair and went to bed. Val slept on the bed in Fiona's room, staying there to avoid Greg. He wasn't home when she went to bed or when she got up. She forgot about him. The girls got on the bus. Her mom was due in an hour, and Valerie saw Greg's truck come flying around the corner. He got out of his truck and hurried inside.

"What did you forget?" she asked him.

"Val, I'm sorry. We were playing cards, and I must have fallen asleep. I'm sorry you couldn't get a hold of me, but—"

"Wait. You didn't come home last night? I slept in Fiona's room. I thought you left early this morning. You never came home? You never CAME HOME? Where were you?"

"I stopped by O'Malley's on the way home. We went back to Bender's and played cards. I fell asleep."

"You know, you must think I'm an idiot or something. You don't come home. You don't call. And I'm too tired to keep track of your bullshit. You have a problem with alcohol. Or maybe I'm the one with the problem. It's starting to sink in. You'd rather hang out in a filthy bar with a bunch of your dumbass boozer friends than come home to me and the kids. Your fucking family, and that's your choice. Your preference." Her voice began to shake, and she started to cry.

"One of these days, it's going to go too far, and it will be all your fucking fault. If I ever catch you driving those kids after you've been drinking, that's the line. If you do that, you'll lose everything: the three girls and me. It's pretty obvious. It's only a matter of time before you go too far. If you can't be bothered to take care of us, I'll do it. The first change I'll make is to cut and lose the dead weight. Don't push me. I'll do anything for those kids, even if you won't. My mom's going to be here soon. I have to get dressed," Valerie said, picked up Fiona, and went to get ready for work.

Greg had a splitting headache. Why does she go off like that? She has to make a big deal out of everything. He searched through the cupboard, looking for aspirin, and the rattle of the pill bottles sounded like rocks crashing around his brain.

Greg figured out a way around it. He would stop at O'Malley's, throw back a couple, and beat Val home. Have one while he waited for her and one with dinner, just two for her count. It worked fine until the bartender called to tell him he left his wallet on the bar, but Val took the message. She asked him point-blank when was the last time he was at O'Malley's. He lied right to her face. Greg told her it was over a week ago.

"Stop by there and pick up your wallet. You left it on the bar when you were there earlier," Valerie told him.

One morning, she was getting the girls ready for the bus, and while zipping her coat, Astrid breathed peppermint in Valerie's face.

"Hey. Where'd you get the candy?"

Astrid pulled a roll of mints out of her pocket. "Daddy says they're magic mints."

"Yeah, magic," said Ingrid.

"He says it will give us fresh breaths when we get home."

"Oh," said Valerie. "Magic mints."

One afternoon, she came home early, and Greg pulled into the driveway right behind her. He picked the girls up from school. She was able to get to them before they got out of his truck. She reached over to Greg to get to Ingrid's backpack and smelled the beer on his breath. Valerie asked him, "Hey, Greg. Need a magic mint?"

His eyes widened, and it gave him away.

"Girls, run and change. I have to talk to Daddy for a second." The girls ran inside, and Greg followed Valerie into their bedroom. Valerie shut the door and turned to face him, flames sparking behind her eyes.

"Okay, Greg. Yes or no. Were you drinking before you picked them up?"

"Well, I—"

"Yes or No."

"Yes, but—"

"That's it." She cut him off. "I'm done. I'm taking the girls and moving to my mother's. I guess it finally sunk in. We aren't enough. We will never be enough. You'd rather drink at O'Malley's with all those morons from high school than come home to us." She made her hands into fists and pounded on his chest.

"How dare you drive those kids when you've been drinking! You lie and sneak around and don't show up, and then you drink and drive? I told you one day you'd go too far, and that was it! You've crossed the line. Not my kids. Now get out. Go sleep on Bender's couch. We'll be out after the school bus comes tomorrow. Get out, you bastard."

"Mommy! What's happening? Why are you yelling?" Astrid called from the other side of the door.

"Get out. Or you'll be lucky to ever see them again."

Greg pushed her over the edge so she would have to act, and she did, just like he knew she would. He was determined to drive her away, and he did. He knew Val loved him. He also knew he didn't deserve her. Greg was a selfish, immature, fucking asshole who used the fact that she still loved him to drive her away.

Greg came out of their bedroom and saw two expectant little faces who wanted his attention and the baby, who stopped trying to get out of her car seat to smile at him. He almost started to cry, looking at those little girls he was walking out on. He leaned over and kissed their heads on his way out of the door.

"I have to go out, girls, and you'll be in bed before I get home, so goodnight. Be good and go to bed when your mom tells you to."

"Daddy!" Astrid called after him. "You need a magic mint!"

The next morning, after her mother came, Valerie went over to see Ellin and gave her side of the story. Greg could say whatever he wanted. She didn't give a shit. Minimizing the damage his drinking would cause the girls was her driving force. She even took a day off from work to smooth out this transition; she forced herself to put some steel in her spine and keep the tears away. Valerie was on a mission.

Ellin greeted her at the door with a smile and a hug, only to look at Valerie and change her greeting to concern.

"Valerie! What's wrong? What happened?" She pulled out a chair and had her sit at the kitchen table. She made them coffee, pulled a chair close, and sat down. "Valerie, honey, talk to me. Let me help." She reached out and put her hand on Valerie's arm.

All of her determination and resolve gave way when Ellin touched her. Valerie let out a huge sob and started to cry. "I'm sorry. I'm sorry." Ellin grabbed the tissues.

"Take your time, honey. It will be okay. It'll be okay."

"It will never be okay," Valerie sobbed. "I have to leave Greg. I told him it was coming. I told him. But he didn't care. He doesn't care about us, and it's about time I faced it."

"Valerie, take your time."

"My time? I can't trust him. He drove the girls after he'd been drinking.

I told him I could work around pretty much anything, but if I ever found out he drank and drove with the kids in the car, that was it. That was my line in the sand. He's lucky I don't have a shotgun. I'm that mad."

She cried a bit more but managed to pull herself together. Greg's father came in when he heard the crying; he stood in the doorway and listened.

"We've been having trouble lately. For a while. We've been fighting a lot over his drinking. He lies. He stays out late. He doesn't come home. He's totally unreliable and, what's worse, unreachable. Greg doesn't answer my calls. He doesn't return my messages. All he wants to do is drink beer at O'Malley's with his old high school buddies and relive their glory days. He was averaging about five beers a night. A night. Then he learned I was counting, so he started hiding the empties. I don't care if it's only beer. It affects his judgment.

"I told him it was too much. I told him something was gonna happen, and he was gonna lose us. He didn't care. Greg did it anyway. I caught him driving the girls, and he'd been drinking. He didn't even deny it. I can't let him drive the kids if he's drinking; I have to keep them safe. I can't trust him. I have to keep them safe from their own father." Her voice broke.

"I'm going to move in with my mom. I'm scared he'll get a DWI or have an accident with the girls in the truck. I don't know what else to do. I'm so scared. I'm scared for him. He let us go. He let us go."

Ellin looked at her husband in desperation. She was at a loss for what to do. He nodded his head and spoke to Valerie.

"Valerie," Dave said.

"Oh, God, Dave. I didn't know you were there. I'm sorry." Valerie sounded embarrassed.

"Don't be sorry. You didn't do anything. Greg's behavior isn't a surprise."

He looked at the bewildered look on his wife's face. "It's no surprise to me. Ellin, I didn't want to worry you. I've had to hunt him down a few times at work. He goes to O'Malley's for lunch and doesn't come back. I've had subs looking for him and calling me. And Valerie's not the only one whose calls don't get answered or returned. Greg's been very irresponsible.

"Drinking and driving his kids around? Valerie, you're right. That's unacceptable. You have to put those kids first, Val. Nobody is going to fault you for that, and we'll help you with whatever you need. Just let Ellin or me know what you need, and we'll be there for you."

"My mom is with the baby now, and I have to go get the kids' things ready to go." Her voice broke again. "I can't go. I love him. I want to help him." She started to cry again. Ellin leaned over and hugged her. "You aren't alone, Val. We'll help you. We'll help with the girls." After a bit, Val stopped crying and stood up.

"I've got to go, really. Dave, have you seen him since last night?"

"No. Why?"

"Because he left before dinner yesterday. I haven't seen or heard from him. I hope he's okay."

"Don't worry about him. I'll keep an eye on him. You just take care of those girls." Valerie stood up and hugged both him and Ellin.

"Thanks. I'm afraid I am going to need you. My mom isn't in the greatest health, and having four more people at her house might be a bit much. I can't see Greg. It took all I had to get to this point. I can't think about him. I have to think about the girls. He can see them as much as he wants, but he can't take them anywhere."

Dave walked Valerie out to her car. "We love you like a daughter, Val. We will always take care of you, and we can be the go-between. We'll do some driving, so don't worry about that. Just go take care of those kids. I'll handle Greg." He watched her pull out and drive away and went inside to get his keys.

"Dave? Where are you going?" his wife asked.

"To find that idiot son of ours and knock some sense into him." Dave knew exactly where to go to find him; he drove directly to O'Malley's.

Dave Wilson sat for a minute and collected his thoughts before he went inside. He had observed some of his son's self-destructive behavior, but he had no idea things were that bad at home. He got out of his car and prepared to go into Dad mode. If his son was going to act like a child, he was going to act like a father. It had been a while. He hoped he remembered how. Dave opened the door and entered O'Malley's. He stopped after a few steps to let his vision adjust to the bar's dark interior. He saw his son alone at the bar, sitting opposite the door, a beer on the bar in front of him.

He went over and was going to sit next to him, but had to switch out the barstool since it had a cracked leather seat, and half the stuffing was gone. He sat down and ordered a beer in an attempt not to appear confrontational. Greg looked at his dad and took a sip of beer.

"Hey, Dad."

"Hey, son." Greg didn't seem to be in a talkative mood, so Dave was going to have to bring it up.

"Aren't you even curious why I'm here?"

"No. I know why you're here. Valerie probably ran right over first thing this morning to give you her side."

"Her side? Of what?"

"You know what. You probably rushed over here after she left to talk some sense into me."

"Yes, I did. Your mother and I are very concerned. Valerie said she was moving with the girls back to her mother's house. She said she was worried about your drinking and how it was going to affect the kids. Valerie was very upset. It seemed like you driving with the kids in the truck after drinking put her in a bad position."

"Valerie," Greg said with a dismissive tone in his voice. "Did she tell you about how she counted my empties? How did she keep track of my drinking? She overreacts all the time. She's probably doing all this to force me to do what she wants."

"Valerie said you left because you didn't love her enough, and you didn't love the kids enough. That when faced with the choice of either giving up drinking or your family, you didn't choose them."

"Yeah, well, Valerie's a drama queen."

"Well, she's not the only one. That truck out there belongs to the company. I can't get behind you drinking and driving, either. If you wreck that truck or, worse, get in an accident and somebody gets hurt, the company is liable. We'll get sued. People haven't invested their whole lives into something only to have some fuck up lose it all."

Greg remained silent. He took another sip. "It's only beer. So, I have a beer or two. I don't see the big deal."

"A breathalyzer doesn't care if it's only beer. Don't you think losing your wife and family is a big deal? When did you become so selfish?"

A man in jeans and a beat-up jean jacket walked by and stopped. "Greg! My man! How the hell are you?"

"Great, Owen. Remember my dad?" Greg replied. "Oh, yeah. Hey, Mr. Wilson. It's me. Owen MacAvoy."

Dave looked at the guy. He played football with Greg in high school. He looked old and used up.

"Yes, hello, Owen. Nice to see you."

"You guys look like you're deep in the middle of something, so I'll leave you alone. Greg, see you at Bender's later." He walked away.

"That's your plan?" his father asked incredulously.

"Well, what's yours?"

"Go home. Beg forgiveness. You don't want to let this get too far. Like her taking the kids and moving in with her mother."

"She's so dramatic," Greg said and took another sip.

"You know, I don't think you realize how off-base you are. Valerie's right! You are a fuck-up. You'd get fired from any other place. I can't believe you would jeopardize everything over that bottle and this barstool. She still believes in you. Valerie won't give up on you. Take that gift and use it to repair things."

Greg stood up. His father did as well, blocking him. "What are you doing?"

"Taking your keys. I'll give you a ride home. You can ask one of your friends to drop you off here later when you're sober. Give." He extended his hand, palm up, and took the keys. They walked to Dave's car, parked next to the truck.

"Get in."

"Fine. But you're making a big deal out of nothing."

He brought him to the familial home. Greg got out and stomped up the stairs, slammed the door, and went inside. Dave followed.

"What's that all about?" asked Ellin.

He explained what happened at the bar. "It's odd, though. I told him I was taking him home, and he just went to his old room. He didn't ask to go to his house."

Valerie went ahead and moved into her mother's. The girls thought it was big fun until they realized they weren't going back to their house. They didn't understand their life as they knew it was no longer.

Astrid put it together first.

"Mommy? Where's Daddy? How come he doesn't live here?" She was sitting at the table, drawing with crayons. She tapped the butt end of her crayon on the table.

Valerie knew this was coming and wasn't sure how to address it. She asked, "Why do you ask?" to buy herself some time.

"I can't remember when I saw him. I don't think he lives here. Does he live at our house?"

"I think so. Do you miss him?"

"Yes. When Amelia's dad moved out, they got a divorce. Are you getting a divorce?"

"I don't know, Astrid. Daddy's sick, and he needs to get better. Let me call Gramma Ellin and see if he's over there."

She dialed the number, and Ellin picked up.

"Ellin. Hi. Um, the girls are missing their dad. Do you know where he's staying?"

"He's in and out. Why don't we take the girls this weekend? He can see them then. You haven't heard from Greg?"

"No." Valerie's voice started shaking. "It's something I learned to live with a long time ago. We're not a priority. It's okay."

"Val, it kills me he's doing this. I don't know what to say other than we're here for you and the kids. There is something wrong with Greg. I'm at a total loss as to why he's acting like this."

Saturday came, and the girls were excited to go over to Gramma Ellin's and see their dad. Dave and Ellin came and expected to take Fiona, too. Valerie figured the baby would stay home with her, but quickly got her things together. After they left, the silence ate at her. Her mother was enjoying the respite, but it agitated Val.

"I'm going to run a few errands, Mom. Need anything while I'm out?" She grabbed her keys.

She just meant to drive aimlessly around, but ended up at the family house. She sat in the driveway but couldn't bring herself to go inside. She looked at the house that would never be their home ever again. It might as well just burn to the ground for all the good it did her. She put her hands on the steering wheel, put her face down, and cried her eyes out.

***

They established a pattern through the end of the school year. She got them on weekdays, and Ellin and Dave got them on Saturdays and Sundays. The girls adjusted reasonably well. It was sad how few of their classmates had intact families. Sometimes, Astrid and then Ingrid would have a meltdown.

"I don't want a divorce!" Astrid screamed. "I want us to live in our house! I want my Daddy back! This is not fair! You didn't ask me! I don't want it!" she would yell, and Ingrid would join in.

Luckily, summer came, and the girls went back and forth with no problem. Everyone fell into an established rhythm, with Greg making drop-in appearances when it was convenient. He drove his father's truck conditionally. If he was going to be out drinking, he had to call or catch a ride with someone. If his father caught him behind the wheel with even the hint of beer on his breath, he was fired. It was non-negotiable.

Her mom was a great support to Valerie. She knew how hard she cried when she thought nobody was listening, but her mother could hear her through the vents of the old house. She knew how devastated Valerie was that Greg never came over to confront her about the situation. He didn't come to beg for another chance; he didn't plead for her not to break up the family. His absence was noticeable. It broke Valerie's heart. Her assertion that he put O'Malley's and drinking buddies ahead of them proved true.

It was a truth that haunted her. What was missing from their life that he had to go outside of it to be happy? What did she lack? What didn't she provide? These and many other questions rolled and bounced around her brain like a pinball machine. What did she do? What didn't she do? How could he just stop loving her and walk away? Greg must not have loved her for a long time. Valerie felt stupid. She missed it, him making her obsolete; he must think she's an idiot for not catching on sooner.

Valerie's job offered her a VP position. It was a great opportunity and a considerable pay increase; the only drawback was it was in the home office, and she'd have to move. They gave her a week to think about it, but she didn't want to relocate for the kids' sake.

Valerie left at lunch to run to the bank and was stopped at a red light. She saw Greg stop going in the opposite direction. She felt a tremor of hope. If only he saw her, he would remember what they had and want it back. Valerie leaned forward in the seat and gripped the steering wheel. The light changed; she had a smile ready for when they made eye contact. As they went through the light, Greg looked her straight in the eyes, and before she had a chance to smile or wave, he looked away.

He looked away. Greg deliberately avoided looking at her. That act was a stake in her heart. It killed the hope she secretly held. Valerie was going to cry, but suddenly felt enraged. How dare he negate their entire past? Like we never existed. I guess his promise to stand by me when Fiona was born was never broken because he never made it, she thought. If he thinks I'm just going to go down easy, well, fuck him.

She pulled over and called her boss about the job offer.

"I'll take it. I need the rest of the summer off to close things out here and find a place to live and get the kids into school there. I'll use up my vacation time." Valerie hung up and drove over to her mom's.

"It hurt like hell to have him pretend I don't exist. I can't go through that again, and he will not do it to my kids. They will not be made to feel less than to allow Greg to feel better about his actions. I need your help, Mom. I hate to ask you, but would you move with me for a little while to figure out the kids' situation? There is an on-site daycare so that the baby will be okay. It's just after school or days off. We'll come back in the summer and let the kids stay with Ellin and Dave, and their father can see them if he wants. I'll use vacation time and wait a few weeks until they adjust."

Next, she talked to Greg's parents, "There's no way I can live here. It hurts too much to have your husband and the father of your kids demonstrate daily he never wants to see you again, that he's sorry he ever got involved with you."

"Valerie, I'm so sorry. I'm stunned by my son's behavior," confessed Ellin. "Greg won't talk to us. I don't understand how he can just walk away from his family."

"I've tried to talk to him myself," Dave added. "He shows up at work sober, and he does his job, but when I bring the up subject, he shuts me down completely. I don't know where he sleeps. Probably back at your house."

"It's not my house. You gave it to us. I'm giving it back and taking my name off the deed. I need to find a divorce lawyer. I can't be married to someone who won't even look at me."

"Oh, Valerie," Ellin said. "Don't do anything hasty."

"Minimizing the damage to my children is my primary motive. How I feel is secondary to that. I never want them to feel what I felt: nonexistent to someone who said he loved me. That's a hole in my heart that I don't think will ever heal. It will hurt me forever, but if there's something I can do to prevent my kids from experiencing it, I'll do it.

"It's the only solution I can think of. Removing us from the situation. Since this promotion came up, I'm taking it. I want him to have custody for the summer. I want these kids to know their grandparents and cousins. I want them to live with you, so if he feels like checking out, maybe the hole he leaves won't be so obvious." She managed to say all that before she crumbled and began sobbing.

"I'm sorry you had to see that, but every time I think about it, I feel like I've been kicked in the chest by a horse. I never knew a broken heart caused such physical pain," she said as she blew her nose.

"Val, whatever you need from Greg, come talk to me first. If you can't see him, don't. Have all communication go through me," Dave offered. "These kids are Wilsons, and they will be taken care of by Wilsons. We don't abandon our own."

"Thank you, Dave and Ellin. I don't know how to do this any other way."

Telling the girls was another story. Astrid, and consequently Ingrid, blew a gasket.

"Move? What are you, crazy? You made us leave our house. Now we have to leave our school and our friends! Just because Daddy's a big jerk! Why doesn't he leave?"

"Yeah," added Ingrid. "Make him go away."

"You'll come back all the time, and in the summers, you'll stay with Gramma El and Grampa Dave. You know they like to take you around to the blue-haired ladies and show you off. They go to fancy lodges and lovely places."

"That's terrible, you trying to buy us off with it because it's all posh and swell. They look like they enjoy showing us off, but it can get really boring. And for old people, they stay up pretty late drinking a lot of booze," Astrid said. Valerie wondered where she heard the words "posh" and "swell."

"Yeah, it's like looking at you guys in twenty years."

"Ingrid!" Valerie said.

"Yeah, Ingrid! Good one!" her sister congratulated her.

"Well, it's happening. Might as well get used to it. You have all summer to think about it."

Greg's sister Caroline came over to help Val organize the move. She was in town and left her kids with Ellin and Dave, showing up with donuts. Val's two were also there, so they had a house full of grandkids. Caroline made them coffee and motioned for Valerie to sit.

"Let's have a cup of coffee before we start. You want to start in the kitchen?" Caroline asked.

"You know," said Valerie, "I don't think I can do this. I don't want to remember anything more than I do. This is the ruins of a family that exists no more."

"Think about it. Any heirlooms you want? We can ask Dad for guys to pack it all up, and we can either donate it or put it in storage."

"Donate it all unless Greg expresses it differently. I'm packing a suitcase for each of the girls, and that's what we're keeping. Donate everything else. I'm ripping the band-aid off quickly. This stuff is from a different lifetime. I'm renting a furnished apartment, so I don't need any of this. It's contaminated. There used to be so much love here. Happiness. Sanctuary. It's all gone, Caroline. Am I doing the right thing? Is it petty to want to avoid someone you still love? I can't believe this happened." Val was breathing high in her chest and made herself light-headed. Caroline reached over to her and hugged her.

"Honey, nobody knows what to do. Greg is such an asshole just to walk away and leave you. He's not talking to anybody. Even my dad. Let me do this. Let's go in your room and get your things together. Your personal things, things specific to you. You've got to pack a bag for when you go away to find a place to live and check out schools."

That was what they did. Valerie focused solely on her things, and anything of Greg's Caroline hid under the bed and in the closet once Valerie's things were out. By the end of the afternoon, the bedroom was vacant of any evidence Valerie had ever lived there. Same with the bathroom and front closet. Caroline loaded everything in her car and brought it to Val's mother's to be put in boxes.

"I know this was hard. The girls' rooms are going to be even harder. How do you want to handle them?"

"I know this sounds terrible, but let's go get a bottle of wine and a couple of sandwiches, take it over there, and do the girls' clothes and things. Their toys and mementos, I don't know what to do. They can't see me break down anymore. I have to put a positive spin on it. We are moving. That's that. Since I don't have a problem with alcohol, I could really use a drink." They left to purchase their items and returned back to the house.

"God, this makes me so angry. I sit and look at the house, and I just want to burn it to the ground with Greg inside it," Valerie said.

"That's it, Valerie. I'll get the matches. Get good and fucking mad. It sure beats crying," Caroline said.

They sat on the floor of the girls' room. Both older girls shared a room; Fiona had her own. Valerie figured there would come a time when Astrid, as the oldest, would demand her own room because she needed more privacy. Val considered that a rite of passage; that was why they shared a room in the first place. It was a carrot extended to make the move a bit more palatable; they each would get their own room. Val would share with Fiona.

There were plenty of things to be donated. Val could remember where each girl wore each outfit, who gave it to them, and whether or not the kid liked it.

"Jesus, this is hard," Valerie said. "So many memories. I just want to get rid of it all and pretend none of this ever happened. I can't get rid of the girls' histories. It's not fair to them."

Caroline looked at Valerie. She wiped the sweat off her forehead with the back of her hand. Valerie was so thin. She was a real trooper, doing it because it must be done, but on the verge of tears when certain outfits came into her hands. The fact that she had two tons of shit land on her head and was still standing was remarkable, considering Greg was MIA. Caroline thought maybe Val could use someone to talk to, or at least a shoulder to cry on.

"Hey. Why don't we have a glass of wine and take a break?" Caroline suggested.

"Sure. Sounds great," Val said and picked up her wine glass. She looked at the glass. "A wedding present from my old roommate," an undisguised tremor in her voice.

"Hey, Valerie, how are you doing? You've put so many priorities ahead of yourself; are you doing that on purpose? You'll get settled, and everything will be done, but you'll be all alone. You'll be in a strange place and won't have any support at all."

"Yeah, that's probably true. I can't think about myself because I don't know what to think. When I think about your brother, part of me wants to strangle him; part of me wants to console him. I can't help it. I still love him. I can't help but think he's mentally ill. Something is wrong with him. Something has to be for him just to disappear like this. Me? Okay, he married the wrong woman. The ultimate rejection. But the kids, his own kids? I can't figure that out at all."

"Well, if you had to guess, what happened? Another woman? Some bar fly?"

"I think when his injury ruined his football career, he never got over it. Greg was used to being someone people sought out, someone everyone wanted to know. He thought it mattered that he wasn't that guy anymore. It didn't matter to me; he got mad because he didn't think I took his loss seriously. It just was, and we needed to work around it. I was pushing us forward, and Greg couldn't leave the past. He can't accept he's not that guy anymore. Every time he saw me, I must have reminded him who he wasn't. He didn't bother to finish school; he stopped going into the office and preferred to go with the crews. I think the older and more grown-up things got, the wider the gap, the farther behind he fell. When I got pregnant with Fiona, that put him over the edge.

"He had a wife and three kids, too much for someone who didn't have any coping skills because he never needed to develop any. I think he wants to eliminate anything that invites comparisons to him after football. Maybe he thinks nobody will notice his limp if he's alone. He won't accept the fact nobody cares but him. He's mentally stuck there, and rather than find a way around it, he'd instead drink and forget about it. But who knows? I've tried to get him to talk, but he gets mean, so I stopped. He doesn't need me constantly reinforcing his perceived faults. The dregs of his family will go one way; he'll go his."

"That makes a lot of sense when you think about it," Caroline said. "He went from hot shit to not shit, not easy to do when your ego is as big as his."

"I wouldn't go to the bank with that, but it is based on over fifteen years of observation. Does it even matter? He wants nothing to do with me. I could cure him of cancer, but he'd want nothing to do with me. Just thinking about it makes me feel like I want to throw up. I need to get us there: Me, my girls, and my mother."

"Let me know, and I'll fly in to help you. That's a lot to manage. I'll meet you there, and I'll stay the week and help you guys get adjusted. Please, I want to do it."

"I'm grateful you want to help me, and I'm scared enough to take you up on it. I don't know why you want to help. Isn't that like fraternizing with the enemy or something? Shouldn't you be pro-Greg and hate me?"

"We all knew something was off, but we didn't want to confront him. Look at what he did when you called him on it. Dad always said, 'Boys will be boys.' Everybody wanted to be standing next to Greg, my father included. When you think about it, that injury was pretty traumatic, both physically and mentally. He was probably so busy pretending to be positive that nobody acknowledged his loss."

"That's what I think, but it doesn't matter, does it? He used to be so happy. I'd give it all up if he could be happy, you know."

"You're too good, Val."

"Not really. I still care. I probably will for the rest of my life. He set the terms. So be it. But you can't decide to stop caring about a person because you want to. Maybe someday."

"I talked to my dad. He said he'll take care of whatever you leave behind. Label the things you want to be sent, and he'll get those out. You have a place already?"

"Corporate handled all that. We have a three-bedroom unit in a condo community. Schools have a good ranking, close to the office. They've arranged for six months of a mother's helper. She'll handle from two to eight p.m. Get the kids' homework done, do their chores, help them with their next-day items together, and give Fiona a bath. There's a pool and recreation complex, and you can join the club at a discount. It looks pretty nice."

"Let me know when you're getting in, I'll get a rental and pick you all up."

"You really don't have to do this, you know. I'm sure they'll have it all set for us on the other end."

"I'll sit by the pool drinking margaritas and watch the kids."

"Make sure he tells Greg to clean out anything he might want because I'm not coming back here. I think we're done here. Literally and figuratively. Done. Over. That's all, folks," Valerie said as she locked the door for the last time. She walked to the car. She turned and looked at her old home. Someone else's new home.

Valerie left later that weekend to spend a few days at the home office. She had her own office with her name engraved on a brass placard outside the door. The on-site daycare was very nice, she thought. Fiona will be happy there. She toured the condo complex. Her place was larger than she thought. It was either brand new or totally updated. The three bedrooms were good-sized. Since the climate was warmer than what they were used to, the pool was a big draw. The complex was shaped in a square, the center an open courtyard where the pool was located.

It was different enough from home. It would give the girls something to focus on besides being new. Lastly, she toured the school. Yes, they would have uniforms, but everyone she talked to seemed to endorse it.

There was nothing left to do here but move. Greg's dad gave them a ride to the airport. He had more than stepped up to compensate for his piss-poor excuse of a son.

"Valerie, if you need anything, you call me. Anything that you need from Greg, you call me. I'll be your contact back here. I'll handle the house and watch your mom's, too. You must be safe and enjoy my grandchildren. We love you. You're like a daughter to us. We're here for you. Don't forget." He kissed the girls and even her mom. He hugged Val hard. His solid presence was maybe what she'd miss the most. He kissed her goodbye and said, "Remember what I said."

The girls waved and yelled, "Bye-bye, Grampa!"

She was leaving with her mother, two kids, and a baby. She pitied her seatmates, but springing for first class must not be a luxury her company provided. Maybe a layover would be good; get those kids out and moving around a bit so they'd burn off some energy. Her mother sat in the middle seat, one girl in the window seat. The row behind sat the other girl at the window with Valerie and Fiona, Val in the middle. The girls waved out the window as the plane left the gate. From the window, they could see the place Valerie and her mom called home all their lives. "Bye, house," said Ingrid. "Bye School. Bye-bye, Grandma and Grampa." She lowered her voice to barely a whisper and said, "Bye, Daddy."

***

Twelve

VAL

EVERYONE SETTLED into their new environment. The girls loved their new school. Every day after school, they went in the pool and swam until dinnertime. Ingrid was like a little fish. She loved the water. They offered swim lessons after school. Valerie signed both girls up. Astrid had her usual excuse. She already knew how to "fill in the blank." In this case, she already knew how to swim.

"If we are going to live where there's a pool, you're taking lessons. It's not negotiable, so don't even start." Even Fiona liked the water. Gramma was happy to sit under an umbrella, drink iced tea, and pretend to read a book.

Valerie was so busy at work that the time flew by. There were a lot of meetings. No matter the department, she had to attend. She hoped it was because she needed to learn the company from a global perspective. Valerie managed to put out a summary of the meeting and the action items needed, and be the liaison between upper management and the department head. Valerie also sent out a monthly email to keep the departments updated on the progress of the action items. She only did that because she wasn't told to do anything, so she created a paper trail of her output that justified her position. Valerie asked her superior what else she needed to do.

"You were hired for your people skills, Valerie. Your 'soft skills.' Departments needed to know their concerns were heard. Feedback was that management was unapproachable, department heads weren't being heard, and their needs were unmet," her boss and friend since they both started at the same time, Marcus said.

"We needed someone from management to be visible and put a face to the kinder, gentler corporate goon."

Valerie laughed. "I'm the poster child for a corporate goon?"

"The kinder, gentler, corporate goon."

"Well, I have skills in other areas. Don't forget that."

The holidays arrived. Val thought her mom might want to go home for Christmas, but that wasn't the case. "Let's go out for Thanksgiving and do something here for Christmas."

Valerie thought maybe Greg might want to see the girls, but when she called Dave, he said Greg wasn't in any shape to see his kids.

"It wouldn't be good for the kids to see him, and if they came all this way only to have their dad refuse to see them, that's not healthy for them; let's plan on the summer. Ellin sent a number of packages, so be on the lookout. Make sure you tip the UPS guy," Dave joked.

They went to the store, bought a smaller tree, and filled up the cart with all the accessories. They decorated the inside even though the weather outside didn't match.

Precisely at noon on Christmas Day, the doorbell rang. When Val opened the door, there were two assembled bikes. Even Fiona got a tricycle. The girls whooped and hollered, every other gift forgotten. Everyone got dressed and went outside to practice riding their new bikes. Val took a video of the kids riding around the parking lot to send to Greg's family.

She had them pull up and recorded them, saying, "Thank you, Gramma and Grampa! Merry Christmas, everyone! We love you!"

"Merry Christmas, Daddy!" added Ingrid.

Even Fiona, who at one year old had no use for a bicycle, sat on that plastic trike and pretended to go like her sisters. They spent the afternoon riding their bikes while the grown-ups mingled as people came and went. When it was dinner time, they heated Gramma's macaroni and cheese with broccoli, which the girls would eat if they were called trees. They pretended to be giraffes and ate the tops of the trees. Then they pretended to be dinosaurs to eat the stalks.

Everyone took their baths, got in their jammies, and watched what Valerie considered her holiday tradition: watching Pee-Wee's Big Adventure.

***

Thirteen

GREG AND VAL

GREG HAD BEEN on a slow downward spiral since Valerie left. He didn't want to talk about it; he made no attempt to contact her, not even when he heard she was moving away. Valerie was leaving and taking the kids. Greg knew a real man would fight her to stay, and if that didn't work, fight for his kids. He was too self-involved to pay attention to his family. When he heard they were leaving, he was too busy feeling sorry for himself to do anything about it. Greg bought a case of beer and retired to his parents' basement, and spent a weekend in the dark until he finished. He honored his father's request not to drive any company vehicles when he'd been drinking. Greg made it through the day okay, but came back to his parents' house with a case of beer to keep him company.

Greg knew he was fucked up in the head. When he thought about how he did nothing to fix things early on, and later, when he heard his family was leaving, he disappeared. If he didn't have the numbness from the alcohol, Greg felt things he didn't want to, ashamed of his family situation and the disappointment in his father's eyes. His dad tried to impress upon him what his inaction was costing him.

"Greg, if you don't want to talk to me, I get it. I'm your dad. But you have to do something. You can't let Valerie leave. She loves you. She wants to help you."

"Valerie? Valerie left me and took my kids."

"Are you sure you didn't drive her away?"

"Do I drive your truck when I've been drinking? No. Do I show up for work on time? Yes. We really don't have anything else to talk about. Are we done?"

"I guess we are," his dad said and walked away.

Christmas afternoon, Greg had his head in the fridge when he heard his mother and sister talking about the video Val sent.

"Here," Caroline said, reaching for the laptop. "Let me watch it again." His ears perked up at the sound of his daughters' voices. He heard them wishing everyone a Merry Christmas and the end; he heard Ingrid say, "Merry Christmas, Daddy."

He felt like he was on a ride at an amusement park he desperately wanted to get off of; he was nauseous and his head was spinning. He quickly ran down the basement stairs to the couch he was living on. He grabbed a beer and drank it as fast as he could and kept drinking until he could obliterate the sound of Ingrid's sweet little voice and the stain it left on his heart.

Spring came, the girls continued to adjust to their new lives. Astrid met her best friend, a girl from her school named Amelia. They were together all the time. Her dad worked at the same place as Valerie, and they lived in the same complex, or gated community might be the correct term, Val figured. Poor Ingrid. She considered Astrid to be her best friend. She moped around. Playing with Fiona was a bore, no matter what the toy, Fiona would say it was hers. The answer to her missing her sister was swim club. She joined and found it consumed her time and consumed her mind. She wanted to swim competitively, so that's what she did. Such determination in a little girl stunned them all. Her mindset reminded Valerie so much of Greg. Ingrid was just starting out, but she could see herself at the Olympics. Fiona turned one and was walking. So much happened since they left.

From what Valerie understood, the company had many long term, and short term hires. Once their project segment was completed, they left, only to be replaced by others doing something else. Valerie was a bit concerned about her position. Was she just a temp, too? She decided to talk to her boss about it. Valerie caught him one day in his office, a rare occurrence. She knocked on his door.

"Morning, Marcus. Got a second?"

"For you, I've got a whole minute. Come on in," he invited. "Shut the door if you need to."

Val entered and shut the door. In Corporate America, she trusted nobody. This company had gone out of its way to accommodate Valerie at each stage in her career. She had been blessed with great people in positions above her. She knew that things could change in a minute, though.

"It's nothing. I was just curious about my living situation. It seems temporary. There are a lot of people who come and go. They work here on a project and leave. I guess my question is, am I on a temporary assignment? Should I make a backup plan to be on the safe side?"

"No. I thought the location and schools, and the many family friendly things would be good for the kids. You are free to move if you want. Why? Is there a problem?"

"Not at all. I was just curious about the turnover. It seemed high, and I was wondering if I should look for a more permanent place to live or wait for a transfer or a pink slip."

"That's why we'll do anything to keep you happy. You see things others don't. Like every project is a puzzle, each department has its own business plan. Marketing has no idea what production is up to— ditto research. If we are trying to capture the 50+ demographic, the design team had no idea the size of the screen mattered for keyless entry. Too much information on too small a screen.

"You know who said that? You. You know what else? You were right. And that was your second week here. So, no, you're not a temp. You are a very valuable employee. Your global view of the company is great, but the practical application of your observations is your strength. That's why you're here. That's why you attend so many meetings."

"Thanks, Marcus. That clears up a lot," Val told him as she stood to exit.

"Any time, Valerie. You can always come to me."

***

School was finishing up, and they were making plans for the summer, returning to their hometown. Astrid cried and didn't want to go, afraid Amelia would find a new best friend. Ingrid didn't care as long as there was water. Fiona was on the move now. Her mother was nearing the end of her time of service, Fiona was a toddler now, and Val's mom, Mary, couldn't keep up. She was looking forward to getting back to her house and her life.

The plan was that Dave would pick them up at the airport and drop them off at Mary's house. Once the grown-ups were settled, he would come back and get the girls. The two older ones weren't sure about staying with the Wilsons, but Valerie said it wasn't fair that Grandma Mary hogged the girls; she had to share. Val was staying a week and then leaving to go back to work. She was mostly there as backup if the girls were miserable. She wasn't sure if they would see their dad at all, but that was out of her hands.

Dave came back to get the girls. They were reluctant to leave.

"You guys come with me," Grampa said. "There's a surprise for you." They got in the car with trepidation, and he took them to their summer home. Valerie drove her mother's car over to check if they had trouble adapting to their new environment, but it seemed not. She and Dave went outside to check.

"Hey, you guys, what are you doing out here?" she called.

"Look, Mom! Our bikes are here!" Astrid yelled. They even had a trike with a handle tall enough for an adult to push, so Fiona got to ride, too.

"Why look at you, you big girl! You rode a bike!"

Fiona smiled, a huge drooly one. She slapped the handlebars. "Bike! Mine!" she yelled.

"Okay, let's see what Gramma Ellin has cooked us for dinner. Hot dogs, or octopus pie?" Grandpa Dave asked.

Astrid was figuring out what humor was, and she thought Grampa made a joke, so she would make a joke back. "Octopus pie? Yum! My favorite!" All the adults laughed; Astrid was pleased they thought it was a good one. Val arranged to meet them at the pool in the morning. Ingrid was taking private swim lessons.

Ingrid couldn't wait to get in the water. She ran out of the locker room, past her mother, with barely a "Hello, Mom!" to get to the teacher. Dave and Valerie sat on a bench to watch her.

"How did it go last night? Was the octopus pie a hit?"

"No, we had burgers and dogs. That little Fiona can really pack it away."

"Yeah, she can eat. How did they sleep? Any trouble at bedtime?"

"None at all. They were exhausted," Dave said and took a breath. "How do you want to handle Greg? He lives in the basement."

"In my heart, I want him to say, 'I'm going to quit drinking. These girls are worth it,' but I don't know. Whatever interaction they have, as long as he's not driving, I'm fine. It's Ingrid I worry about. She asks about him. 'Where's Daddy? Why doesn't he live with us?' I hope my explanation is close to the truth. I just tell her he's sick. He can't be with us until he's better. The little one will never even know him, which makes me incredibly sad.

"I don't know how this is going to go over, but I have the divorce papers. I'm not asking for any money, no child support, nothing. If he wants to sue me for half my retirement IRA, he can. He can have whatever he wants. My only issue is no unsupervised visitation. I don't trust him. I feel bad saying that; he's their dad. Whatever the house sold for, he can have it. I'm not going to get into a whole custody battle about visitation. I don't think he'll do that. He may hate me, but I think deep down, he knows his situation would be unhealthy for his children."

"I didn't give him the proceeds from the sale of the house. I opened three college accounts for the girls," Dave told Val.

Valerie started to tear up. "Dave, you've done more than enough. You don't have to be so kind."

"Like I said, Wilsons take care of their own. I am not going to miss out on having a relationship with my grandchildren because my son is an idiot." He turned and watched Ingrid with the teacher. "She's a natural. If she sticks with it, she's going to be really good."

"I know. She reminds me of Greg when he was healthy. He had such natural talent and ability, but it was how hard he worked. He was going to be the best. I think that's his problem. He can't be the best, so he has to be the worst. He's not comfortable in the middle."

"That's very wise, Val. It's true. If he's going to do something, he's going to be the best at it, so he's decided he's going to be the very best alcoholic he can."

"Why couldn't he want to be the best husband and father?"

"I wish I knew why, Val." He put his arm over her shoulder and hugged her. "But don't worry. You'll always have a place at our table, and if he doesn't like it, he can eat in the garage."

"Thanks, Dave. I lost my father, at times, I really miss him. I worry the girls will never have that, and they'll always pick the wrong guy because that's all they know. As far as my father goes, he was one of the good ones. You are, too. Sometimes I think of you like that, as a dad. I probably shouldn't; who knows what Greg will do once he gets the divorce papers, but why should he care? He found more comfort on a barstool than he did in my arms. We'll always be connected because of the kids. He didn't care about our marriage; why should he care about our divorce?" Val looked at Dave. "Sorry about that. He's still your son."

"Yes, he is, Valerie, and his mother's heart aches like yours. I am furious at him for a number of reasons. I'm his father; I'll always love him, but the hurt he's caused the people I love infuriates me. The damage those little girls are going to suffer isn't even apparent, but when they grow up, well..." They sat quietly and watched Ingrid in the pool. Ingrid finished her lesson; she came over, wrapped in a towel, her long blond eyelashes stuck together with drops of water. "Did you see me, Mom? Did you?" she asked excitedly.

"Yes, I did. You're my little fishy."

"No." Ingrid shook her head at the idea. "Shark?" Ingrid shook her head again. "Whale?" Ingrid made a face like she was getting further away.

Val looked at Dave with a little smile. "I know." Ingrid looked at her mom with a look of expectation.

"A mermaid?"

"Yes, finally." Ingrid laughed.

"I know," Dave said. "A mermaid with teeth like a shark."

"You got it, Grampa!" Ingrid danced around.

"Why don't you change out of that wet suit? Then we can go," Val told her. "Am I coming back tomorrow?"

"No. Your lessons are Monday, Wednesday, and Friday."

"I want to come back tomorrow." Ingrid dug in.

"I don't think they have them. I think tomorrow morning it's the old lady water aerobics class."

"But I want to swim," Ingrid insisted.

"Those old ladies and their upper arms flapping like pancakes might get in your way," Val said.

"You go and get changed, and let me check the schedule," Dave said as he walked towards the lifeguard.

Ingrid changed in record time. She had her bathing suit wrapped in her wet towel and handed her mother the wet ball.

"What am I supposed to do with this?" Val asked her, but Ingrid's attention was diverted to her grandpa.

He walked back to them after his consultation. "Well, Grampa?"

"You can come on Tuesday and Thursday at eleven."

"Yay, Grampa!"

They left and walked to the parking lot; they each drove. Val walked them to their car. She handed Ingrid back her wad of wet clothes.

"Goodbye, Ariel the shark," she said. Ingrid laughed and opened her mouth wide to show her teeth.

"You're scaring me. Don't forget to hang up your wet things when you get back, or tomorrow you'll have to put your bottom in a wet suit." She turned to Dave. "Thank you for everything. How did you find her lessons on Tuesdays and Thursdays? When I signed her up, they didn't offer them."

"They don't. I hired the instructor to be Ingrid's private coach. Remember, Wilsons take care of their own. If swimming is what makes her happy, she'll come home ready to train for the Olympics."

Val hugged Ingrid goodbye. "If you have any time in your schedule later, ride your bike over and say hello to Gramma Mary and me."

"Okay, Mommy. Bye." She got in and buckled her seat belt. They watched Val walk to her car, and Dave beeped as they exited.

Valerie smiled to herself and drove to her mother's house. Ariel with teeth. She must take after her mother, she thought. It was time for her mother's soap; there was no need to hurry home. She drove around aimlessly.

Dave brought Ingrid back and went inside. Ellin had prepared peanut butter and jelly sandwiches and sliced oranges for lunch. Ingrid took an orange wedge and bit into it. She held it in her teeth so when she smiled, all you could see was the rind. She closed her lips and tapped her grandpa on the arm. He turned to her, and she smiled a big, orange smile on his face. He smiled a big orange smile back at her. Ingrid giggled and took the orange out of her mouth.

"Grandpa! You're silly!"

He took the orange wedge out his mouth. "What? You think you're the only kid ever to do that?" He stood up. "Here. You take the plates to the counter, I'll take glasses." He threw the napkins in the trash can. "I'm going to find Gramma. You hang your wet things on the line, or your mommy will yell at me. Deal?"

"Deal," Ingrid said and gathered up her things. She scampered out the door, humming a tune only she heard in her head. She wasn't tall enough to hang them up. Ingrid thought maybe she could throw them over the clothesline, but they missed, only to land on the ground. She tried to think of another way when she heard a car pull up the drive. Ingrid hid around the side of the garage and watched. A white truck parked, and a man opened the door and got out.

"Daddy?" Daddy?" Ingrid said quietly. He looked up and smiled. The little girl's voice trembled as if she might cry.

"Fiona? Is that you?" he said back to her. He meant only to tease her, but the little girl's face fell, and two large tears ran down her cheeks. She looked crestfallen her own father didn't recognize her. Greg left the truck door open and sat on the floor of the truck, his work boots on the ground.

"Why, I'd know that little girl anywhere. That's my girl, Ingrid," he said. "Daddy!" she said and ran into his open arms. "It is you!"

"Look how big you are! I'm glad I didn't call you Astrid! Anyway, I was teasing. I remember you. I could be at the very top of a Ferris wheel and still be able to pick you out of the crowd."

"Oh, Daddy, I miss you so much. Are you all better?"

"All better? What do you mean?"

"Mommy said you were sick. That's why you couldn't be with us."

"That's what your mom said, huh? What else did she say?" Greg felt bad, pumping his little girl for information.

"Nothing, just she was sad and hoped you could find a good doctor to help you."

Greg felt the tears threaten his eyes. Even after it all, she wasn't throwing him under the bus. That only reinforced his position that she deserved better than his sorry ass.

"I'm sorry, Jelly." He called her his pet name for her. Astrid was peanut buddy. "I'm still looking for a good doctor."

"I hope you find one soon. We want you back, Daddy."

A car pulled in behind the truck. There was a woman behind the wheel.

"Who is that lady, Daddy?"

"Nobody, sweetie. Just my ride. Listen, I know I shouldn't ask you to keep a secret, but would you not tell anyone you saw me? I don't want Astrid to be upset that you saw me, and I didn't have time to come inside to see her."

"It's okay, Daddy. We're here all summer, so you can do it later," she said, kissing his cheek. "I miss your scratchy face."

"Well, I miss your face, too." He stood up and closed the door. "Let me help you hang up your stuff before I go." After he took care of her swimsuit and towel, he said goodbye and got in the car. He waved at his little girl, and she waved until he pulled out of sight.

"Who's that girl?" asked the driver, a girl named Sherri. "My sister's kid," he answered.

"She looks just like you," Sherri said and looked at him out of the side of her eye. "You should see her sister. Let's stop at the pub and have one," he said.

God, I really am a piece of shit, he thought. I could look at it like she took my kids and left me, or I drove her away and gave her no reason to stay. He knew where the truth lay. He couldn't get a drink soon enough.

Valerie drove around for a while, past the houses of her old friends. She drove over to the high school and looked at the football field, empty in the summer heat. She smiled at the memory of Greg. He looked so tall and handsome out there.

Valerie headed home but stopped for gas. She slid her card through the reader and started pumping, leaning against the car as it filled. A car pulled in on the opposite side, and a girl who was pretty ten years ago got out. She was now only barely pleasant-looking, a little short and squat. She walked by Val and said hello, and Val returned with her own hello. She hung the pump up and got back in the car.

She put her sunglasses on, pulled out into traffic, and drove away. Greg looked over his shoulder at her car until it faded from his view.

He marveled at how she looked almost unchanged from high school. Long, tall, and lean. Greg's eyes watered at the thought of Valerie. She was so beautiful. He didn't notice Sherri when she got in the car.

"Who was that girl?" she asked.

"Who?"

"The one pumping gas," Sherri pointed out.

"Oh. Her? I think she was ahead of me in high school."

Huh, he thought. I should write some of these lies down if I'm going to start telling so many.

"She's kind of scrawny," Sherri said, mostly to see what his response would be.

"Yeah. I guess. I didn't notice."

Sherri put her car in drive and headed over to the pub. Greg got a beer and downed it. He ordered another one, and as he sat on a barstool, he thought about his family, even though he tried not to.

He thought about Ingrid. She was such a sweet, loving kid. He could see her greeting him every night he came home, like she did today. He worried about how she seemed like an empty vessel, desperate for love. If she didn't have a dad define for her what real, healthy love was, how would she recognize it as she grew and went out in the world? She'd be a sitting duck for awful men with bad intentions and not even know it.

Astrid. She ran hotter than Ingrid. He could see her give him a rash of shit and never speak to him again. She'd forever hold it against him, how he hurt them all. Astrid would demand he crawl on his hands and knees through hot coals and still not forgive him.

And Fiona. She could pass him on the street and have no idea he was her father when she grew up. Who knew what kind of father figure she'd seek out? He finished his beer and ordered another. He would need a full one when he considered Valerie. Seeing her at the gas station really rocked him to his core.

She looked as good as she did the first time he saw her. Back then, it was like she deliberately tried to go unnoticed. She stuck with her two friends and hid out in the library. Not his type. He should have known back then to pass. No, that wasn't true. It was only later that things went bad.

What happened? She didn't change; I did, he thought. It was the third child. Not Fiona specifically, but the responsibility of a third child pushed me over the edge. That was a load of bricks he couldn't get out from under. He didn't have the emotional or physical resources to figure it out. That was another great big lie he told himself. He didn't have the courage. He was a coward. He failed Valerie the most. A third child scared her, too. Greg promised her he'd be there for her—another lie.

Valerie rose up and met the challenge alone. He ran like a little bitch. First, into a bottle of beer, then into the ether. He ordered another beer, trying to blur the faces of his family so it didn't hurt so much. So, the fact that he was a coward didn't eat at him, so he could get far enough away he could live with himself.

They sat together and had a few beers. Greg, who was never much of a talker, was silent. Sherri decided she would be the one he turned to if he needed comfort. His wife and kids lived out of state, a divorce should soon follow, she figured. He was a couple years older than she was. She remembered when he was the star quarterback, and every girl in school wanted him. Of all those girls, she probably wasn't even on the list. That didn't matter. All those girls moved on to other things; she was the one next to him now. It didn't matter he wasn't interested in her romantically; just like she waited those other girls out, she'd wait him out too. Then, when he was too deep in the gutter and completely broken, it would be her turn. She would fix him up and make him hers.

"Hey, Sherri. Would you give me a ride home after this beer?"

"What's the rush?"

"I think I'm coming down with something. I don't feel so good," Greg said.

"Why don't you come back to my place? I'll stop and get some ginger ale and soup. I'll take care of you," she offered.

"No, it's more like a migraine. I need a dark room and silence. But thanks." Close, but no cigar, she thought. Next time.

Soon it was time for Valerie to leave. She planned in bringing Fiona back with her, but Dave and Ellin wanted her to stay, so Val was returning alone. The night before she left, they all went out for pizza for a going-away party. Afterward, she went back to Dave and Ellin's to tuck them in. Astrid was in the bathroom, and Val was with Ingrid in the room she shared with her sister.

"Mom? Can I talk to you?" Ingrid asked. "Sure. What's up?"

"I have a secret. I don't like secrets, they're too hard not to tell. Are you good at keeping secrets?"

"Not really. I forget they're supposed to be secrets, so I usually blab about it and get in trouble. Aren't you a little young to keep secrets? I mean, most grownups can't keep secrets. Who is it a secret from?"

"Astrid. She's not supposed to know because it might hurt her feelings."

"That's a pretty good reason to keep a secret, so you don't hurt somebody's feelings. Would it help if you told me? I'd keep it a secret, and you won't worry about it so much. Want to whisper in my ear?"

Ingrid nodded, and Valerie lowered her head. She cupped her hand around her mother's ear.

"I saw Daddy. He said not to tell because it might hurt Astrid's feelings. He parked his truck, and some lady picked him up. He didn't have time to go inside and say hello to her and didn't want to hurt her feelings."

"You saw Daddy? How is he?"

"He's still sick and looking for a good doctor."

"Oh, I'm sorry he's still sick."

"I told him to hurry up. I miss him and want him to come back home." Poor Ingrid, Val thought. There is no home to come back to.

"Yes, we all want him better. It's okay that you miss him. There is no reason why if you see him you can't talk to him. Astrid too. He's always going to be your dad. He's always going to love you. But no worries, your secret is safe with me."

Ingrid wrapped her arms around her mom. "I'm going to miss you, too. I wish you could stay."

"I'll be back before you know it, and that means summer will be over. Make sure you enjoy every day. Don't forget to visit Gramma Mary. She's staying."

"You'll be all alone, Mommy? Will you be okay?"

"I think I'll try to get a lot of work done so when you come back, I'll have plenty of time to play with you."

"Please? Try hard, Mommy. You don't play enough."

"I agree," said Val. "I'm leaving early in the morning, so kiss me goodbye now."

Astrid entered the room. "What? You're leaving?"

"Yes, I am, so get in bed so I can say goodbye to you."

Valerie said goodbye to Dave and Ellin. She planned on walking, but Dave offered her a ride. She preferred to walk, but got the impression Dave wanted to talk to her, so she accepted. Valerie was right. He pulled into her mother's driveway and turned the car off. She looked at him and waited for him to speak.

"I've enjoyed your visit, Val, and those kids just kill me with the stuff they come out with. They keep us laughing."

"It's very nice of you to take them for the whole summer. If they're too much, just call and I'll come get them."

"No need. They'll be fine. I am curious on your position about Greg. How involved do you want him to be?"

"As involved as he wants. Ingrid was out in the yard when he brought the truck back. She was so happy to see him. Now, Astrid, I have a feeling she's furious at him, and she will give it to him with both barrels, but Ingrid is more sensitive. She views his absence as a direct rejection of her.

"Ingrid said a lady picked him up. Is he involved with anyone? That might be a different conversation. He's not even divorced, and I want no strange women around them. Oh shit. I forgot the divorce papers. I'll send them to you." Valerie pushed some of the hair the wind blew loose from her ponytail out of her face and tucked it behind her ear.

"I don't think he's seeing anybody, but sometimes girls think differently. I'll find out. Since none of the legal issues have been worked out, I'll ask him to not bring anyone around, so as not to confuse the kids.

"But you. You'll be all alone. You haven't been by yourself in ages. What are you going to do?"

"I'm not sure what I'll do; I'll probably just work, although others will be on vacation, so I don't know how much I'll actually get done."

"Make sure you get some rest. You've been under a lot of stress, take some time to relax. We'll have the kids under control, between Ellin and I. What time do you want me to pick you up tomorrow morning?"

"For what?"

"Your ride to the airport?"

"Oh, it's early. I'll call a cab. I won't make my mom get up and bring me; I won't make you either."

"No. What time?" Dave insisted.

Valerie knew he wouldn't stop until she said yes. "Five thirty. You want to get up that early?"

"That's not early. Back in the day, I was on the job by six. Have a good night, Valerie. See you in the morning. Just cream in your coffee, right?"

"You're too kind, Dave. Would you make the girls ride their bikes over to my mom's every so often, just to say hello?"

"Done. See you in the morning."

Valerie got out of his car, leaned in and told him, "Thanks for everything. See you bright and early." She closed the door and walked up to the door. Val turned and waved as he left; she went inside. Her mom was sitting in her favorite chair, watching TV.

"How's it going, Mom? Enjoying the peace?"

"Very much. I have to ask you, Val, about your long-term plans."

"How so?"

"I think this is going to be my last time staying. Even with the help, it's hard. Just having Fiona climb all over me is exhausting. She's very mobile. I'm not fast enough to catch her. Not that it will be an issue, I hope, but she's entering the terrible twos, and I won't be able to handle a toddler. I like being home. I miss my house."

"Yeah, I can see that. We agreed it was only going to be a short-term fix. Could you help the fall through Christmas? I'll check and see about getting Fiona in a full-time preschool. Astrid and Ingrid will be in school all day. Ingrid swims every day, and Astrid has piano lessons. She wants to be a rock star."

Ingrid looked so much like her dad. She had that natural ability combined with grace. Valerie felt tears flood her eyes. She could see why Greg's loss of this gift he once possessed caused him such trauma. She could hear Greg's sneakers as they squeaked on the gym floor up and back, playing basketball for hours. Valerie smiled inwardly. He was such a gifted athlete, she thought. Football, basketball, it didn't matter.

Ingrid felt better telling her mom the secret. Holding it left her conflicted. What was her involvement supposed to be? How long was she supposed to keep it? Anyway, Valerie thought it was okay Greg stayed in the basement. Everyone was nice to each other. Astrid was sort of mad Ingrid saw him first. She was happy to see her dad in the end. Fiona cried, and he had to put her down. Ingrid never knew when he was here, that lady came for him often. He left with her.

"Daddy," Ingrid asked one Saturday morning, "who is that lady who picks you up? Do you like her better than Mom?"

"That lady?" he asked.

"Yes. You leave the truck here and go in her car."

"Oh. Her. You mean Sherri. No, I don't like her more than your mom. We go the same places, so she drives. There's nobody better than your mom."

"Then come home," she said. The solution seemed pretty simple to her. "Come home."

"I'm trying, Jelly," he said, another lie. "I'm trying."

***

Fourteen

VAL

VALERIE GOT HOME FRIDAY NIGHT. She only had one bag, no kids, and a house that hadn't been this quiet since they moved in. She was tired from her trip and sick of airport food. She found some ice cream and filled up a bowl. Val took it to her room, turned the TV on and looked for the trashiest show on cable.

Val changed into her pajamas and took the ice cream to eat in bed. It was odd not to have Fiona in the room. It was very nice to be alone. Valerie had forgotten the joy of not being responsible for anybody other than herself. She finished the ice cream, set the timer on the TV, and fell sound asleep. Val slept until late the next morning.

It was a beautiful day. Valerie took her coffee and toast outside on the balcony. It wasn't a huge space, and she put baby gates up to keep Fiona off the balcony, so consequently nobody went out there, but today it was not a concern. Valerie was on the third floor. She felt like a ghost haunting the place, it was so quiet with her family gone.

From her balcony, she could see the pool area. Already, families were laying claim to lounge chairs. She had one on her balcony and decided to do nothing more than read that stupid book. She wasn't answering the phone unless it was her family. Peaceful, blessed, silence.

"Hello?" a male voice called over the balcony.

Val stood up and looked over the railing. "Is someone calling me?" she asked loudly.

"Yes. Pardon me," he said, but knocked over a flowerpot and was momentarily distracted. "I was hoping you'd invite me over for coffee."

"What? Do you want me to invite you over for coffee? Why would I do that?" Val asked him.

"Because I really want a cup of coffee, and I'm out. I don't feel like getting in my car and driving to the store or Starbucks."

Valerie looked at him. He was older than she, his smile didn't look false, and he looked like he just wanted coffee.

"Do you expect to drink it here?" she asked.

"Only if you invite me to."

"I'm not sure about the invite, but you can get a cup of coffee. Come on over."

She left her cup out on the balcony, went to the door, and let him in.

"Cups. Coffee. Cream and sugar," she pointed out. "Help yourself. I'm not making it for you." She went back out on the balcony to finish hers. He stuck his head out. "Would you like another one?"

If someone was going to wait on her, she was going to say yes. "Just cream, please," she answered and handed him her cup. He came out, handed her back her cup, set his cup on the table, and took a seat.

He reached for his cup, took a sip and made a contented sigh afterwards and said, "Delicious. Thank you so very much. I should introduce myself. Walter Granger."

"Valerie Wilson. Nice to meet you, although I remember inviting you over for coffee, I don't remember asking you to stay."

"I'm sorry, excuse me. I didn't mean to be presumptuous. I thought I might spill it or it would get cold on the way back. I'll go," he said, and stood up.

"Don't bother, sit back down. You don't need to ruin a good cup of coffee over your bad manners."

" Hey," he said and frowned.

Valerie laughed. "My bad. I was just kidding. Enjoy your coffee. I'm feeling generous. Have a second cup."

Valerie looked at him. Walter Granger was older than she was, maybe about ten years. He wore rimless glasses, and his dark hair was cut close to his head. Walter looked taut. Short hair, little body fat, muscular. His eyes were dark brown, unobstructed by eyeglass frames. He must have recently shaved, his chin and cheeks looked smooth. Walter Granger smiled without guile or threat. He appeared harmless.

"Where's the rest of your crew?" he asked.

"Who?"

"All those girls who live with you. Your sorority. They're kind of loud."

"Well, the older lady is my mom, and the kids are with my in-laws for the summer. My mom's back home recovering from her time here, and I, for the first time in a long time, don't have to think about anybody but myself," Valerie said..

"Not to be nosy, but you didn't mention a man. Not either a husband or father. I imagine there had to be one once."

"My husband, well, he made his choice, and it wasn't us. The kids are staying at his parents' for the summer. I'm trying to preserve whatever thread there is so the kids maintain some resemblance of a relationship with their dad. His parents are great people; they love those girls. That's the connection I want to preserve. I don't have any responsibilities but my own for the next six weeks. It's been so long since I've been alone, I don't know what to do, so I decided right now I'm going to do nothing. It's quite a luxury. I'm still working, but because a lot of people are on vacation, everything is on pause, so I guess I get to destress for the rest of the summer."

"That's where I've seen you. Do you work for the Lambert Development Group?"

"Yes, I do. What's your connection?"

"The hotel project. I'm an electrical engineer. I think you sat in on one of our meetings. You're not the typical suit."

"How so?"

"For starters, you don't get up and waste ten minutes of our time introducing yourself and your goals and objectives, when the meeting isn't about what management can do for us, it's what we need from management. Two weeks later, we get a report from Valerie Wilson, outlining what we requested and who's going to get it for us. With names of the people responsible. Naming names. I'm surprised nobody's fired you yet."

"That's why they hired me. To drop the hammer with velvet gloves, I guess. Surveys showed management was unresponsive to departmental needs. So, I go to meetings. Observe. Take notes. Follow up. If there's a problem, the person whose job it is to handle such things, you have the name. I think I'm supposed to keep an audit trail to cover everyone's ass, but I mostly do it to cover my own. Since nobody ever gave me a job description, I created my own. What session were you there?"

"Oh, HR's responsibility to contract workers. Which is basically none, because we file 1099s. We are considered independent contractors, and we all know it."

"Yeah. I remember that one. It was hard to stay awake," she said. He laughed.

"Now that you know all my stats, tell me a few of yours."

"I'm one month into a three-month assignment. I report directly to James DiSiva. I was born in Tulsa. Went to Penn State, originally for meteorology, but switched. Settled in Philadelphia for most of my working career and moved to Boston five years ago. I've never been married, no children that I can recall. In my free time, I golf. I'm the middle child, I have an older brother and a younger sister. Good Irish Catholics. Not too many in Tulsa."

"Are you gay? In the closet?"

"No, but why do you ask?"

"You have no baggage: ex-wife or children. No immature man child searching for his bliss while living in your basement. Not tied to any one place. Are you kinky? Some kind of pervert?"

He laughed again. "You didn't ask me if I was a serial killer or a domestic terrorist."

"Well, are you?" she probed.

"Absolutely not. Ignore the duct tape and zip ties in the trunk."

"What's wrong with you? How come you never got married?"

"I guess that old tried and true 'I've never met the right one' applies here. Or maybe I just never met the one that was right enough. Why are you so nosy?"

"We have to talk about something. I apologize. I've not had a casual conversation with anybody in like ten years that didn't end with 'you better not get jelly on my new sofa.'"

"Is it hard? Being a single mother?"

"That's what I am? Yeah, I guess I am a single mother. Which line is for the government cheese? Sorry. Bad joke. My apologies to single moms everywhere. At the moment, it's easy as pie. When they're here, I am very lucky. I have my mom plus the nanny."

"May I ask what the situation is with their dad? He doesn't seem that dominant in the picture."

Valerie sat back, took another sip of her coffee and narrowed her eyes at him. She evaluated the risk in telling him anything, or everything. Valerie decided to tell him it all, and maybe it would scare him away.

"Don't you wish you asked the people on the other side for coffee?" Valerie sipped her coffee.

"No. Just to let you know, my dad was an alcoholic. He was a mean drunk. I wanted so badly for my mother to take us and escape, but she didn't. Maybe she had no place to go. She got married right after high school, so she never developed any skills as far as being able to get a job. It's probably because she was scared about supporting herself and three kids, about what my father would do if she left. He was a domineering prick. My mom lived in fear most of her life, and any nerve she was born with, he probably beat it out of her, and she couldn't fight back.

"It's hard to be a little kid with an alcoholic in the house. We had to play outside because if we woke him up, he was brutal. It would be freezing rain or a tornado, still we were thrown outside to play. You're just being a kid, and your brother takes your toy, you yell and get in a fight. Typical sibling stuff.

"If he got out of bed because of you, he would walk by, and it was a backhand to the face. He never said anything. You'd be sitting there on the floor, playing with your cars, and suddenly he'd smack you. It came out of nowhere. I can see why my mother was afraid. He wasn't the kind of guy who beat her on the regular, but he wasn't afraid to put his hands on her. My brother—he was two years older—as soon as he graduated high school, he took off. He left me, my mother, and sister and didn't look back.

About this time, I had grown into a man.

"I wasn't a skinny, wimpy teenager anymore. I had some bulk to me. My sister was sitting at the kitchen table doing her homework, and I think she took the last soda or something, but my dad smacked her one good and knocked her so hard she fell out of the chair. I snapped and punched him as hard as I could. He hit the wall and went down. I told him if I ever saw him lay a hand on my mother or my sister again, he'd get the beatdown of his life.

"I graduated high school and went to work. I stayed home for three years to make sure my sister was safe. When she graduated, I gave her the money I saved from working and told her to go to college and don't look back, and I joined the Marines. I re-upped once. I didn't know if I was college material. I decided I was, so when the second tour was over, I left and went to school. I initially thought of meteorology, but I trained in the military in electrical operations, so I just continued on that path. I wasn't your typical college kid. I was older and worked full-time, but I got through it. So, the moral of the story is growing up with an alcoholic parent sucks and causes a lot of damage, so don't question yourself if you did the right thing. Getting them out of a bad situation is what a responsible parent does," he finished.

"I told the kids the reason he's not with us is he's sick, and he needs to find a good doctor to get better, and when he's not sick anymore, he can come back. The longer this goes on, the less likely things are going to get better."

Valerie clamped down on her feelings to prevent any evidence of emotion, but was only partially successful. She couldn't help the tears that insisted on pricking in her eyes. She was loathe to have them fall, so she looked away to put her focus somewhere, anywhere else.

Walter Granger looked at his neighbor, who shared more than a cup of coffee, she pretty much told him her life story. The unshed tears in her eyes meant the wound was still fresh. He decided to change the subject, but he couldn't help but ask her if she still loved him. She was quiet a minute or two before she answered.

"The short answer is yes, I do. He's the only man I ever loved, the father of my kids and all that. We have grown so far apart, I don't think there's any way the relationship could be salvaged. To be honest, I don't want him back. He had more than his share of second chances."

"Where is he? I can go beat the shit out of him for you if you like."

"Didn't your father teach you violence is never the answer?"

"Point taken. I just thought it might make you feel better. I'd get nothing out of it." he paused. "Would you like another cup of coffee?"

"Thank you, but no. Help yourself, though."

He stood and took her cup into the kitchen. He came out empty handed. "Are you in the mood for more company, or shall I go home?"

"You can stay, although I have no idea why you'd want to. I just told you about my mess of a life. Why aren't you screaming, 'This chick's fucked up!' and running for the door?"

"Because I have nothing better to do," he said.

"Well, points for honesty. But I have nothing more to say. If you're going to stay, you have to talk. Tell me about your broken engagement."

"What broken engagement?"

"It's obvious. If you aren't gay or extremely screwed up, there had to be at least one serious relationship. Even if you are too screwed up, there are women out there into that," Valerie pointed out.

"You're not too far off the mark. Because I was in the military before college, I felt so much older. I was so much older. When I went out into the working world, I didn't have much in common with other kids. They were kids, overgrown boys. I felt being a man was instilled in me in the Marines. A boy went in, and the output was a man.

"I worked, went to the gym, and went home. Even when I traveled, I stuck to that schedule. So, meeting someone at work didn't fit; I wasn't around long enough to establish more than a casual hello. I did meet a woman at the gym. We had that in common. She was very nice looking, fit, healthy. I found that attractive. When I was home, we were pretty serious. We were serious for a long time, too long.

"She said put a ring on it or move out, and I was gone by noon. I never gave up my apartment. That should have been a big red flag. After her, unless God himself picked her out, I wasn't interested. God must have been busy in the Middle East because other than a casual lunch, I found nobody worth a second look.

"I put it down to my parents. Not having seen a healthy marriage growing up kind of soured me to the whole idea. Unfortunately, it gives credence to your fears about your daughter's prospects. I didn't have a mother like you. A mother who communicated the message that I was worth saving."

"Your sister. How did things work out for her?"

"She's a happily married mom of two kids."

"Maybe because you stayed to see her through high school, she had a sense of her own value. Maybe you came to her defense and laid out your old man, she knew there were good men out there."

"If that's true, and those three years helped my sister to grow up to be the person she is now, it wasn't a sacrifice. She's worth it. Enlisting was a good thing. The discipline and structure helped a lot. I craved it; I was making decisions for other people since I was fifteen. I was glad to let someone else tell me what to do."

"Huh," she answered. "It was nice to have someone to talk to over a cup of coffee. Come back tomorrow if you want."

"Perhaps I will. We talked so long it's now lunchtime. Are you hungry? Interested in a casual lunch?"

"Yes and no. I'm hungry and there's no food in the house, so a casual lunch sounds good. I really need to go grocery shopping, though. So that's the no."

"They say you should never go grocery shopping hungry," Walt said. "How about this: We go to lunch and then go to the grocery store."

"It's good, but I should drive myself so you can skip the store."

"I'll drive. I have to pick up a few things myself."

"That's fine. For the rest of the summer, I think I will agree to pretty much anything and defer the decisions. It seems when you have kids, they are so needy and want stuff, and I always have to figure out how to get Ingrid to her swim club and Astrid to piano, while balancing Fiona, who is overdue for her nap."

"Those are some interesting names."

"You should talk, Walter."

"My full name is William Walter Granger. I don't use William. I was named after my bastard of a father. Professionally, it's W. Walter Granger, but I refuse to give my father the pleasure of using his name. As bad as Walter is, that's it."

"Are you a junior?"

"Not that I'll admit."

"Well, Walter it is. You tell me what our plans are."

"I think, Valerie, I'd like to take you to lunch and then do some grocery shopping."

"Fine. Let me grab my bag and take me to your favorite lunch spot." The place he chose was a nondescript restaurant off of Main. It was named Fat Linda's, and Valerie had never been there. When she mentioned that, he smiled to himself. He was delighted he could show her something new, and he didn't want to think too deeply about why. Walter parked in the back, and they went in the back door. It opened right next to the kitchen, and the waitstaff used that area as a station. They had to cut between the servers to get to the dining room.

He led, and most of the people knew him. They called him Ranger. He took her hand so they could pass single file. Once they passed the bottleneck, he didn't release her hand. Walter held it until he ushered her to a booth. Val sat on one side, and he the other. Walter looked at her and smiled. She smiled back at him.

"You held my hand," she said.

"Did I? I guess I did. How tall are you?" he asked.

"Five-foot-nine. When we have those management meetings, I always wear three-inch heels. Maybe nobody knows, but I like to play head games with those dolts. If I'm six feet tall, it's intimidating for some of the shorties. How tall are you?"

"Five-eleven. If you wear three-inch heels, you'll be taller than me."

"Does that bother you?"

"Hell no. If I bring you anywhere formal, you'd have to wear those heels. I'd be the envy of all the other guys because I landed a supermodel. That would be quite a score. It's hard not to want to show it off. You have skills. Mad skills. What a waste if they're never acknowledged."

"Are you goofing on me? Since when are high heels considered a skill? Where would we go that I needed heels? I don't go places if heels are required."

"What about a wedding?"

"You have any on your calendar?"

"No, but maybe we could crash one. Or New Year's Eve," Walter said, looking her in the eye.

"You'll be long gone by New Year's Eve."

"What if we go to a wedding on New Year's Eve?"

"Uncle! I'll go to a wedding on New Year's Eve. I'll even wear four-inch heels."

"Four-inch? Okay, now you're talking."

"Who's your friend, Ranger?" the waitress asked as she approached with menus. "This is my friend, Valerie. Valerie, this is Linda."

"Linda? Fat Linda? You're Fat Linda?" Valerie said to the rather slim Linda. "Yes. It's creative license. Would you stop at Skinny Linda's?"

"No."

"Nobody would."

Valerie ordered the Greek chicken salad sandwich in a pita. He ordered the turkey club and fries. Linda left, and Valerie looked at Walter; he looked back at her. "Are you enjoying yourself, Valerie?"

"I am. Simple pleasures, I guess. I'm pretty easy to get along with. I usually don't demand much. I'm self-sufficient and I can take care of myself."

"That's good. I haven't had a casual lunch in some time. Women like you make men nervous."

"What does that mean?" Valerie asked him, not sure she wanted to hear the answer.

"You wouldn't hesitate to cut off my balls and serve them to me for lunch. I bet there are lots of tricks you use to make people do what you want."

"Whoa," she said and pushed her hands out. "I'm not sure that's a fair assessment. I don't do anything to make people do what I want."

"That's the thing. You don't have to do anything. People must think there's more going on than there appears, so they better not fuck around."

"You give me way more credit than I deserve."

"Not at all. There's a head table of corporate suits. Seven. Five men, all replicants of each other. One woman of color, and you. You're quiet and serene. You know everyone there by name. Nobody in the room has one bad thing to say about you except the short guys. The fact that you don't speak loudly and call attention to yourself makes you easy to overlook. People like you strike like a scorpion. Nobody sees it coming, and it stings like hell."

"Do you read cards, too? I'm none of those things. When did you even have time to think about all that?"

"Last year, I was here and sat in through one of those mind-numbing presentations. My mind wandered, and I stopped when I saw you. So I created this whole backstory for you. I do that a lot when I'm in those meetings. Otherwise, I tend to get up to go to the men's room and stop at the bar. I wander around the lobby. When I hear applause, I go back in. Nobody's caught on yet."

"Yeah, I know what you mean. My mind wanders, and I do the same thing. Like the speaker. What's his deal? Does he cheat on his wife? Sneak outside to smoke? It's easy to do. But me. I'm a cypher, an enigma, wrapped in riddle. Is that how that goes?"

Their food came. She removed the sliced red onions. She took the chicken salad out of the pita and looked at its contents.

He laughed at her. "Something wrong?"

"No, it looks good." She took a bite. "It tastes very good. Nice choice."

They ate their lunch and made innocuous small talk. Walter paid the check, and they left the way they came in. He reached for her hand and escorted her out the back door, and held her hand until he reached the car. Walt let go and searched his pockets for the keys. He opened the door for her, and once she was inside, he closed her door. Walt got in and started the car, pulled out, and reached again for her hand.

She looked at their entwined fingers but said nothing. Walter stopped at the grocery store, and they completed their errands.

They arrived back at the complex, he parked the car but made no move to exit. "What do you want to do now? We have some time to kill until dinner."

"What are you doing? We have coffee, lunch, and now you want to hang out and have dinner? I have groceries I need to put away."

"Isn't it obvious? I enjoy your company. It's a Saturday afternoon, the sun is shining, and I have no plans. Do you?"

"Um, no. Other than the grocery store. I'm trying to figure out your intent. I'm a married woman with a whole lot of baggage. There's no point to any of this," Valerie said, looking him straight in the eye.

"You're right. There is no point, but I still enjoy your company. I thought because it was all about you for the next few weeks, we could hang around and do stuff."

"Yeah, like going to the store. Otherwise, I planned just lying on the couch and binge-watching Intervention while eating cold pizza in the dark."

"Are you wearing pants?"

"What? Why?"

"If you're not wearing pants, that means you have no plans to leave the couch."

"Maybe PJs. Or shorts. Or just underwear. I haven't thought that far ahead. Why are you interested?"

"When I'm out on a job I never talk to women. It always happens after you spend some time with a woman; they want to follow you to the next job or figure out how you hook up again. Your baggage is the attraction. You can't follow me anywhere."

"That's true. Why would I want to? Follow you, I mean?

"This is why." He picked up her hand. "What do you feel?"

She looked down and wrinkled her forehead. "It's nice. Warm. Smooth. Secure."

"Anything else?" She looked at him. "Okay. I like it. I'm comfortable. It's going to make me cry."

"Why would it make you cry? It's not supposed to."

"It symbolizes that I've moved on. If I were still hung up on my husband, I'd take it back. I'd tell you to go away. But I'm not doing anything, other than sitting here waiting to see what happens next."

"What do you want to see happen?"

"It doesn't matter what I want. The ball's in your court. I told you I was taking the rest of the summer off when it comes to decisions. I'm tired of being in charge. But your hand. It makes me realize how long it's been since anybody touched me without grubby fingers. It makes me accept that my husband checked out of our marriage a long time ago. But again, your hand. It's nice. I bet you didn't expect all that, did you?"

"I don't expect anything. I was wondering if you felt what I did. I wouldn't consider it a connection, but more like a mutually pleasant reaction. It's enjoyable. Your hand fits my hand like a missing puzzle piece. It fits perfectly."

"It's been even longer since I've had a conversation with someone and not get interrupted by someone who wants something from me. You don't want anything from me, do you?"

"Just to be your friend. I think you need one."

"Probably. I have a couple of good friends, but we communicate through email. They're spread out all over."

"I'm right here. Do you want to go get some sweats on and watch TV? We can order a pizza. If you want it cold, I'll put a few slices in the fridge. Tomorrow is supposed to be nice, too. We can go somewhere if you want."

"Yes. Let's go get our sweats on and go watch some TV. We can just hang out. That's all I want to do right now. It's all I'm capable of at this point."

They decided to change into more comfortable clothes. He went home, changed and came over to her place. She sat next to him and tucked her feet under herself. Walter had his on the coffee table and found a movie that they both agreed was acceptable. As the movie played, he noticed she was getting heavier, leaning into him. Walter looked over, and she was asleep. He moved a bit to give her his shoulder to rest her head. While she was asleep, he was able to get a good look at her close up.

Her face showed few wrinkles, complexion smooth and even. Her eyelashes were long enough to cast shadows on her cheeks. Her face was absent a visible seam of make-up. She probably wears very little, he thought.

Valerie, are you a complicated woman, or a woman with complications? I don't do complicated women. There's always some drama with girls like that. For instance, her divorce. Is it going to be as quick and clean like she thinks, or will her dumb-ass-soon-to-be-ex-husband wake up and realize what he's losing and beg for a second chance? Would she probably decide to try again for the kids' sake? Dating a freshly divorced woman is dangerous. I always end up as a shoulder to cry on to mourn the death of her marriage, when all I want to do is to fuck.

I don't know her well enough to be thinking about these things. Yet here he was, thinking such things. Women like Valerie don't climb the corporate ladder if they were dithering idiots. Walter looked at her again. She looked so young. She had kids. What he thought would be a carefree summer romp was morphing into something yet unnamed. I should wake her up and run like hell. Instead, I move to make her more comfortable. It won't matter. In two months, I'll be gone.

Valerie stirred and woke up. She blinked a few times to shake the sleep from her eyes. She realized her head was on his shoulder; she pushed herself off and straightened herself up.

"Oh, geez," she said and wiped her mouth with the back of her hand. "Sorry. I fell asleep. I hope I didn't drool all over you."

"No problem. The movie wasn't that great. You didn't miss much."

"Oh. What should we do now?"

Fuck your brains out. Instead, he smiled at her and said, "Valerie. What are you going to do if your husband pushes back and contests the divorce?"

"You mean, what if he sobers up and tries to change my mind?"

"Yes."

"Nothing. I've hired the best divorce lawyer in town, and she can figure it out." Valerie sat back and considered his question like she never realized he might do that. "I don't hate Greg and hope he gets hit by a bus. I hope he sobers up for the girls' sake, and his own. I want them to have a dad. I mean, he is their dad, but I want them to have a dad who's present in their lives.

"I loved him. A part of me always will, but the opportunity to fix things is long past. Even if he heals from his trauma and is able to have a healthy relationship, it's not going to be with me. It's going to be with his kids. Does that answer your question?"

"Yeah. That's enough. I happened to think about it while you were asleep."

"What else were you thinking about me?"

"That your resume is very impressive, and about what type of woman it takes to claw their way up to be a contender for the corner office. You seem to be too nice a person to step all over people on your way up."

She laughed. "You know, part of it might be because I really don't give a shit. When I started, I had an ancient metal desk, a phone, and about a two-foot-tall pile of accounts. I did what they told me to do the way they told me to do it. I worked my way through the pile, so they gave me another pile, and I worked my way through that. I guess I was consistent. I always met my numbers. I never made any enemies. I was steady, someone you didn't have to worry about.

"Who knows? Usually, people who are really good at their jobs get stuck there. No reason to move them. Who is going to produce like they do? Some moron gets the job or promotion, and the one who produces moves on to someplace else that will treat them better. So, if you look at it now, you're down two people. The one who produces and the moron who is useless. Maybe I was in the right place at the right time. Maybe they wanted a woman for diversity's sake.

"Maybe they want to communicate to the rest of the employees there's room for growth, so they bring up a woman who's been around a while. Maybe it was to show those good employees who leave, you too can be rewarded, a way to improve employee retention. Or maybe I was the only one willing to relocate. A million things that don't have anything to do with me, I don't know."

"Did you wear three-inch heels to the interview?"

"Yup."

"You just scared the guy enough to promote you."

"There was that." She smiled.

"Valerie, you should write a book. 'How To Succeed In Business Without Really Trying.'"

"I think somebody already did."

"How To Climb The Corporate Ladder In Stilettos?"

"That's good. Or 'How To Swim With The Sharks and Not Ruin Your Blowout.'" "What's a blowout?"

"A hairstyle. How about 'How To Make Your Numbers Without Losing Your Dignity?'"

"I like that one. Are you hungry? Want me to order the pizza now?" he asked.

"No. I already ate today."

"What? That lunch? A piece of chicken and some lettuce? No wonder you're so thin. Do you have some sort of eating disorder?"

"No, I just got into the habit of not eating. I always plan on eating something, but something distracts me, and I'm in the car on the way home, thinking about what to make for dinner, and I realize I didn't have lunch. I think Americans eat too much anyway, so it's no big deal."

"Maybe not, but it's not healthy."

"Says who?"

"Your doctor. And me. A bag of bones isn't very attractive. Nobody wants to cuddle with a bag of bones." She laughed at him.

"Are you a closet cuddler? A guy who admits he likes to cuddle. You should have your testosterone checked."

"I might enjoy a little one-on-one with a pretty girl. So what do you like on your pizza?"

"I like black olives, but nobody else does, so either cheese or sausage, depending on who I'm eating it with."

"Sausage? What do the girls like?"

"Usually just cheese. Or half black olives. Fiona likes olives. She calls them ollips."

"That's cute. You have nice ollips," Walter said.

"So do you," Valerie answered.

"I have wonderful lips, full and soft," he bragged.

"I can see that."

"You need to feel them to really appreciate them."

Valerie moved fast. She had her mouth millimeters from his. She barely grazed his lips with hers. He felt her breath mingle with his, and if her lips came any closer, she would be giving him mouth-to-mouth resuscitation. Walter was afraid to kiss her. Once he started, he didn't think he'd be able to stop. It didn't matter because she took her tongue and licked his bottom lip. Valerie placed her lips on his and stopped.

Walter wasn't sure what to do, but while he was considering his options, he felt her mouth move on his, and he had to play catch-up. He was confused by what she was doing. Her tongue moved so fast he couldn't predict where or when it would pop up next; he just had to wait for it to appear and try to respond, but she was on to the next place before he could answer.

Walter suddenly felt like all the air from his lungs was gone, and his chest collapsed. If he didn't take control of the situation soon, he'd be nothing but a drooling idiot when she was done. The next time she put her lips on his, he didn't wait. He answered her with some pressure of his own. She was momentarily confused; she thought she was running the show, but he slid in the gap and kissed her.

It was now her turn to follow his mouth, to react and chase his lips with hers. He had her in his arms and was going to kiss the living shit out of her until she was breathless and stuttering. It was only then he'd release his embrace and let her go. She pulled her head back and sank into him. She wasn't a bag of bones but a quivering mass of Jell-O.

They both just sat there, neither speaking. Finally, Walter said, "Valerie. We have to talk." The hair on the back of her neck stood up. Good news never started with those four words.

"Why? Can't we just sit here and be quiet?"

"I want you to listen. I don't know how you feel about what just happened, but it can't happen again. You're married. I don't take up with married women, and I don't usually see women recently divorced. They always have underlying issues they need to work through. That never works because you always say the wrong thing, but it's a trap. There never is a right thing to say. I don't stay in one place long enough to get involved with an emotionally fragile woman."

"Is that what I am? Emotionally fragile?"

"I don't know. You don't know. You only find out when it's too late and feelings get hurt. I'm not going to be here to help you get over your divorce. I'm not going to be here to help you manage your emotions. Whatever happens, you deal with the fallout alone, and you have three kids that need you. That's where you should put your energy. That's what you need, not driving to some soccer game crying over my absence."

"Huh," Valerie responded and then was silent.

"What does that mean? 'Huh.'"

"It means I heard you. That's your position. I'm not going to talk you out of it. You're old enough to have gone through this a few times. I'll defer to your expertise."

"That's it? You're not going to tell me I'm wrong? That you're the one that'll be different?"

"Nope."

He clenched his jaw. He expected her to thank him for his unselfish nobility; instead, she said, "Don't let the door hit you in the ass on your way out." That irritated him to no end.

"What's the matter?" Valerie asked him. "Isn't that what you wanted to hear?"

"It's what I wanted to hear, but I didn't like the way it sounded coming out of your mouth."

"What if I said summer was all I was good for? Once my kids come back, I'll be too busy to hang out with you. I don't want to break your heart. Being with me is a dead end. I wouldn't want any guy not related to us within five miles of my girls. I didn't expect you to ask me to go steady."

"So, you'd be content to have a summer fling? That's enough for you?"

"I might have, but not anymore," Valerie replied.

"B-But," Walter stuttered.

"But nothing. Go. You're just a rambling man, so just ramble on home."

"What about the pizza?" he asked.

Valerie stood up and looked down at him. "Get up. I have a frozen one in the freezer. Out." She went to the door and opened it. "See you."

He stood up. "You're making me leave?"

"Yeah. I'm making you walk home. Good thing it's only next door."

He didn't believe she actually threw him out. He was too stunned to react and followed her pointed finger to the door. Women didn't dump him. He did the dumping.

"Valerie—" he started to say, but she shut him down.

"Out." He went through the doorway but turned around and looked at her as if there was some sort of mistake. He stood outside her door and looked at her dumbfounded.

"Walter?" she said.

"What?"

"Fuck you." She slammed the door in his face.

The next day, he sat on his balcony and waited for Valerie to appear, but she didn't come out. He knocked on her door, but she didn't answer. He didn't know her phone number, so he couldn't call her. Walter wanted to talk to her and clear up any misunderstanding, but she apparently felt there was no miscommunication.

Her message came through loud and clear. He was puzzled about what exactly he should do. Walter couldn't work things out with her if she wouldn't talk to him. He told her why it was a lost cause, and she agreed. She didn't cry or look at him with unshed tears in her eyes.

In all his years of dating, he could not recall a woman acting like her. He didn't see her all day, and when he got up the next morning, her car was gone. Fuck, he thought. She turned the tables on me and tossed me out. Well, Ms. Valerie Wilson. Game on.

***

Valerie had an early morning meeting scheduled. She had a special place in her heart for these dopes who scheduled meetings for six a.m. on a Monday in July or August. It was to illustrate how hungry the employee was to demonstrate their dedication to the job. Valerie didn't care. She'd show up and listen to their issues. She'd draw up an action plan. She'd dictate it to her admin. Copy everybody. Assign task-specific corporate bullshit, and kick it up to the president, whose admin will toss it.

To have Valerie Wilson's whole attention the entire time, was a worthy bullet point to have on your resume. Plus, she was nice and approachable, not the seething dragon lady people made her out to be. She was known to pick a junior rep and let them shadow her for a bit. She might pick a project she liked and give it the green light for the summer, that person answered directly to her. It was too funny how seriously they took her. It made her think back to her career. She'd be back there slugging away at that never-ending two-foot pile, wasting the opportunity to network with a higher-up.

Once she went in the back looking for a certain girl who she saw most mornings, but quickly dropped off the radar once she entered the building. Valerie was bored one day and went through the cubicles looking for her. She wondered where her desk was located, but Valerie couldn't find her. She wandered around and introduced herself to the support staff. Val met everyone and talked a bit, giving management a friendly face instead of the ego-driven personalities that made people hide when it rippled through the floor. After a while, she said she had to go. Valerie set off through the maze to wander back to her office.

Most upper management wanted to work Tuesday, Wednesday, and Thursday and had that second family to take on vacation during the summer. Someone from corporate needed to be available, and Valerie volunteered. Everybody won. Val got more time off during the school year.

She made her way back to her desk, noticing her administrative assistant had flowers on her desk. How sweet, Val thought. She entered her office and looked around. She sat and glanced at the pile requiring her signature. She pulled a bunch over. A knock on the door broke her focus. It was Jackie, her AA, with the flowers. Valerie looked at them and tilted her head. "Very nice. Special occasion?" she said to Jackie.

"I should ask you. They're not for me."

"Well, they're certainly not for me."

"Yes, they are," Jackie insisted.

"Oooh, flowers. Gimme." Valerie motioned with her arms. "Is there a card?" Jackie pulled the spike out that held the card. On the card was written a single word. "WILL."

"What does that mean?" Valerie asked.

"Does some guy named Will have a crush on you? Otherwise, I can't imagine. I don't run in the same circles as you. The delivery guy said to keep the stick."

"Huh," Val said to herself. She sat down and admired the flowers.

After a while, Jackie came with a deli bag. "Lunch."

"I didn't order anything."

"I don't know. It was mistakenly left on seven. They brought it up."

It was a turkey sandwich and a bottle of water. The original seal was intact, so she ate it. It was a good sandwich.

The next morning, Walter left for work, and her car was still parked.

He looked up, but the drapes were drawn. He went to work. After lunch, he gave the mail guy twenty bucks to see what was happening in her office. Walter came back and reported these ladies all gathered around her door, but he didn't know why. Another bouquet had arrived, and the ladies were all debating what the card signed "YOU" meant.

The next couple of days, he was on-site and not able to keep tabs on his experiment. He wouldn't be home until Saturday.

Jackie brought over the flowers that downstairs had sent up. She had in her hands another vase of flowers. Valerie asked Jackie to line up the vases from oldest to newest. The cards read, "WILL YOU BE."

"Be what, Valerie? Do you have any idea?" Jackie asked.

"No. I'm stumped," she said as she shook her head.

Jackie came back later with another deli bag. "They delivered it to seven again," she said. Valerie looked inside the bag but only found a bottle of water and a wrapped sandwich. She ate the sandwich and drank the water. That was twice this week when she had lunch. Twice. Lunch. Huh. It couldn't be him, could it?

Thursday, another delivery from the florist came. Jackie and all the staff were taking bets on who could be Valerie's secret admirer. Val stayed seated and looked at the flowers, all lined up; they read, "WILL YOU BE MY." Jackie peered at Valerie and saw the smile she was trying to hide.

"You know who it is! Who is it, Val?" Jackie begged.

"'Neighbor?' Will you be my neighbor? Mr. Rogers? I think I know who it is, but I want to wait for tomorrow to be sure."

"Who? Please," said Jackie. "Does he work here, at least?"

"No," Val said. "I think it's my next-door neighbor. The sandwich gave it away."

"Is he good-looking?" Jackie asked.

"Yeah, I guess so. Did I ever show you a picture of my husband?" Jackie shook her head no. She could not believe Ms. Wilson was sharing so much info about her personal life. Valerie opened a drawer and rooted it around the back. She pulled a frame out. It was a picture of her with Greg and the two older girls.

"Now this guy," Val said, "he was a thing of beauty."

Jackie said, "This is your family?"

"Yes, before the little one was born."

"You guys look so happy. If you have to have an ex-husband, I guess this one's pretty good." Jackie thought she overstepped the boss/underling relationship. "I'm sorry. I shouldn't have said anything."

"Well, he was the most beautiful man I've ever seen. You're not out of line admiring him. He lived for it."

"What happened? I'm sorry. I didn't mean to blurt that out, either. It's none of my business. I forget you're my boss."

"Didn't I tell you summer hours until Labor Day?"

"I think there's no such thing."

"Ah, I'll write some motivational crap and send it out early in the month." Val lifted up the picture and looked at her formerly happy family. "Long story short, he had an accident he never dealt with, and instead of seeking professional help to get over it, he pickled his pain with booze. He wasn't safe around the kids."

She put the picture back on her desk. "Ah, back to work. Jackie, if you could close the door behind you, that'd be great."

When she got there on Friday, everyone was abuzz about her flowers. She thought that she might send them to herself next summer, and the office seemed to enjoy them. They had to wait until Friday afternoon for the florist delivery. When nothing happened before lunchtime, they all thought the game was over, only to have Jackie race back to Valerie's office about two o'clock, everyone following her.

"What does it say? Did you see it?" the crowd murmured.

"Line them up, Jackie, and see what it says," Val said. Lined up, the beautiful riot of colors and attached cards read, "WILL YOU BE MY GIRL?" It was pretty impressive.

All eyes turned towards Val. She was a bit stunned about how to react to all the flowers. He told her why he couldn't see her, she agreed and showed him the door. What's the point of all this? she thought. Why the public display of affection? Is it affection? Is he mad I slammed the door in his face, and he's doing it as payback? Does he want to embarrass me in front of the staff? Asshole.

She didn't care if they knew about him. By Labor Day, he'd be in the distant past.

After work, she went home and poured herself a glass of wine. She wanted to sit on her balcony and enjoy the summer evening, and read her book in peace. There sure were a lot of handsome, hunky, hungry men in this town. The lawyer? The plumber? A veritable buffet of available well-adjusted men. This is truly a work of fiction.

She let her mind wander, and it wandered over to her neighbor. She couldn't decide whether to speak to him or not. Even at her age and having three kids, she didn't have a lot of experience with men. It was Greg, and some fling she had in college. She never dated around. Walter gave her a certain thrill, he lit up a part of her brain that she had not experienced before and was unsure how to process.

It was linked to sexual tension, flirtation, romance, all these unfamiliar feelings she wasn't sure she wanted to explore, but her mind kept pulling her back there. Valerie went inside and got ready for bed. The wine made her sleepy. She awoke in the middle of the night and turned off the TV, and fell back asleep.

Val was having her morning coffee outside the next day, her back to his unit. It wasn't until late that morning she heard sounds of activity, the squeak in his sliding door, the scrape of patio furniture being rearranged. The way he put the mug down on the glass table with a heavy thud. She thought one of these days it was going to go right through the tabletop, and shattered glass would fly everywhere, get in those tiny cracks in the stone you couldn't get with the vacuum, but a bare foot would catch one of those minuscule shards of glass and draw blood.

"Good morning!" he yelled over to her. "Mind if I come over? She waited a bit and yelled back, "Sure. The door's open."

It took him a bit to come over, but he did. He got a cup of coffee and sat down.

He looked at her and smiled. She looked back, her expression totally blank.

"Thank you for the flowers. They were beautiful, and the staff got a kick out of solving the puzzle. It was fun." Her face relaxed and she smiled.

"When did you figure out it was me?"

"After the second sandwich. That was confusing. It was always found on the seventh floor and brought up. That was very creative. A real red herring. I remembered telling you I didn't eat lunch because I didn't think about it, so somebody brought it up especially for me, and the admin looked for me deliberately in case I was waiting for it, genius. You made sure it would definitely get my attention. The flowers, it wasn't until the last word. The phrase, though, didn't make any sense."

"I thought it was direct and to the point."

"What was that big speech about the many ways I'm totally wrong for you? What was that all about? 'Be your girl.' Yeah, right."

"Well, sorry about that. You kissed me. I liked it. I'd like to do it again. There was a clause in there. If you kissed me and I liked it, you have to be my summer girlfriend," Walter explained.

"Oh. I didn't get to where I am by not reading the small print. What clause? What if I don't want to be your girlfriend?"

"You'll be my summer girl. Come on. Let's just see what happens. There's not enough time to get anything going."

"Yeah, but I have an issue with not being divorced. A married woman shouldn't have a boyfriend. I've never gotten divorced before. There could be major pitfalls or drama. I know I don't want him back. I don't know what he wants. I don't care, either, but he could cause you stress you've never considered."

"Then you absolutely shouldn't be my girlfriend."

"Although, I actually may be divorced. I signed the papers and sent them off. I don't know if he signed yet." Valerie scratched her forearm, and Walter watched her. He found her arm incredibly sexy.

"We seem to be in a gray area."

"Yes, yes, we are."

"Please? You're divorced. You signed. His signature is needed. He's the one that's not divorced," Walt told her.

"That is true. I'm getting the kids the weekend before Labor Day. You'll be gone the next week. It is doable."

"Yes. Let's just keep it on the down low. The less people involved, the better."

"What if I feel things aren't working out? Or it's going too far too fast for me."

"It's done. Over."

"Okay, summer boy, what do you want to do now?"

"Kiss some more."

"No. It's customary for the male to bring the female something to eat if he wants her to consider him as a mate. That's across species," Valerie informed him.

"You want some worms? Small rodents?" Walt asked her.

"I never said I wanted to mate with you. Anyway, that's a problem for me."

"How so?"

"My experience is minimal. I haven't been anyone's girl in ages. My sexual history is minor. You have never been married, correct? You've been screwing around for years. That concerns me. If I get involved with you, that means I get involved with all your prior partners. What am I exposing myself to?"

"Jesus. You want a note from my doctor? A sexual history report?" Walter said.

"Am I wrong?" Valerie asked him. "I don't know a lot about you. You were in the army. You've been all over the world. How do I know where you've scattered your seed?"

"You know, if I didn't find this conversation funny, I think I'd leave. 'Scattered my seed.' You're crazy."

"Look, I'm telling you I'm inexperienced. How do you have this conversation? Don't you have this discussion with possible partners? I think having sex nowadays is pretty risky."

"Yet we continue to do so. I think you're right to be concerned. As far as it pertains to me, I think I told you about how I grew up. Having a partner looked way too complicated and scary to me, so I don't think I've had as many as you think. But I am not a virgin, and there have been a few over the years. I'll bring a note from my doctor. I'm disease-free."

"I'm concerned I might get pregnant," Valerie confessed, "as much I worry about the STDs. I'm pretty good at that. Getting pregnant, I mean."

"Let's table this right now, we can revisit it in the future if needed. It's too early to talk about it. We can just make out. It's too late to worry about that, we've already done it. So do you want something to eat or not?"

"No. I can make myself toast if I get hungry."

What a ballbuster. Maybe that's why he liked her. She was so open and honest. Val defined what she wanted. It was up to him to decide if he could work within her parameters.

"What if I told you I understood how you managed to move up in corporate America. I was impressed with the way you tossed me out of here. You dropped a hammer on me, and I didn't feel the lump until later."

"Practice, Ranger, practice."

"It's a nice day. Let me take you on a date. I don't know if we even get along. What do people do when it's an afternoon date?"

"Go to the zoo. A movie? Brunch?" Valerie answered. "Yes. The zoo. Why not?" Walter said.

That's what they did. It was nice because there was plenty to talk about that wasn't person-specific, like penguins. She liked them because they came from so far away, he because he thought they looked like little waiters.

Afterwards, they went to the cafe/gift shop and split a sandwich. Val ordered a chocolate shake, and he wanted one too. It was so thick you couldn't suck it up until it thawed a bit. They were forced to talk while the shakes softened up. "So, Ranger, is this what you do on a date?"

"Yeah. This was a good date. Interesting. You learn who's afraid of what. I would swear you'd say alligators, but you said it's bats."

"Well, duh. All girls are afraid of bats getting tangled up in their hair. Everybody knows that."

"Not alligators?"

"No. So what animal are you afraid of, not that you'd admit to being afraid of anything."

"Camels."

"Camels? Why camels?"

"Have you ever been bit by one? Hurts like hell. It's also quite painful when they step on your foot. And they spit. Pretty nasty beasts all the way around."

"What kind of zoo allows you to get up close and personal with a camel?"

"They're pretty common in the Middle East. I was over there for a while when I was in the service."

She nodded, deep in thought.

"What shall I call you? You know, Ranger sounds sort of military, and Walter. Well, Walter sounds like someone's grandpa. Walt? Wally? What one do you prefer?" Valerie asked him.

Walter sucked on the straw until his cheeks were hollowed out and he was squinting. She sat and evaluated her options. "Walt, no. Walter, eh. Granger or Ranger? Stranger Danger. How about that?"

Valerie took her turn, trying to suck her milkshake. She looked at him and took her mouth off the straw. "Mysterious Stranger. That's you. If anybody asks me who you are, I'll say you're the 'Mysterious Stranger.'"

"Yes. Please call me that. By the way, the Army has the Rangers. 'Mysterious Stranger Danger Ranger Granger.' That works. You won't, though. It's too stupid for even you."

"You realize I find the stupider the better. I appreciate a full-on view of unadulterated stupidity."

"Okay, Val. What do you want to do now?"

"Go back to your place so you can try to score on me."

"Let's go." He stood up and grabbed her by the wrist. "Come along. I was taking notes on the primates. I saw a number of males copulating with the females. I saw a couple of things we could try."

They were soon back at the complex. They stood outside their doors, and he pointed at each one. She pointed at his. He opened his door and ushered her in.

"A glass of wine?" he offered. She accepted. They sat on the couch, and she kept giggling and acting kind of goofy.

"What's wrong with you? You're acting all weird," Walter said. "What do you mean?" she asked him and made a face.

"Well, you're bouncing in your seat. You're all flirty and weird. What's wrong with you?" Walter asked her.

"I thought the whole point of coming back here was so we could be alone and you could try to have your way with me. I guess I'm a little self-conscious. Aren't you going to kiss me?"

He laughed.

"Have my 'way with you'? You read too many romance novels, doll face."

"'Doll face'? You read too many pulp fiction novels from the '50s, buddy."

"Well, I need to figure out a name for you if you're going to call me Stranger? The only thing I can think of is 'Valerie the magnificent,'" he said, smiling at her.

"Besides, there is no law that says you can't kiss me."

"That's true." She slid closer to him on the couch. "Would you mind filling my glass?"

"Why? I thought you weren't a big drinker?"

"I'm not. I thought it would relax me."

Val's face was right there, he tried to listen, but he could only look at her mouth and lips move. Walter stopped listening and focused on her mouth. Her lips looked plump and ripe, juicy like berries, and she occasionally poked her tongue out to moisten them. The appearance of her tongue tipped the scales in his favor. Walt remembered how good a kisser she was and wished she'd bring her mouth over here and shut up. He was hypnotized by her lips moving. He knew she wanted to start something, and he most certainly was interested in finishing it. Walter wanted her to make her the first move, that way, any regrets she might have would be her own.

He decided she did make the first move. By coming over here, it was her choice. Valerie could have kissed him and said goodnight, gone in her door, and that would be that, but she didn't. It must be the moon or the tides or something like that, but he never met a girl who stirred up so many emotions at once; it was hard to know what was the correct one. I want her bad, he thought.

The pull towards her was overwhelming. He felt himself get sucked in until he had no choice but to get involved with her. Walter was going to fuck her husband right out of her head. He'd worry about her kids later. He looked at Valerie. She had stopped talking and was looking at him, a slight smile on her face as if she was reading his mind. Walter pulled her over until she was practically in his lap. He looked down at her, and she looked back at him. Valerie took off his glasses and put them on the coffee table, and looked back up at him.

Walter looked at her, calculated the risk one last time, and decided all this thinking was overthinking. She was here. So was he. That was all he needed, and gathered her in his arms. Valerie still had that Mona Lisa smile on her face.

Walter was going to kiss that smile right off her face. He was going to kiss her until the only thing in her head was the anticipation of what came next. Walt felt the heat radiating off her. Valerie was on fire and needed him to put it out. He pulled her face to his and kissed her.

Walt started out slow. Her mouth was soft and warm and yielded to him. When he moved his lips, she moved hers. He crushed Valerie to him and kissed her, only this wasn't soft and sweet. It was urgent and firm, filled with desire. He felt her mouth open and invite him in, she was waiting for him to accept. Walter held her fast in his arms. When her mouth opened, his did as well.

Valerie teased, and he danced around, taking it further until he felt her relax. Walter kissed her with an intensity he didn't know he possessed, and she kissed him back the same way. Soon it was hard for him to tell who was doing what.

Was that her tongue or his? His air or hers? Ranger felt as if their lips were fused with lust and desire. He pulled his mouth away and sought out other places where she found pleasure. He licked her earlobe and said whatever thought popped in his head. Walt told her how absolutely her touch thrilled him. How hot she made him, how desperately he needed her. He mumbled all these things while exploring her neck; her head tilted back, giving him access to her throat and the place where her collarbones almost met.

As he kissed her throat, he could feel the vibration of the sounds of satisfaction she made deep down. Walt kissed his way back to her mouth only to have her place both hands in his hair and pull his mouth to hers. She kissed him, and it went so deep he thought he would die from lack of oxygen. He stood up only to scoop her up in his arms and carry her to his bed. Walter stopped in the doorway and asked her if this was what she wanted.

"Last chance, Valerie. If you want to change your mind, it's now or never."

Valerie answered him by pulling his head down and gave him another one of those kisses that made him squirm and caused such a riot of sensations he thought he might drop her. Walt carried her over and dropped her on his bed, hurried back to get the wine and glasses. He came back into the room and stopped in the doorway. Valerie was a vision come to life, and she was waiting for him. She was waiting for him.

He brought the glasses over and poured them each one. "What is this for?" she asked.

"In case you get thirsty."

"Oh," Valerie said and took a sip. She put her glass down. He did the same, and they met in the middle. The next phase was almost dream-like. They were out of their heads with desire. Ranger was relentless in his pursuit of her and made sure she was aware of his efforts. She let him in. Valerie gave herself away; this wasn't like her.

Walter held her hips exactly how he wanted them, and they crashed into each other like waves hit the shore before a storm and only stopped when they were exhausted and depleted.

"Well, I didn't see that coming," Valerie said. She was sort of embarrassed at her abandon, her wildness at one of life's most basic functions, but he kept urging her forward, and her body would not listen to anything but the sound of his voice.

"I will never meet another Valerie Wilson." Valerie heard and turned towards his voice. "Come here," he said and asked her to move closer to him under the covers. She did as he asked. He snuggled up against her.

"What are you doing?" Valerie asked.

"Cuddling. I'm a cuddler. But you already knew that." He tucked himself in any of the gaps between them. He had soft black hairs covering his chest and legs. She could feel them brush up against her skin. She thought it felt nice. He felt nice, a wonderfully solid body. Mass. Density. Boulder versus sand.

He wasn't a cuddler at all; he only said that for a moment, such as this. A moment he wanted to stretch out and make last as long as possible.

"Okay, Val, what is it? I can sense your agitation. Do you want to leave? You can. If you think this was a mistake, tell me and I won't mention it again. But just so you know, no one has ever invaded my consciousness like you. Nobody has ever loved me like that. I'm blown away. How did it feel to you?"

"I'm shocked, to be honest. I'm only going to say this once. I'm sure you were worried that my mind would invite all these comparisons between you and Greg, but that didn't happen. After the first thirty seconds, I didn't have time to think about it. It was you. Just you. Only you. You even wore a condom, and I didn't need to ask you. My insides finally feel settled. They haven't been that in a long time. I keep waiting for something bad to happen. So what if it does? I just had sex and it was a 7.5 on the Richter Scale. I feel like we should turn on the TV and see if anybody else felt an earthquake like we did. If anyone lost power or sinkholes appeared," Valerie said.

"I know I did. That was it. Earth-shattering. I have no idea where we go from here. Do you?"

"No. There's no hurry."

He held on to her like she was that door in Titanic. Val was so soft and smooth. Walter was sure he shouldn't be thinking about her, but why not? In a couple of weeks, the kids would come back, and he'd be on a "hi neighbor!" status. At least he could look at her.

"Oh, look. It's late. I need to go next door and get home and resume my life." Walter walked her to the door and then the extra ten steps to her door.

"Goodnight, Stranger," Valerie said.

He grabbed her face, kissed her a good one, and let her go. "Goodnight, Valerie." He walked back to his door, waved to her, and went inside.

Valerie didn't see him for a couple of days. On Thursday, she was seated at her desk, and she heard a knock on her door. She looked up, and in walked Walter, Jackie, right behind him.

"Valerie. I tried to tell him he can't just walk in here, but he—"

"That's okay, Jackie. He has trouble with boundaries." She left, scratching her head, and Valerie looked at him.

"Hi, Valerie. I've come to see your office. It's very nice," Walter said.

"It probably looks the exact same as the one you're in. You look good in a suit." There was something different about him besides that, though. "Where are your glasses?"

"Thank you. You look good in a suit yourself. I don't need them all the time, but 20/20 vision is another casualty of old age," he answered. "I can say I got lost; all the offices look the same."

"You have to go. I don't need a professional misconduct charge." She moved to the door. "I'm sure your meeting is this way," she said and pointed down the hall.

"Thank you, Ms. Wilson," he said as he walked back to the office, where a number of people spilled out.

Jackie watched him walk away. She approached Valerie's office and knocked on her door. "Val," she asked, "is that him?"

"Who?"

"The guy who sent the flowers."

Val looked at Jackie, puzzled. "Flowers?"

"The ones that came this summer? The neighbor."

"Oh, oh, oh. That neighbor. Yeah, that's him."

"He's cute!" Jackie said.

"Are you sure?" Valerie asked her. "Sometimes I question my judgment."

"Yeah, for an old guy." Valerie's eyes widened. "I mean, an older guy. He has it bad for you." Jackie looked around the office and saw him in the group outside of Mr. Melcher's office. Valerie followed Jackie's eyes.

"Can't Melcher reserve a conference room? We all have been alerted that Melcher's on the job. Why do you think he's that into me?"

"Mr. Melcher?"

"No, the neighbor."

"Oh, as soon as he came in the door, he wanted to know where your office was, then he lagged behind so he could come to say hi."

"You know, anybody that wants to know anything that goes on around here doesn't need the boardroom, they need to go in the break room. Yeah, he's growing on me, but he's leaving the end of the month."

"Aw, that's too bad. Who knows if you'll ever see him again?" Jackie said mournfully.

"Who knows? He was nice to have around this summer, but now's not the time.

Maybe next year."

Walter was due to leave next Saturday. Caroline, Greg's sister, was in town visiting her parents. She offered to fly the girls back with Valerie's mom. It saved Valerie the trip home. Little Fiona needed her own handler. Caroline spent the whole time wrangling her.

She was over at Walter's, in bed, wrapped in his sheets and his arms. "Well, Stranger, this has been one of those summers," she said. "Are you going to miss me?"

"Yes. More than you realize."

"What does that mean?"

"It means I'm not looking forward to not seeing you again. I have a question for you. If, instead of going back to Boston, I was thinking about extending the lease and work from here, how would you feel about that? If this is your turf and not where I belong, tell me. Even if we were reduced to coffee on Sunday, that would be enough for me. I just don't like the idea of being so far away from you. Maybe it's a guy thing. You don't need me, I know that. I don't have any reason to be here. I just want to be where you are."

"Really? You'd relocate just to be closer? Even though you can't be anything more than my neighbor?"

"Yes. In a heartbeat. Would it bother you?"

"I want to say yes, but I don't think so. I think I'd like running into you here and there. But wouldn't it be too hard to not be involved if we're in such close proximity to each other?"

"It would be worse not to see you at all," he said honestly.

"What am I to you?"

"Do you want the truth?" She nodded.

"I've been around a bit, and I know what I want and what I don't want. You know about my home life growing up, and all my adult life, I've tried to avoid a sense of permanence. There has always been an exit plan on the table. Any woman involved with me knows that going in. That's been a deliberate action on my part. Never stay too long in one place, never give her time to become attached. To be honest, there has never been a girl who made me question it. Until you.

"There are a million reasons for you not to be involved with me, starting with your kids. I don't want to become 'Uncle Wally' to them. Your mom. She's here to help you, not babysit while you're out having a good time. If you have that kind of free time, send the poor lady home. Your job keeps you here. I travel during the week. I guess if someone asked me who's the girl I'm with, I'd have to say the most important person in the world to me. That's what you are—the most important person in the world to me. If I stayed, would it cramp your style?"

"It's kind of funny, you talking about the roadblocks you throw up to discourage what? Emotional intimacy? Long-term commitment? Falling in love? If you want to avoid all that, wear a wedding band. I've used mine that way. I still wear it, but it's not why you think. It's not for sentimental reasons. It's so guys will leave me alone. Nobody even knew my marriage was on the rocks except my boss and my admin. Now, because I received all those flowers this summer, every female in the office knows I'm hanging out with some dude."

"Yeah, I probably should have been more subtle."

"No, the flowers, they were fun. I sort of took the summer work schedule and redefined it. I don't care what you do, just don't get caught was my attitude. I would never have done that before, I would have clung to my Ms. Wilson persona. The grim Ms. Wilson. She can get you fired, so stay out of her way. Don't let Ms. Wilson catch you. I relaxed the Ms. Wilson and just became Valerie. I threw the whole hierarchy thing out the window. I hope I can reel them all in once management comes back from their summer vacations."

"Nobody knows you're divorced?"

"To be fair, I don't really know if I am divorced. But if you think you can accept that my children come first, and you'll be respectful of that, and understand the most you'll get is Sunday morning coffee, I'd like it if you were my neighbor. I can't believe I just said that, but yes. If you can handle all the strings attached, stay here."

He was on his back, and Valerie had her head on his chest. She was smoothing his chest hair so it all lay in the same direction, but the whorls it formed as it grew wouldn't cooperate. Her fingers stroking his chest, he found very pleasant. Her hair fanned out all around him. He picked up a bunch and draped it over his chest. He picked up another handful and did the same. By the time he had covered himself in her hair, it covered most of her face as well.

"Can you still hear me?" she asked.

"Yes, but I stopped listening a while ago. I love your hair and wanted to see what it felt like to be covered in it."

"Too bad you weren't listening. I gave you the okay to stay, but since you didn't hear me, I can pretend I didn't say anything." He rolled her off his chest so she was on her back, and he looked down at her face.

"There's only one way I can think of to get you to be quiet." He looked her in the eye, but she couldn't read his expression. He started to kiss her quite savagely. He put his hand between her legs and stroked her softly. He kept kissing her until the moment. The moment where her body took over and she gave herself to him. It didn't take very long, she trusted him completely.

Valerie sighed and opened herself to him. In this moment, she was totally his. Her body responded immediately. Her hips started to buck and roll independently. She moved against his fingers. When he tried to remove his hand, she brought it back. Ranger learned what she liked over the summer. His touch needed to be as soft as air. You couldn't manhandle Valerie and expect her to respond.

Now that Walt crossed that threshold, he could do anything he wanted to her, but the only thing he wanted was to be inside her. He could feel the wetness her body created to welcome him, but he needed to finish what he started. Her body moved against his fingers, and his fingers knew exactly what to do to get her to the edge.

He decided to get her off first and join in at the end. Valerie started to moan, and her legs trembled as she looked for release. Walt didn't stop when she told him she wanted him inside her. Walter kept up the friction and heat until she was rolling around on the bed, grasping at the sheets or his shoulders. He didn't move his hand, he used her own lubrication. Walt knew exactly where to place his thumb so she could rub against him. Valerie didn't know where his thumb was, or even that it was his thumb, but it was right where she wanted it.

"Oh yeah," she said, "right there. Don't stop. Please, oh please!"

Walt stopped and looked at her. He saw the look of a woman getting ready to orgasm, to go off somewhere in her mind without him. Walter was not down with that. He quickly grabbed a condom and plunged into her. Walter ground his pelvis into hers, and Valerie arched her back and did the same.

He could not believe her response. He grabbed her by her ass and set the contact points. Walter pushed into her as she cried out his name, and he pressed her shoulders down as if to impale her with his dick. She never had this kind of sex before. Urgent and thick with need. This sex was the humidity at 100% and a mushroom cloud on the horizon.

"If this is the last day of my life, am I going to regret what I did? Or am I going to say, 'Hell yeah!' When I'm with you, it doesn't matter," he said as they lay next to each other, spent and sated.

She rolled over until she was right up against him. She had her head tucked below his chin and threw her leg over him. He had his arm come around and cupped her butt cheek. They watched TV for a while like this; he had his other hand on her leg, unwilling to release his hold on her to the very last second.

***

Fifteen

GREG AND VAL

THE GIRLS SPENT the summer with the Wilsons. Mr. Wilson ended up taking the summer off, but being semi-retired, it wasn't that big an impact on the company. If Greg had played things out differently, he would be in charge, but his choices left him only qualified to work/supervise field contractors, so that's all he did. Someone else was up front running the business as a whole. Greg was lucky his father owned the company. Anybody else would have fired him a long time ago.

His father insisted he be home when his kids arrived. His father was picking them up at the airport, as well as Valerie and her mom. Greg said he would only if he took Val and her mom home first. He did not want to see her. His father looked at his son with an odd expression on his face, but said nothing.

His son had lost his shine. He gained weight in his face and waist. He developed quite a beer gut. The blue eyes that he inherited from his mother were cloudy and dim from the alcohol. The golden boy from ten years ago was just a memory now. Greg looked like a guy who spent his free time in a dark bar: pasty and yellow. All his free time. His dad told him to be sober when he saw the kids, when a beer was exactly what he needed to calm his nerves. Greg tried to prepare himself for three little girls who'd be climbing all over him. He tried to get ready for the noise three screeching girls would make. Greg figured he'd hang out a bit and go to O'Malley's to see what was going on down there afterwards.

Greg heard them when they pulled in. The squeals and chatter felt like a spike right between the eyes. He wished they would shut up. He heard his father say, "Come on in and see your dad," and he immediately felt his stomach knot up. Greg took a deep breath and prayed it would go okay. He had not seen his kids in a year, and he was curious to see how they were growing up.

They ran up the stairs and found Greg sitting at the kitchen table. "Daddy! Daddy!" they screamed. Ingrid ran over and hugged him, and she wouldn't let go. Greg hauled her up on his lap. She immediately threw her arms around her father's neck and wouldn't let go. Astrid came over, lacking the enthusiasm of her sister. She walked over and kissed him on the cheek and said, "Hello, Daddy. Are you going to the beach with us?"

"Beach?" he said and looked at his dad with raised eyebrows. "Beach? What beach?"

"Your mother and I are taking the kids to the Cape the first two weeks of August. You're more than welcome. We rented a house, there's plenty of room," his father told him.

He wasn't going to the Cape, and his father knew it. Why does he want to make me look bad?

"I'm not sure, Astrid. This is the first I heard about going to the beach. I'll check and see if I can get the time off from work."

"Okay, Daddy," Astrid said, not quite sure he really wanted to go with them, but something deep inside told her he wouldn't. Greg read the truth in her eyes, but it wasn't anger or sadness, it was indifference. He wondered if Val told them not to get their hopes up when it came to him. Greg felt a flash of anger at Valerie, she should mind her own business. What is Astrid? Seven? Eight? How did a little girl get so jaded at her age?

His mother brought the little one over. He leaned over, with his elbows on his knees and looked at her.

"Hello, Princess Fiona. How are you today?" Fiona was a carbon copy of her mom, whereas the other two favored his side. Greg wondered if it was God's idea of a cruel joke. Fiona wouldn't know him from Moses and had no interest in him or who he was. She looked him in the face and screamed, "NO!"

Greg was surprised she had such a visceral response to him. He anticipated disinterest or boredom, but it was like a mini-Valerie possessed her and told him in that one word exactly what she thought.

"NO" to having her whole life upended by his selfishness, "NO" to his boozing that broke them apart, and "NO" making up for lost time. This was how his behavior affected his family. They were lost to him. God, I really need a drink, he thought. Those feelings he thought were gone were just numbed by alcohol and threatened to rise to the surface. Greg was agitated and fidgeting, waiting for his first opportunity to escape his kids and crawl headfirst into a bottle of Bud.

"Daddy! You remembered to call her Princess!" Ingrid said with glee. Her daddy remembered! Maybe he didn't forget them! She tightened her arms around his neck.

Princess Fiona scowled and looked at him and said "NO!" again. She looked just like Valerie when she spoke with a frown on her face. She looked just like Valerie regardless of her expression. "Let her go," he told his mom. "She just needs some time to warm up to me."

The moment Ellin released Fiona, she ran after Astrid. His mother looked at him, sadness filling her. How did my son become such a fuck up? He has a daughter that he doesn't even know.

Greg still had Ingrid in his lap. She favored him, and that made him happy. It proved that once in his life, he had a happy family. Once, he was someone who had it all. Greg had it all and walked away from it. He didn't want to think about these things. His thoughts just snowballed over him, and he felt the anxiety shrink-wrap his brain. All these thoughts. All these answers. All these things, Greg didn't want to think about. Ingrid was sitting on his lap, touching his hair.

"I have hair just like you, Daddy. Just like Gramma El."

"That's right. Astrid does, too."

"Maybe the reason Princess Fiona is so angry all the time because she has Mommy's hair."

"You think so? I think Mommy's hair is pretty. I think Princess is younger than you, and she's angry about everything. I think she's mad because she can't keep up with her sisters."

"Was I mad when I was two?"

"I don't think so. You were trying to keep up with Astrid, and she was only one year older, so it was a lot easier. You probably ride bikes without training wheels, and Princess is stuck riding a tricycle."

"How come Fiona's so little?"

"She was born later than you two."

"Why, Daddy?" she asked him.

He exhaled—ten minutes into their visit, and all these questions. Greg didn't think he could handle a whole summer of this. Ingrid kept him looking into the past for answers, and he didn't want to consider the truths or their alternatives to her deadly "But why, Daddy?"

"That's just the way it happened. You and your sister said if it were a boy, we had to leave him at the hospital, so it's a good thing the baby was a girl."

"Astrid!" she yelled into his ear. "Did you want Fiona to be a baby boy? Did we want a brother?"

"NO!" Astrid yelled back. "No boys allowed!"

"Is that why you left, Daddy? Because you're a boy?"

Greg looked from his mother to his father; their expression told him he was on his own. They weren't going to help him at all.

"I think we should go get your bikes out of the garage!" Greg said. "Let's go! Astrid! Let's go and get your bike."

The two girls danced around the kitchen and out the door to the garage. Greg looked at his parents. "Do they have bikes?"

"You're lucky we do. In the back of the garage," his father said with an unreadable expression on his face.

Greg followed after his girls into the garage and got their bikes. He brought the bikes out. This would be the last year for these. They would outgrow them over the winter. The girls looked at the dust and accumulated grime. Astrid wrinkled her nose at the dirty bike. She was not going to ride that.

"Daddy, the bikes are all dirty," Ingrid told him.

"Well, let's wash them." Greg went into the garage and came out with a bucket, soap, and a couple of sponges. Ingrid was dragging the hose over, Astrid at the spigot.

"Okay, Astrid, turn it on," he called to her. She turned the water on, but the water's force caused the hose to fill and snap out of Ingrid's little hands and sprayed Greg. The little girls laughed and laughed at their father's dripping face.

"Hey!" he yelled. He picked up the hose and swept it over them. They squealed and ran. He filled the bucket up with soap and water, took a couple of sponges and put them in the bucket.

"Get over here, you two! These bikes aren't going to wash themselves."

"No! You're going to spray us again!" Astrid yelled.

"No, I won't. I promise."

They cautiously approached him. Greg handed them each sponges. "Here you go, girls." They wiped down the bikes and hosed them off. "One of you turn the water off, and then we'll put the hose away."

Ingrid went to turn the water off, and Astrid picked up the hose and deliberately sprayed her father.

Greg stood there, dripping wet, and listened to Astrid laugh. It was worth getting soaked to hear her. Ingrid turned the water off. She laughed, too.

"Hey, you girls! That's war! I'll get you back! Now I have to go change!" he yelled as he went inside.

They rode their bikes around the backyard driveway. It was paved on the side of the garage because of the basketball court. Soon, a car pulled up, and a woman got out.

She leaned on the open door and said, "Hey, kids, is Greg here?" The girls stopped their bike riding and assessed the lady. She was dressed young, but her face looked like she spent too much time in the sun, thin and wrinkly.

Ingrid whispered, "She wants Daddy."

"I'll take care of it," Astrid said, sounding older than she was. "Just a minute, ma'am." She went in the house.

The lady looked at Ingrid and said, "Hi." Ingrid said, "Hello."

Astrid returned, and Ingrid heard her sister's voice say, "Greg will be right out."

Her father came around the side of the house and said, "Oh hi, Lisa." He jumped into the passenger side. "Bye, girls," he said before he shut the car door and drove off.

Ingrid went inside. She didn't know why her dad left. They just got here. She found her Grandpa. Maybe he could help her understand.

"Hi, Grandpa. It's me, Ingrid. I was hoping you could help me."

"Ingrid who?"

"Ingrid me," she said, but knew Grandpa was just joking.

"Shoot. Ask me anything," he said.

"Where did Daddy go? We just got here, and he left with some old lady. Astrid called him Greg. Something's not right."

"Did your mom tell you why you moved and your dad stayed here?"

"Yes. She said Daddy was sick and until he found the right doctor and got better, he had to stay here. But he just left with some lady. Why didn't he stay with us? We just got here." Damn it all to hell, Greg. They're your kids. They're your family. What the fuck is wrong with you? And you just left? You left your own kids, you asshole, Dave thought.

"Well, the problem with your daddy is he doesn't think he's sick. Someone can't get better if they don't think they have a problem. We keep hoping he will decide it's time to get better. In the meantime, the rest of us are going to have fun. We are going to the ocean in a couple of weeks, and I signed you up for swim club again."

"Yay!" said Ingrid, her questions about her father fading from the foreground but still not answered.

"C'mon. Let's go get Grams and go out to eat. Your sister outside? Go fetch her."

When they got back, Ingrid snuck down downstairs to check for her dad, but he wasn't there. They soon went upstairs to bed. She kept her eye out for him all summer. Sometimes he was there and played with them, but other times he wasn't there for days. Ingrid tried to talk to her grandpa. He said it was up to her dad to decide if he wanted to be around. He wasn't even going to the ocean with them. Why did they make her come here to see her dad if he was never here?

Caroline came at the end of the summer. She visited with her parents for a while and planned to make the return trip with Valerie's mom, so she didn't have to handle all three. The two older ones were fine, but Fiona required her own escort. When they were in line at the bookstore, she took a pack of gum displayed under the cash register. She ripped into it and put a piece in her mouth. She offered some to her sisters. "Gum. Gum," she said.

Caroline looked down and said, "Hey, give me that." She threw an extra dollar down, and said, "C'mon girls. Let's get your sister," and ran after the little girl with a wrapper in her fist yelling, "Gum! Gum!"

Sunday morning, Valerie enjoyed her last peaceful cup of coffee. Walter came out with his own cup.

"Can I get you anything?" he asked her.

"No, I'm good. I'm enjoying the calm before the storm. It's been nice not to have to worry about them, but I do miss them. I hope they had a nice visit, but I can't pry. Greg has to define their relationship. I can't do it for them, but being girls, I hope he doesn't disappoint them and they go through life thinking it's always their fault, or at best, men are always going to disappoint them and turn them into lesbians."

"Is this how women think? How do you get out of bed in the morning?" Walter asked.

"You guys don't make it easy for us. On the one hand, we're fighting off backstabbing bitches and their sneak attacks, and a full frontal assault on our persons from horny old goats. It's easiest to stay above the fray and keep your hands clean. I spend my whole day pretending to be ignorant of anything that goes on."

"What time do the girls get in?" he asked.

"Late this afternoon. Why?"

"No reason. Just trying to see if there's a chance of getting it in one more time."

"No, my horny friend. Summer's over, so is the sexual part. It's just neighbors now. You still cool with that? Besides, wasn't yesterday enough? I gave you a farewell fuck that was supposed to last all winter."

"Yes, yes, you did. Twice. I shall have to rely on the memory of us to get me by. Maybe you could sunbathe in the nude, and I could spy on you through the potted plants."

"I could, but I'm not gonna. Use your imagination. Please don't talk about this anymore. I might change my mind. I don't have to worry about you, do I? My own personal Peeping Tom? The stalker next door?"

"If I retire, maybe, but not anytime soon. I'm too busy."

They sat and enjoyed their coffee in silence. Every time she looked up, he was

smiling at her. Finally, she said, "What?"

"Nothing. Just storing up images of your beautiful face for future reference," he told her, still smiling.

"Well, hurry up. I'm done with my coffee and need to shower." They went inside. Walt took both cups and put them in the sink, and then came over to her. She was just wearing a cotton terry bathrobe. Walter undid her belt and pulled her close, put his arms inside, and ran his hands all over her naked body, making sounds of contentment.

"I'm not kidding," Valerie said. "I'm all done with that. Besides, aren't you kind of old? Shouldn't you be taking a nap or something? No, really. I always thought things slowed down after fifty."

"I'll let you know. It's been a while; I've been saving it up."

"Okay, now," she said. "That's enough."

Ranger removed his arms and retied her robe. "That was for me." He spun her around and put his arms around her and held her tight. "This for you," referring to his reverse hug. "I want you to know I've got your back. Always." He kissed the back of her head and let her go. "See you next summer," Walt said as he opened the door. He turned to look back at her. "Promise me you'll call if you have a problem. Promise."

"I promise."

Walter went over to the golf course and had dinner. When he got back, there was a lot of noise coming from the pool. He went out on his balcony and discreetly tried to spy on her. The girls grew and were excellent swimmers, especially the younger blond girl. Valerie had the youngest, and they blocked the stairs. People could pass by them, but you had to go single file.

Valerie picked up the youngest and moved to the wall to get out the way. She talked to her sister? His sister? The conversation unspooled as she moved around, not bothered by motion. He could see Valerie's bare shoulders and went inside rather than risk seeing more. He left the door open so he could hear them.

Caroline and Valerie gabbed and gabbed. The unavoidable topic that was Greg came up. "I'm not sure I want to know. If I know, I feel obligated to fix it, or him, and don't want that burden. I finally feel like I can breathe. I have room to move. But, you know, I still care. I'll keep hoping he'll come to his senses."

"Yeah, but it's starting to catch up to him. He's put on weight. He's bloated. He's not so pretty anymore," Caroline replied.

"That makes me sad. I always thought his beauty was ethereal and everlasting, but I guess I was wrong. Things are ephemeral. Here until it's not."

"Don't get all moody. I know you don't know what half those words mean! He's had a bunch of people step up and try to help. He's happy. Or he's not unhappy. He's right where he wants to be. Numb."

"How did he do with the girls? Are they okay? Should I expect nightmares?"

"He did good in the beginning. He was home most nights. They had dinner. My dad took them to the Cape for a couple of weeks, and afterwards, he barely saw them. Poor Ingrid. It was so sad when she kept asking about him. It broke my heart when she stopped. Overall, they had a busy summer. Astrid started tennis; Ingrid barely dried off."

"That's good. I want them to know their grandparents and give them a chance to know their cousins. I think this arrangement works out pretty well. This way, I can see you a bit when you bring them back.

"My mom is done after this trip. When she goes home at Christmas, she's not coming back. Fiona's tough. She moves so quickly it's scary. That's okay. The older two are good, and I can take care of her, so things will get better." They both looked at Valerie's mom, sacked out in a lounge chair, her mouth partway open, dead to the world.

They went inside to see about supper. Caroline got ready to leave; she was taking the rental and returning it. She couldn't stay for dinner, good old macaroni and cheese, but she kissed them goodbye on her way out. The girls got their jammies on and had some TV time. Mary was tired and went to bed. The girls soon went down, Fiona too. Soon, Valerie's phone buzzed. It said: balcony? She went out and said hello to Walter.

"Everyone adjusting okay?" he called over the rail.

"Yes, yes. How are you doing?"

"I'm okay. I miss you, but I expected that."

"This will be okay for you?"

"Yes. Now go to bed. Just watching those kids made me tired. See you around."

"Yeah," she said. "See you around."

That's how their relationship, if you considered it one, went. Most nights, they just met to say goodnight over the railings. Late in the fall, there was a corporate dinner to celebrate the hotel project's end. There was a ribbon-cutting ceremony the day after. The dinner was a dry run for the hotel, and how close it would perform for the upcoming holiday season.

Lambert sent over a sitter, usually an unpaid intern who was willing to suffer any indignity to go over to Ms. Wilson's house and suck up to her. Valerie was on her way to her car when she heard somebody yell her name. Valerie turned behind her to see Walter. She stopped and waited for him. Walt offered her a ride, so they went together. They valet-parked the car. Right before they entered, he offered her his arm.

"Please allow a poor but humble engineer to escort the cold fish known as Ms. Wilson."

"Hey," she said as she took his arm. "Who said I was a cold fish?"

"I did. You have a reputation to uphold." They entered the atrium and soon split apart to the opposite sides of the room. There was a cocktail party before dinner. She did the old meet-and-greet corporate schmooze so much her mouth was dry. Walt swooped in with a bottle of water.

"Hey, thank you." She smiled at him.

"Gotta take care of my girl," he said and moved off.

Valerie entered the ballroom, stunned. It was beautiful. She looked around at all the special touches— the marble pillars and floor, the whole ceiling hung with chandeliers that bathed every attendee in a warm glow and made everyone look much better than they did in real life.

Walter walked over to Valerie to see her impression of the place. "Very nice." She waved her hand to the ceiling. "My compliments to the engineer. This lighting is gorgeous."

"Hello, Walter. I didn't know you had such friends in high places." Somebody from middle management came over to throw his weight around and remind her that Walter was "just a sub, as in contractor."

Walter watched Valerie go to work. She inhaled and spread out to her full height. She dwarfed him. "I'm very familiar with the concept of subs, as in contractors. Are you with the subs, too?"

"No. Field Sales Manager."

"Too bad. I was just telling Mr. Granger I thought the lighting was my favorite part. They did a wonderful job."

"How did you meet Walter?" The guy wasn't giving up.

"In the garage. He was kind enough to offer to escort me."

"Walter, you sly SOB. Picking up girls in the garage."

"Excuse me," Valerie asked. "What's your name?"

"James Orwell." Valerie nodded as if her knowing your name wasn't in your best interest.

"Walter. Thanks for coming over to say hello." Valerie took a look at the other man. "Mr. Orwell." She walked away.

"Geez, it's true. She really is the ice queen."

"Really? I thought she was very nice," Walter said.

Corporate liked to assign a board member to each individual table. They were there to show all the people who worked on the project how grateful the Lambert Development Group was for their hard work and dedication. Valerie was surprised she was sitting at the same table as Walter.

When it came time to be seated, Valerie went to her table. Walter met her and held her chair for her. As she sat down, she commented on how coincidental it was she was seated at their table, and how she didn't believe in coincidences.

"That's why they pay you the big bucks."

"Huh?" she said, confused.

"The universe can't fool you. You figured it out. I switched you with the other suit who was supposed to sit here. I wanted to watch you decimate Orwell up close."

Walter enjoyed watching Valerie work. Her voice was the same voice she used with her kids. It was quiet and soothing, almost hypnotic. She turned to speak to the person on the other side. His name was Bryan something, a temp who got hired as a permanent employee. He was probably the newest person there, and he looked a bit uncomfortable in his suit.

Valerie asked him a few questions and let him talk. He was grateful to be invited, being such a new hire. He was the lowest of the low, a laborer with one of Walter's crew. Bryan was so new he hadn't learned that he was not supposed to engage with the bigwigs. He didn't know what being a bigwig meant. Or who they were. Bryan should answer all questions briefly and succinctly, not widely and as expansively as he did. Valerie smiled at him as he talked.

"You there?" Mr. Orwell said to the guy who spoke to Valerie. It was obvious he lacked the discipline to learn his employees' names, and Valerie thought his management style was lacking. How could he expect to get his people to work their best when he couldn't be bothered to learn their names? That's management 101.

"His name is Bryan. He works out in the field as an assistant to the men on the job." Valerie had, in one sentence, illustrated why nobody liked Orwell. Orwell leveled a hard stare at this guy who dared to speak to their guest.

Bryan sensed tension at the table and thought Mr. Orwell was mad he misrepresented himself to Ms. Wilson. "Oh, no. I'm not an assistant. I'm a laborer."

Valerie smiled at him. "If I'm not mistaken, they do all the thinking"—she waved her hand at the others seated—"and you do all the work." Bryan felt his face grow hot and red.

"Yes, ma'am." Bryan decided to only give short answers.

"Please call me Valerie. Let me brief you on corporate etiquette, Bryan. Unless someone from upper management invites you to use their first name, they are always addressed by Mr. or Ms. Even if I invite you to call me Valerie, I haven't extended the invitation to the whole table. Just you. Isn't that right, Walter?"

"Yes, Ms. Wilson," he agreed.

"Well, get ready. Try not to fall asleep. Time to look sharp," she said, referring to the speakers. They served the salad during the first address. The whole table waited for Valerie to pick up her fork. Once the first speaker finished, she picked up her silverware. Someone else came to the podium.

"Well, I'm starving. They may have speakers for the next couple of hours, but I'm not waiting. I'm hungry." Once her fork stabbed a piece of lettuce, everyone else exhaled and began to eat. "I wonder what's for dessert?" she asked the table.

"Chocolate cake," said one of the engineers, a woman named Audrey.

"I like chocolate cake, the real dense type with a ganache frosting," Valerie agreed.

"That's the best," said Audrey.

"Cheesecake," one of the guys, Jack something, said.

Valerie looked at everyone. "Chocolate sauce or raspberry drizzle? If it's either the cake or cheesecake, I'll be happy."

"Cheesecake," Walter added. "One vote from me." Valerie laughed.

She lifted up her water glass. "Here's hoping." All relaxed and resumed their respective conversations.

"I wish I could just order the desserts first. I wouldn't need to eat dinner," Valerie told Walter.

"I can try," he offered.

"No need," said Valerie. "But thanks."

The dessert was cheesecake with mixed berries. "Close enough," she told the table and ate a bite. Everyone else went to work and ate their desserts. Walter, just because he was humorous and bored, reached over and snagged the last raspberry from her plate. The table held their breath, waiting for Valerie to rip him a new one.

"You're very lucky," she told Walter. "The last guy who did that lost his arm. I was saving that raspberry for last. It is nice doing business with you, Mr. Granger."

The rest of the table started talking about what happened between Valerie and Walter. Taking food off of someone else's plate was verboten at business functions, as well as most other places. Walter didn't look too concerned, and Valerie dropped the subject with a smile. Dessert was finished, and Valerie stood up. All the men started to stand, but Val told them to sit.

"I'd like to thank everyone here for showing me such a good time at dinner. I hope you enjoyed it as much as I did. It was nice to meet everybody." She smiled at Bryan. "Granger Garbage and Waste Removal is lucky to have such a great group of employees. Too bad you'll never work in this town again. I declare this dinner officially over."

The rest of the table stood, murmuring about Valerie's address. Why did she call them garbage men?

"Touché," Walter said under his breath. "Let me know when you're ready."

"Nine thirty. Meet me at the front desk. See you then."

"Copy that."

They waited for the valet together with a few other attendees out front. They saw Valerie Wilson get in a car with the guy she was sitting with at dinner, but nobody knew who he was.

When he parked back at the complex, they sat for a minute. Ranger held her hand. He marveled at her people skills. He was more impressed with her shoes.

"Your shoes. The three-inch heels ones. You were very impressive. You don't talk over people. You automatically stop talking. People think you're listening, but they lost you," Walt said.

"True. I use the time to commit your name and face to memory. If I ever hear that name again, I automatically call up a negative first impression."

"You're so cognizant of the younger staff."

"The future of the company is in their hands. These white-haired old men are going to die off sooner or later. That's the talent you need to groom. Invest in. My approach is to be plugged in. I know what's going on everywhere, and it's like tape I queue up. I know everything from the mail room to the boardroom. I know who in production is doing Liz in special accounts. It's taken years to develop these relationships. I do like the people I talk to, they are very interesting. My job isn't that hard. It takes finesse, though. I'm good at finesse."

"I wish you'd come over and finesse me," he said. She put her elbows on the console and grabbed him by the lapels and kissed him. His lips lit up, and he was it was like a former alcoholic who was accidentally served vodka, and after the first sip, he should run from the glass instead of slamming it down like he did. He was so dry for her attention, and her kiss was just the tip of the iceberg. She let him go.

"No. More, please," he begged. "One more." She leaned over and let him kiss her a bit. "Oh, God."

"How are you holding up? Are you doing okay? Are you going to be able to survive the drought?" Valerie asked him.

"Yes, it's all fine unless I'm within ten feet of you. So go away."

"Yes. It's time," she said and opened her door. He got out and rushed to her side. "Allow me," he said and took her arm. "Let me escort you home."

They reached their doors. She took his hand. "Shall we expect you tomorrow morning?"

"Yes, I'll be by. Is nine a.m. too early? I know the kids need to eat."

"That's fine.

"They get up around seven."

"I know."

"Is this too hard, Ranger? You are an eligible single man. You should go out and fuck any girl that will have you. We aren't even good neighbors. We're loud and noisy."

"Um, 'fuck any girl that'll have me'? I'll pass. I want you." He kissed her. "Now, goodnight, Valerie.

"Are you sure? This may go on a couple of years, at least until the baby starts school."

"I understand. If you make me wait too long, I'll just have to marry you. Goodnight, Val."

"Goodnight, Ranger. See you tomorrow."

"Oh, yes," he said. "Granger Garbage and Waste Removal? I'm printing up T-shirts. Expect one. Goodnight."

Valerie went inside. Everyone was asleep. She got ready and went to bed. She tried to read her book, but her mind kept wandering over to Walter. She wondered if he had a serious mental illness. Otherwise, what was the point of her being in his life? So what? Fiona starts school. There are still fifteen more years of parenting. It made no sense to her.

Valerie thought, what if the situation were reversed? Could she wait for him? She didn't like the answer. Yes, she probably would. She liked him. They always had fun. It wasn't just sex. They enjoyed each other. If he had confidence in his ability to hang out, why was she concerned about it? Because he's never dealt with an ex-husband or hormonal teenagers. What was he thinking? She tossed fitfully and finally fell asleep.

Valerie woke the next morning and rolled over to look at Fiona. She was sitting in her crib, playing with her stuffed animals. She had them lined up and was speaking to them. Valerie looked at her youngest. She was so sweet, sitting there with her "babies." Val just watched her and smiled. As if she knew she was being watched, she looked up.

"Hi, Mama," Fiona said.

"Hello, Fiona." Val got up and grabbed her and a diaper. Fiona looked at her mother and pointed at the diaper with her index finger. "No."

"No diaper, Fi?"

"No." She took her index finger and pointed at her chest. "Big girl. Big girl pants." She pointed at the diaper and shook her head no. "Baby."

"Okay." Just for luck, she grabbed a pair of underwear with the ogre on it. Val leaned over and put her hair over the baby. "Where's my baby? Where's Fiona?"

"I here, Mama." Fiona parted Valerie's hair and laughed.

"Big girl pants means the potty. If you want to go pee, you have to sit on the potty. Understand?"

"Okay," Fiona said, but she said that to everything. They left the bedroom to see what everybody else was doing.

"Morning, girls."

"Hi, Mommy! Did you have fun on your date last night?" Astrid asked her.

"Date? No date. Work dinner."

"What's for breakfast? We're hungry," Ingrid said.

"Today's Sunday, right? Mr. Stranger comes for coffee. Sometimes, he brings you guys something special."

"Mr. Stranger? Yay!" Ingrid said. "I hope he brings donuts!"

Walter got his name from the one time he waved to them from the parking lot. The girls wanted to know who he was. "He lives next door. He's a mysterious stranger," Valerie told them.

"Oh. Mr. Stranger."

"No. A mysterious stranger."

But he was stuck as Mr. Stranger.

They invited Mr. Stranger for Christmas, and he came bearing gifts. He gave Valerie a sterling silver marcasite key on a silver chain.

***

Before they knew it, it was summer again, and time to go for their visit. The girls pushed back. There were things they wanted to attend at home, but Valerie was adamant they needed to spend time with their grandparents; Grandma Mary went home after Christmas, so there were plenty of people to visit. Astrid grumbled the most, but being the oldest, she was developing a preference for friends over family. Ingrid grumbled because Astrid did, but she didn't care where she went as long as there was a pool. Fiona was feeling her grown-up self. She walked, talked, and potty trained herself, trying to catch up to her sisters.

After she dropped the kids off, she came back and picked up Walter where they had left off, like it was yesterday. He was pleased to have her all to himself. They never talked about feelings or labels and mostly hung out. The closest they got was the Christmas gift he gave her. When she opened the box, she got the necklace out to admire.

"I love it," Val held the key up to catch the light. "What's it to?" She looked at Walter. He pointed at his chest and mouthed, "My heart."

"You are such a cheeseball," she mouthed back.

He called it the "Summers of Love," and she laughed. Sometimes he slept at her place, or she at his or alone if they felt like some space. He held her hand any time he could, and she laughed at him.

"I have to hold it. I'm afraid you're going to make a break for it," he told her.

"Yes, all the way next door."

Halfway through the summer, she got a call from Caroline. She was going to be bringing the girls home early. Ellin was ill.

***

Sixteen

GREG AND VAL

CAROLINE STAYED OVERNIGHT the day she brought the girls home. The news wasn't good. Ellin was diagnosed with ovarian cancer, and the prognosis was grim.

Greg was devastated. He was very close to his mother. Where his father was more inclined to be hard on Greg, he thought the root of his problem was Greg's choice not to grow up. Being a husband and father was too much responsibility, and Greg coped by drinking. Dave felt Greg should simply stop drinking and repair his relationship with his family. Greg interpreted his inability to stop as a weakness, another thing to add to his list of failings.

Greg came after work every day and sat with his mother. He visited with her before he left for the night. Greg left the work truck behind, and whoever he was with the night before brought him back in the morning so he could take it to work. Ellin had chemo, and it made her feel awful. She went to the doctor and got the news the chemo wasn't working, and radiation might be next. Greg cried and held her hand.

"Mom, if you need anything, ask me. Like bone marrow or blood or a kidney, ask me."

"Honey, there is only one thing you could do for me. I worry about you. When you were born, they put you in my arms, and I cried. My beautiful baby boy is so strong and healthy. My heart melted. Your brother was my first, and I had no idea what I was doing, so as his mom, I was really tense all the time. I practiced on him, and then you were born. I was a much better mother to you. Jason had me as a new mom, and with your sister, I was a new mom again because she was a girl. But you got the best mom. You were lucky.

"That's why it hurts so badly to watch you destroy yourself. Everybody talks about what you're doing to your kids and Valerie, but what about you? You're on a bad path, and there's nothing I can do but watch. Please, save my boy. If you want to do something for me, go to rehab. Give me back my son." Greg took her hand.

"I don't know how Mom. I don't know how to get started. I don't know how to stop. I don't know how it got this bad. It's all fucked up. None of this is how it was supposed to be," he cried on his mother's hand.

"Call your father, please, Greg? I need you to tell him to come home." Greg didn't ask questions and did as he was told. His father showed up immediately.

"What do you need, El?" he asked her. "Are you okay?"

"Yes, I'm feeling better, Dave. Greg has something he needs help with."

"What's that?"

"He needs us to get him into rehab. He said he'll go."

Dave looked at his son. Greg could barely look at him. He needed a beer. Badly. "Greg, I need to hear it from you. I don't know much about rehab, but I do know it's not going to work if you're doing it for your mom or anybody else. If it's not for you, it's not going to work."

"Dad," Greg started, his voice cracking. "Help me. Please. I don't want to live like this. I don't want to be like the people I hang around with, a bunch of losers. I want to get clean and stay clean. For me." He broke down in tears. His father took him in his arms and hugged him while he cried. After Greg stopped crying, his father let go and made some calls.

"I pulled a few strings and got you in tonight. Are you ready to walk away from it? Do you want to? Look deep down."

"Yeah, Dad. I can't do this anymore. I don't want to do it anymore."

"Well, grab a bag with your things. We have an appointment at six thirty."

When he was ready, he went over and gave his mom a hug and a kiss. "I love you, Mom. I'm scared shitless. I have no idea what's on the other side. It's got to be better than this. Pray for me, Mom. I'm gonna need all the help I can get."

He followed his dad out and got in the car. Before his father started the car, he looked at Greg.

"You know, Greg, you are enough. I probably don't say it as much as I should, but I love you, and I'm proud of you. You may have lost your way here, but you will find your way back if you want to. You have a lot of support here."

"I know. I made the mess. I have to clean it up. I bet that's the first thing they must teach in rehab. You have to own it before you can fix it. Let's go."

His father drove and took him to a nondescript brick building. It looked like a reappointed Catholic school, built in the sixties, but no longer used for education. His father parked and got all the insurance cards and paperwork. He handed it to his son. "Don't lose hope. Keep the faith. You are here for you. Focus on you. You're worth it."

"Thanks, Dad. Really. I want this. Love you," he said and got out of the car. He knocked on the hood with his knuckle, just like he used to do with Valerie, and headed into the building. Dave watched his boy and tamped down the hope of his son's success. He knew he could physically handle the heavy lifting. He was unsure of his ability to do it emotionally.

Thirty days later, Dave picked up his son. He looked good. He was still heavy, but his eyes were whiter, and his color looked better. He looked at his son.

He always heard stories about how addicts lie and steal, but he wasn't sure it applied to alcoholics. It certainly applied to Greg. He was addicted to alcohol. Dave brought him home to his mother.

"Greg, seeing as how things needed to change, I wanted to run something by you. I'm afraid if I put you back to work with the crews, you might consider evaluating it as not a workable plan right now. Stay on leave until after the New Year and come work in the office for a bit. Spend time with your mom and keep each other company while you both heal."

Greg kept his mom company; they guessed the answers on game shows and watched soaps. He left her soap channel on while she dozed. Journaling was one of the ways to help a person with addiction issues cope by putting things on paper rather than stuffing them down internally. Burn the papers if the thoughts grip your inside in knots. It may help release the hold they have. He wrote while she slept, and he found it very therapeutic. He gave his father his phone, got a new one and number, and told no one but family.

Greg was sincere in what he told his parents. He needed to dry out and grow up. He dried out. Now what?

Greg had to acknowledge how selfish he'd been all this time. He went to AA and did the thirty meetings in thirty days. He saw a lot of people who looked like him or the people next door. If he was looking for skid row bums, he was disappointed. It seemed alcohol had a way of infiltrating a lot of other people's lives, too, like several women who started out having a glass of wine with friends and ended up hiding wine bottles in the laundry room and would have a drink with every load. One started doing the laundry at ten a.m.

"We never had such clean clothes in our lives. I washed everything we owned. Because a wine glass would be an obvious sign I had been drinking, I put it in a to-go cup, and if I forgot that, I would drink wine right out of the bottle. Imagine trying to time your drinking around a school bus," one woman confessed.

"I know. I was like that. I'd serve the kids lemonade, but mine always had a shot of vodka. Then I stopped measuring and just poured it into the glass and added a splash of lemonade. I thought I was so smart until I got pulled over and popped for a DUI. I was on my way to pick up the kids. Imagine if I had them in the car," another woman said.

That could have been him. He was still trying to figure out why one beer ended up almost drowning him. Greg had an addiction counselor, a sponsor, and a therapist who might help him figure it out. Greg was a common, everyday drunk. There was nothing special about him. The why would be nice to know, but the behavior had to stop. Everyone had a different reason, but they all led here.

I could spend ten years trying to figure out why, he thought, *but the secret was I had to do it sober. The man behind the curtain is me. The curtain was the booze. I am totally exposed. Naked in front of all these other people in various stages of undress.* Exposing his soul to strangers left him with an odd sense of relief. *I could vomit words all over these people, and they would respond with their own version of the story.* There was nothing special about him. That was the first truth he'd have to accept.

Greg spent time with his mom, running errands and trying to contribute to the household. He even cooked dinner. Greg had to find a new hobby. His old one, drinking beer at O'Malley's, was no longer an option. He found any time he was idle, the thought of the last ten years ran through his head, and the only cure for that was having a beer or ten.

Greg watched the cooking channel with Ellin, looking for meal ideas. Nothing appealed to her. She was in a constant state of nausea, but she watched for Greg's sake; he was trying so hard to stay sober. He felt like his skin was rubbed raw, trying to distract himself.

Greg continued with the discharge plan. He wanted to change it or eliminate parts, but knew that his alcoholic self wanted to do so because that meant it was invalid, and if it was invalid, he didn't have to follow it. If he didn't have to follow it, he could drink. So, he kept to the plan, worked the program, and avoided places like O'Malley's. His mother suggested he get a personal trainer and work out.

"Go to physical therapy and have them create a program around your knee. Don't look back and compare yourself to an earlier version. Start where you are now. Look forward to the future, Greg."

Greg didn't want to. He was in terrible shape. Part of removing the alcoholic haze meant you had to deal with what was in front of you as it really was, and the shape he was in made him sad. He told his mother that. His mother told him he needed to be present now as is.

"You know, Greg, think about it. You were a top-notch athlete, and you felt robbed when you got hurt. You were so busy in your head comparing yourself to your previous self. Then you drank because you couldn't accept the change. So now, comparing yourself to the alcoholic version of yourself is painful, so stop doing it. Just think about it now. Start where you are today, and fuck everything else."

"Mom! I can't believe you just said that!"

"Look at me. I could compare myself, the cancer patient, to the soccer mom or football mom. All that would do is bum me out. I'm not that woman anymore. I'm not even the same as I was a year ago. If I wanted to, I could pop pain pills like candy to escape it, and who could blame me? But I don't. I need to be here for my family. But believe me, I understand the desire to escape who you are or even where you are. All that does is drag you down. So, don't. Today is the first day of the rest of your life, that's what they say. Embrace that. Start an exercise program. Your liver isn't the only thing you sacrificed with your drinking. It affected the rest of you. Work on the physical part as well as the mental."

He took his mother's advice and started working out. Greg didn't try harder because that was what he always did in the past. Try harder to be better. He had to let go of that. Now, when he felt like he couldn't let go of harmful things or patterns, he would go to a meeting. They made it through the holidays. The mood was somber, or as somber as it could be, with little kids and Santa around. His mom was failing but put on a brave face. His sister Caroline and her kids were there.

It made Greg laugh how, as soon as she crossed through the doorway, her husband was in charge of the kids. Any time her kids spoke to her, the answer was, "Go ask your father."

"Greg," she said, "no pressure and this will be all I'll say, but congratulations. Welcome back. We missed you."

"Thanks, Caroline. One day at a time, as they say. It's been hard. Really hard. One thing I have been struggling with is my black or white mentality. Things are rarely one or the other. Most of life is like that. I think having a purpose helps, like being with Mom. That would've never happened if I didn't dry out. She'd be all by herself, and I'd be at O'Malley's. Or you. I'd avoid you. I'd be too afraid you'd judge me."

"No judgment, Greg. Nobody's perfect. Everyone's allowed to screw up, but you have to clean up the mess yourself."

Later, he heard voices and squealing. Val's kids FaceTimed to wish everyone a Merry Christmas.

They passed the phone around, and Caroline brought it over to Greg.

He heard Val say, "Look right there. That's Daddy. What did we practice?" The three girls lined up and said, "Merry Christmas, Daddy! We love you—Ow! Fiona just tried to bite me!" Then a shove and, "Ow, she's pulling my hair!" They disappeared, and he heard Fiona crying. Valerie took the phone and looked at it. Greg was holding the phone, and his face appeared.

"Hi, Val," he said. Val was so shocked she almost dropped the phone. "Oh. Greg. Merry Christmas."

"Merry Christmas to you, too," he said, smiling at her.

"I gotta go now," she said, and the screen went black.

Caroline sat next to him and witnessed the call. She wondered how he felt the first time he faced his family sober. How stable was his sobriety? Would the sight of his family cause him to spiral?

"Greg. How are you doing? You want to go somewhere and talk this out? It must have been tough seeing the kids," she said. She omitted Valerie's name; careful of the impact of seeing her might have been too much, too soon. Instead, he smiled at her.

"Those kids are getting so big. That little one sounds like a handful, though."

"She is. Her biggest problem is she wants to be big like her sisters and gets mad she's little. Val said she potty trained herself at two because only babies wear diapers." Shit, she thought to herself. I wasn't going to mention Valerie's name, but ruined it the first chance I got. Caroline looked at her brother, waiting for him react, but he just smiled.

"Those kids. Two look like me, and one looks just like Val. I'm not supposed to look back because I can't change what happened, and the only thing that matters is to go forward. If I think about how much I've missed and what a jerk I was, I start feeling guilty. My therapist warned me that it would hurt and make me want to drink to blunt my feelings. I have to feel things, good and bad. She said I need to be aware of my reaction to things, where drinking was my go-to coping mechanism. I needed to take myself out of the situation and reframe it. I need to focus on the good that is present. I could go on for days with a list of things I've done that hurt them, things I missed, things they learned that I should have taught them. I..I...I.....”

"So, what I have to learn is to take myself out of it. Now it's, 'Those girls are the cutest things. Look how big they are, even the little ones. Valerie sure has done a great job raising them.'"

Caroline looked at her brother. She hoped he wasn't just regurgitating some step to make himself feel better, but actually practiced it. She did notice self-awareness, but not selfishness. It sounded to her like he had made some changes, but in order to succeed, he had to rewrite his inner dialogue, a huge challenge a lot of people face, whether they drink or not.

"I'm proud of you, brother. That is the key. Everybody lies to themselves. They're taller, smarter, better looking, whatever. Yeah, I can see where she is going. She wants you to forgive yourself. You have to accept the truth of who you are. Maybe it's ugly, I don't know, but I do know you have to fix yourself before you can fix anything else."

"Thanks, Caroline. I think this is the first time I've ever talked to you and didn't want anything. You were the one that always knew I was a big phony. You knew it ages ago."

"Don't give me too much credit. Besides being a phony, you were my older brother. You were an asshole and terribly mean to me. You being a big phony was the least of my worries."

Valerie was in shock seeing Greg. First, she didn't expect to see him at all, and second, his appearance. He looked like he put on a lot of weight. Greg looked old. He also looked sober for the first time in a long time.

"Okay, you guys. You wanted to try out your new bikes, let's go!" The girls danced around, screaming.

Walter went out the door. "Anybody who wants me to carry their bikes down better follow me."

"Okay, Walt, if you grab the girls' bikes, I'll carry Fiona's," she said on her way out. "They can ride around the parking lot. It's pretty empty. I think we're the only people here."

"Good. I was afraid you were going to make me go caroling next."

They sat at a couple of plastic chairs outside a floor unit that looked empty. They watched the girls ride around. Even Fiona was working the pedals, trying to keep up.

"How are you doing? You've been pretty quiet since you got off the phone." Walter observed.

"You saw your ex. Did it upset you?"

Valerie looked at Walter with a thoughtful expression. "He was sober. Maybe it's not too late for him to have a healthy, honest relationship with the kids. He still has a long road in front of him if he wants a quality life."

"You said a lot about him and nothing about you. Again, how do you feel about him?"

"I can't reconcile that guy as my ex-husband. He didn't look like that. He did have Greg's smile, but that's about it. He didn't inspire hate or love. Or pain. Or anger. He was just some regular guy I knew a long time ago. That's about it. He's some guy I used to know."

"Just checking. Look at Fiona go!" Walt yelled.

"What about me, Mr. Stranger? Look at me ride!" Ingrid yelled.

"Wow! Ingrid! Look at you," he called to her.

"Mr. Stranger! Look at me!" Astrid yelled.

"Astrid! You look like you were born on a bicycle!" he told her. "I'm glad you only have three kids. It's hard to be positive out loud all the time. Not only do you have to see it, but you also have to acknowledge it."

"Oh, well, Mr. Stranger. It seems you're a natural at it. All those years of flattering cocktail waitresses served you well. Every fifteen minutes, just yell, 'Good job, sweetie.'"

"Why am I calling them sweetie?" he asked.

"Call them 'champ,' I don't care. If you use their names, they keep count. A generic champ or sweetie works best."

"How much longer are they going to be calling me Mr. Stranger?"

"Why?

"What's wrong with Mr. Stranger? I think it's funny. At least it's polite."

Later that night, after Pee Wee was done and the kids were asleep and in bed, Walter sat next to Valerie, his arm stretched out along the back of the couch. He periodically put his arm around her and pulled her close. After he did that a couple times, she laughed.

"What are you trying to do? I can't get any closer. Well, that's not true. I could, but the kids are here. Where did you celebrate Christmas last year?"

"Last year?"

"Yes. Last year."

"I won't lie. There have been many years I lied and said I'm going home to see family. I would sit in the dark, hiding out. A lot of time, friends included me, but that's usually because they have a single female friend or relation in mind that I'd be 'perfect for.' It was best to lie and stay home in the dark."

"Are you alone in the dark this year?"

"Why? You offering?"

"Depends. Are you wearing pants?"

"No. I'm wearing Depends."

"You crack me up," she said.

"I don't want to. I want you to swoon when you see me, not laugh."

She laughed some more. "How old are you? I've never met a man who said swoon before, let alone knew what it meant."

"Never mind. Talk to me about us," Walter said.

"About us? Is there an us?"

"That's what I'm trying to figure out. Are we an us?"

"Are we a we? When did that happen? If we're a we, then we are an us," Valerie said.

"What do I get if we're a we? If I'm part of an us. I don't know. What's it cost to be an us?" Walter asked.

"In cash?"

"Stop it. Do I get to stay here if the kids are gone? Do I get a date on Saturday night? Do you introduce me as your boyfriend? Do I get a girlfriend out of it?"

"Do you want a girlfriend? There's a lot to be implied if you have a girlfriend. You know, like birthdays and shit. I have to meet your family. I get to know your friends. I can tell you I don't like the shirt you're wearing, and you have to go change it."

"Really? What if it's my favorite shirt?" he inquired.

"Sacrificed on the altar of couplehood."

"Do I get a say in what you're wearing? If you can tell me to put on another shirt, I should be able to tell you to take yours off and leave it off. It's only fair."

"Yes, it's only fair," she agreed. Valerie snuggled into him and fell asleep to the noise of guns and tanks; he was watching the Military Channel.

The week between Christmas and New Year's passed quietly. Valerie spent most of the time sitting in the plastic chair, trying to read a book between calling out "Atta Girl!! Way to go!"

Walt opened his door, his intent was to go next door for coffee. He heard Valerie periodically call out some ambiguous form of praise. He went back inside and made a couple of cups, and put them in to-go cups. He brought them down to the parking lot.

"Here you go, I thought you might be a little dry from all the praise your mouth has doled out this morning," he said as he pulled up the other chair. She took a sip.

"Thank you. A cup of coffee is just what I need."

"I've been thinking. If part of us wants to take the other part out for New Year's Eve, does that part have to go?"

"Are you asking me out for New Year's Eve?"

"Yes. I want to take you out to fantastic dinner, visit a few parties downtown, and go back to our room so I can get laid. You'd have to dress up and wear those killer heels."

"Where's our room?"

"Downtown. At the hotel."

"Do I really have to wear those shoes?"

"No. You have to wear the four-inch ones."

"Isn't it too late? We need reservations. A babysitter."

"I took care of it all. I called your assistant to find out what agency you guys use, and she offered to come. She made a few calls and found out what it would cost. If I'd pay her that, she'd do it, so I hired her. You don't have to worry. The kids aren't with a stranger."

"Sounds like you covered everything. You must really want to get laid."

"You have no idea. So, how about it?"

"How can I say no? It seems like Mr. Stranger took care of everything."

"Then say yes."

"Yes. It's a date."

The older girls knew that grown-up people made a big deal about New Year's Eve. When Valerie told them she had a date, they were very excited. Their mom on a date?

"Do old people go out on dates? Where do they go? What exactly is a date, anyway?" Ingrid asked her mom.

"This date is simple. Mr. Stranger has plans with his friends, and they all have dates. If he went alone, he said he'd be the only one without someone to talk to during dinner. He said if he goes alone, all the ladies have friends they want to fix him up with, and that's annoying. He'd rather find his own date so he'll be left alone so people won't bother him. So, it's a friendship kind of date."

"That's different than a romantic date. That's the kind of date when two people like each other and want to be alone so they can hug and kiss. Those kinds of dates give you information about how much you like each other and if you want to go on another date with that person."

"Ew," said Ingrid. "Old people do that too?"

Astrid stuck a finger down her throat, imitating vomiting.

"Yes, but they usually go out early in the day so they can be home in time to go to bed."

Valerie was getting ready for her date as three little faces watched. She blew out her hair until it was sleek and shiny. The girls kept touching it saying, "Oooh, it's so pretty." They watched her put on makeup, mostly her eyes. The final step was lipstick. She looked at herself in the mirror. She wore minimal makeup to work. To see herself all glammed out, she had to admit she looked pretty good.

"You look like a movie star," Astrid said.

"Do you think Mr. Stranger's friends will be sad because he'll have the prettiest date?" Val asked. "Could one of you girls go get me my shoes?"

All three ran to the closet, and Fiona got knocked down and pulled Astrid down with her. "Mom!" Astrid yelled from the depths of the closet. Ingrid used the time to grab some shoes and raced back.

"These ones?"

"No, sweetie, I wear those to work. I need fancy shoes. High heels. Party shoes. Date shoes." Ingrid raced back and came back with another pair. "These? They are the fanciest I could find." She brought a pair of black patent-leather pumps with a very high heel, so high that Valerie couldn't remember buying them. She tried them on and stood up.

"Mommy, you look beautiful," Ingrid said.

"Get off of me, Fiona. I want to see Mommy!" a voice said from the closet. Valerie shut the bedroom door to see herself in the full-length mirror that hung there. Even she was impressed at the outcome.

She wore a simple black wrap dress. The sleeves and hem were trimmed in ruffles to add a little interest. The exposed skin of her chest had several silver chains of different lengths decorating it, a few had chains had small pendants, but the key he gave her was the longest and threatened to get lost in her cleavage.

The shoes made her legs look incredibly long. Valerie had long silver and rhinestone earrings that caught the light as she moved her head. Astrid had finally freed herself from the closet and said, "Mommy, you look so pretty you could be somebody else."

"Well, thank you, honey. I don't look like I usually do, do I? I hear a knock. Will you get it?"

Astrid ran out of the room and answered the door. "Yay! It's Jackie, Mommy!" Valerie came out of her room to greet her.

"Wow, Ms. Wilson, you look hot," Jackie told her. "Thank you, Jackie, but outside the office, it's Valerie." There was another knock at the door. Astrid let Walter in.

"Hello, girls. I'm supposed to pick up your mother. Would one of you girls please tell her I'm here?"

"Haha, Mr. Stranger! Good one," said Astrid. "That's her right there!"

"That's not your mother. That's some model or movie star. I'm looking for your mother."

"That's her!" Ingrid yelled.

Walt looked at Valerie up and down, and then whistled. "Why, girls, I do believe that is your mother. She looks gorgeous." He looked at her shoes and nodded. "You look lovely, Valerie."

"Why thank you, Walter." She smiled at him, and he felt his heart take an extra beat.

"Astrid, please go get Mommy's bag off the bed."

Valerie went into the front closet and grabbed a black fur stole. She gave it to Walter to place on her shoulders. "Fur and high heels? You brought the big guns out tonight," he murmured in her ear.

"Mommy! Look what Fiona did!" Astrid dragged her sister out with her.

Fiona had gotten into Valerie's makeup bag and tried to copy her mother, but instead looked like a drunken clown. She was frowning. Her sister interrupted her, she wasn't finished yet, and Astrid took the makeup bag away. The grownups were very careful not to laugh, but it was hard to hold it in.

"Why look at you, Fi," Val told her. "You're pretty like Mommy. Walt, get a picture before she starts crying."

Everybody started laughing, and Fiona's face crumpled once she realized everyone laughed at her.

Jackie swooped in and lifted Fiona up. "Maybe Mommy has special makeup wipes. Valerie?"

"Yes, Jackie. The top drawer in the bathroom. Thanks. Kiss me goodbye," Val said to the girls. "See you next year!"

"Bye. Mommy! Goodbye, Mr. Stranger," the girls yelled. "See you next year!" They dissolved into piles of laughter. "Next year!"

"Good luck, Jackie. You have my cell if you need me."

Walter opened the door for Valerie and ushered her out. He walked beside her until they reached his car. He made her stand next to him to decide who was taller. She was, and it excited him more than he believed possible.

He kissed her. "Thanks for doing this. You're a good sport, but I gotta say, you look stunning. I should make you dress like this once a week."

"I'm not sure about that."

"Lose the clothes, but wear the shoes?"

"We can talk."

"Here. Hold my hand," he said. "If you are going out like that, don't let go. I don't want to lose you. You look good enough to kidnap and sell into white slavery."

"I'm afraid I've aged out of white slavery."

"I'm sure you could do their laundry."

He parked the car in the garage. "I was going to suggest, since we're early, we could take a walk around, but I'm not sure you'd make it in those shoes. We could go inside and have a drink while we wait."

"Thank you, Ranger. My feet thank you."

"I'm saving your feet for later. And those shoes."

"Can I sit down if I'm wearing these shoes?"

"Or lay. Lie? Kneel, Yes. Have I told you look stunning?"

"Oh yes," Valerie said as they entered the atrium, all glass.

There was the ebb and flow of the party guests, all done up in a spandex and crystal splash. She couldn't help up look up at the ceiling.

"My compliments to the lighting guys. You managed to make everyone look better than in real life."

"Let me tell you a secret. It's not the lighting; it's the booze," he whispered in her ear. "Over there." He pointed to a couple leaving. "Quick. Run over and get that table while I get our drinks."

"I can't run anywhere in these shoes."

"Okay. I'll get the seats and you meet me there," he said, and rushed to grab the table. He beat another couple by ten seconds. Valerie carefully made her way over and sat down.

"I'm off to get the drinks."

He came back after a bit and handed her a glass of wine and sat down. It was a little table between two overstuffed chairs. Behind it, to make it seem more intimate, was a large potted plant. When Walt sat down, his view of Valerie was obscured by foliage. He got up, pushed the plant back, and sat back down.

"What was that all about?" she asked.

"I couldn't see your pretty face, and nobody else's face interests me."

"It's loud in here. I can barely hear you."

He got up again and dragged his chair right next to her. Walt smiled. "Fixed that, too."

They sat there and made small talk, mostly observations of the other guests. They sipped their drinks.

Valerie sat with her legs crossed; the dress parted a bit, so a little bit above the knee. She noticed him looking and said, "Enjoying the view?"

"I'd have to say yes. That leg in those shoes are deadly. You could make a guy do anything for that leg and the chance to explore it further north."

Valerie opened the split until it showed her upper thigh in response. Walter sat there looking at her leg.

"Are you going to be like this all night?" he asked.

"Like what?"

"Sexy as hell and trying a man's patience?"

"Yes, I am. I'll expose myself in public as much as I can; I'm going to flirt with you shamelessly, I'm going to hang off your neck like a drunken floozy, and at midnight, I'm going to let your balls drop."

"You kill me. You say the most inappropriate things, and then there's a punchline, so a person doesn't know if you're kidding or not. You should never joke about a man's balls."

She started laughing. "You'll have to wait until midnight to see if I'm joking."

"Wait here. I'm going to see if our table is ready. Don't talk to anybody, and don't move."

As soon as he left, some guy came over, attracted by her shoes.

Only fucking sexpots wear shoes like that, he thought.

"Hello. I thought I'd pass the time with you until your date comes back. My name's Ed, what's yours?"

"Wilbur," she said, referring to the TV show.

"That's not your name. So, you like to play games. I do, too. I like girls that play."

"Who said I'm playing?"

"If your date really cared, he wouldn't leave you alone. He would know there'd be a feeding frenzy around you, and he could lose you right out from under his nose."

"Is that right? He gives me more credit than that. He knows I can handle a feeding frenzy among a bunch of minnows."

"A hard-to-get wise ass? Now I'm really interested."

"A waste of your time, junior. What if I told you my date was an ex-Marine who would pound you right into the ground if I asked him to?"

"I don't believe you."

"Take your chances if you want."

He stood there and looked at her. She glanced up at him, wondering if he was crazy. He saw Walter leave. Walter looked like an ex-Marine in a suit.

"Are you harassing my girlfriend?" Walt asked, behind him.

The guy mumbled something about how he just came over to say hello and left. Walt peered at Val.

"Let's go, our table's ready. Didn't I tell you not to talk to anybody?" he said as he helped her out of the chair.

"He came up to me. It was the shoes. And hey, you called me your girlfriend."

"You are my girlfriend, and I am your boyfriend, so get used to it."

"Okay," she said, putting her arms around his neck. "I'm all yours."

"Good. Keep it that way. Now let go of my neck. I can't walk."

The hostess showed them to a quiet table in the back. The server took their drink order and left the menus. Val took a brief look and set it down.

"Know what you're getting so soon? You barely looked at the menu."

"When you have little kids, you eat a lot of kid-friendly food, like macaroni and cheese or a grilled cheese sandwich. Tonight, I'm getting grown-up food. A steak. Baked potato. Green beans."

"Sounds good. I'll have the same."

The server came back with their drinks and took their order. They smiled at each other as they each took a sip. She burst out laughing.

"What?" he asked.

"Nothing. I feel like I'm playing dress-up. You're looking me deep in the eyes, like I'm what's for dinner. It feels like you're seducing me, but I can't say how."

"Yes. I am seducing you subliminally, and if you want to take your clothes off, we can skip dinner and go right to the room."

"Oh. Subliminally. I have to eat first."

Walt sat there and complimented every single thing about her. The way her hair looked, the way the candlelight shone in her eyes, the smoothness of her skin.

"I have to share an observation. Men look at women; that's no secret. I'm with the best-looking girl in the place."

"Thank you. That was a nice thing to say."

The check came, and he paid. She offered to pay half, but he said he was taking his girlfriend out, so it was on him. He took two neon green wristbands out of his pocket.

"Want to go check out some parties?"

"You got the whole package?"

The hotel had different parties going on in different banquet rooms, and you could buy only the party package, or you could include dinner and a room.

"They gave them to me at the desk. They're good for all the rooms. There's a rave in the ballroom at ten if you're interested."

They went into the oldies room, but they were the youngest people there. They checked out the disco room. They went into the big band/orchestra room, and it inspired Walter to dance. He pulled Valerie out on the dance floor. She tried to escape.

"I don't know how to dance," she said.

"Here. It's easy. If I move you forward, step forward. If I move you back, step back."

"I don't think so."

"Too bad. We got in here for free, so I want a free dance. I'll use any chance to squeeze you."

The band played some slow songs, and Walter pulled her back to dance. "Just lean into me and shut your eyes," he said. "Relax. It'll be fun. You're supposed to put your face on my chest, but that's not gonna work. Here. Put your face next to mine, and we'll dance cheek to cheek. That's a thing, you know. It's in a song."

She did as she was told and shut her eyes. She relaxed and let him pull her around. It was very nice. The music was soothing, she felt lighter than air, and his hand spread warmth throughout her lower back. The music stopped, and he looked at her, smiling.

"There. Wasn't that nice? You didn't do too bad."

"That was very nice. What's next?"

"Check out more parties." They wandered around and danced a bit more, and went out down to check out the ballroom; they decided to pass on the rave. They walked by a little alcove, and he pulled her in and started kissing her until she was panting.

"Have you had enough of New Year's Eve? Want to go upstairs and continue the celebration?"

Ranger stopped by one of the bars, gave the guy fifty bucks, and got a bottle of Pinot Grigio and two glasses. They grabbed a plate of desserts and headed toward the elevator. He kept trying to kiss her even though their arms were full. They made it into the room and set their haul down.

"How do you want it? Sweet and light or down and dirty?" Valerie asked him. Walter got close and said, "Both."

"Okay, here's how it's going down. We're two people who meet. You're like James Bond. I'm the spy with the State Secrets. You need to fuck those secrets out of me. We meet at a bar, you're gonna seduce the truth out of me. The spy, me, says never. 'Give me the best you got. I won't crack.' Right now, this is the part where you pick me up and bring me to your room. You shove me against the wall, overwrought with desire, and start kissing me, and then we rip each other's clothes off. It's very physical and carnal. You follow?"

He grabbed her and pushed her against the wall. He held her by her arms and pinned her, all the while kissing her, hotter and more urgent. He took possession of her and continued to kiss her into oblivion. When they paused, their breathing hot and ragged, she pulled off his jacket and tie while he worked on his shirt buttons. She undid the outer tie to her dress.

"Hey," she whispered. "Pull this string." He did, and she shrugged. The dress fell to her feet in a black puddle.

She had purchased new lingerie for tonight, a black push-up bra, and a matching thong. He grabbed her ass and ground himself into her. He let go of her to finish taking his shirt off. She walked to the bed and, on purpose, bent at the waist as if picking up loose change. It showcased her legs in those shoes, and the thong left her behind totally exposed. She figured he might be into it the way he was into her shoes. He looked up from his belt and saw her teasing him with the view of her backside. He couldn't get out of his clothes fast enough. She wandered away from the bed to get a glass of wine. He rushed over and led her back to the bed.

He pushed her down on the bed and put her glass on the nightstand. He got naked and slid next to her. He unsnapped her bra to expose her breasts. He caressed her exposed nipples, smiling when he coached them to their erect state. He pulled her bottoms off as well. He felt for her readiness; she was wet and slippery at his touch, and she started to lift her hips to get him to go further inside her.

"You want it? How bad?"

"I want it now," she said, pushing her pelvis into him.

He dove on her. Walt liked how strong she was; sometimes they'd be fooling around, and suddenly he'd get her to push back against him, and her strength surprised him. Valerie did it now. They weren't having sex; they were wrestling each other for power. He could take her down in about two seconds; after all, he was an ex-marine, but this wrestling excited him, so he continued to grapple with her.

"Tell me," he growled at her.

"Never," she answered and struggled against him, but he held her fast.

"Tell me now. Or else," he threatened.

"Never," she said, struggling once more.

He moved so fast; she was flat on her back, her hands pinned over her head with one hand, and he was between her legs in less than a second. Walter used his free hand and gently stroked between her legs. As he teased and tickled her, he could feel her trade her combatant pose for one of a femme fatale. She moved against his fingers, and her hips responded. She started to moan and beg.

"Oh, please. Please. Do it, do it now."

"Tell me," he said, still roleplaying.

"I don't know anything. I don't know anything, honest. The only thing I know is I want you." She raised her hips in invitation.

Walter enjoyed the foreplay, but she wanted it now, and so did he. "Last chance," he said. "Ready or not."

"I'm ready. God, I'm ready. Give it to me," she begged. He let go of her hands and put his on each side of her head, and rested his weight on his elbows. She put her hands on his ass, guiding him into her when he plunged in as deep as her body would allow. Valerie moved against him as he entered her, making sure her pace matched his.

The switch from her resistance to soft and accommodating, matching him stroke for stroke, was enough to send him over, but she wasn't there yet. Walt held out until he heard her moan, which let him know she was ready. He exploded, and she exploded, too. He collapsed next to her, both of them sweaty and panting.

"Whew. That was something," Walt said.

"You suck as a secret agent," Valerie said. "You never got the information, and while you were otherwise involved, I stuck a knife in your back."

"You are good—what a way to die. I've heard of men dying from a heart attack while having sex, but a knife in the back? Genius." She sat up and asked Walt to pass her wine. He did and got up, returning with dessert. "I thought you might like something sweet now." He handed her the plate and got back into bed.

Val looked over to him and said tenderly, "I don't need something sweet. I have you."

Walter looked at her with an unreadable expression on his face. He took a fork, had a bite of the cheesecake, and smiled contentedly.

"I have to ask you a question. It's none of my business, but I have to ask."

"If it's about the State Secrets, don't bother. I'm taking those to the grave."

"No, but I'll get to those later, I promise. It's about your husband. What the fuck is wrong with him?"

"What? Where did that come from?"

"You. From what I can tell, you're one in a million. You're smart as hell, you can pay your own way, you're beautiful, and a ten in the sack. How could he let you go?"

"I guess you have to put it down to the behavior of an addict. Addicts are incredibly selfish. It was always about him. I could see him looking at the clock, wondering if he'd stayed long enough to be able to leave without an argument. Usually, he would sneak out, so there was no way to argue with him. As far as sex went, it was pretty vanilla. The most daring of it was probably having sex in the shower.

"I've matured a lot. He has to start where he was when he busted up his leg. He's been so self-absorbed since then, trying to get back what he lost. It's never coming back. Greg couldn't accept it. That's why he drank, to numb the pain that changed him. After a while, I think he drank just to drink. He didn't know what else to do. Now he's sober, or sober right now, we'll see. I don't want to be pessimistic, but he's got a lot of work to do. I hope he realizes he can't just show up and say, 'It's all good, Daddy's home.' He has to go back to when he broke his leg, and he has to process all that and make his peace with it. I wish him the best of luck, but I'm not going backward. For anybody."

"Walking away from you makes me question his mental stability," Walter maintained.

"Why stay? I'm old. Used up. Another side of forty with stretch marks and saggy boobs. Why are you here? You could do better."

He laughed at that. "That's funny. I think you're a perfect ten. Some perky young thing may have cosmetic benefits, true, but in no way would she be able to do what you did tonight. It takes a real woman to love a man like that; an overgrown teenager wouldn't know where to begin."

"Enough about that," she said. "The ball's going to drop; get your glass and the wine. Get ready to toast to the New Year." After they were done, they got under the covers and cuddled. She was on her side, drifting off to sleep, when he rolled next to her to spoon.

"Val. Valerie. You awake?" he whispered to her; she did not answer. Confident, she was asleep. He whispered in her ear, "I love you."

She wasn't asleep. Valerie heard him. She smiled and drifted off.

The next day, she suggested they say goodbye at the hotel. Valerie would bet the kids are out there riding their bikes waiting for her.

"Let's stop and grab some donuts somewhere to deflect any questions about us. I don't think I'll be able not to laugh if you acted like my boyfriend." He kissed her.

"Happy New Year!" She kissed him back. "It was a pleasure watching your balls—I mean, the ball drop with you. Thanks. I had a great time."

He pulled into the complex and could see her kids riding their bikes in the parking lot.

"Well, goodbye then," she whispered. "Don't you want to know what the State Secret is?" He put the car in park.

"What? What was it?" he asked as he watched her kids swarm them. "It's 'I love you, too.'"

Seventeen

VAL

TIME PASSED. He had a number of out-of-town projects, so when he was in town, they got together at lunch. The kids were away at summer day camp, and Fiona was at preschool. Her place was empty, his too. They would eat lunch at his place, make out a bit, and she'd go back to work. Usually, if the desire was drenched in a cloud of lust, they would make that what was for lunch. He would have a turkey sandwich ready for her to grab so she could eat in her car on her way back to work.

This plan was enough for right now. They shared certain intimate details regarding how they felt about each other on New Year's Eve. However, he didn't push and seemed not to care as long as they saw each other a few times a week. Walter never said it again, and neither did she.

Mr. Stranger still came on Sunday with donuts, so things coasted along through the year. They still never discussed what exactly each defined as love. Val decided not to go home for Christmas; her mother was with her older brother in Chicago. The girls wanted to invite Mr. Stranger for dinner; they felt terrible he would be alone on Christmas Day. They even made him gifts. Astrid was at that age into horses, so she drew him a picture of a horse. Ingrid drew him a picture of balls in markers. Soccer, basketball, volleyball, beach, and all other balls filled this piece of paper, so you could barely see the color of the blank paper she started with. Fiona drew him a picture of what he thought was Valerie.

She got a little carried away with the markers, mashing the tips so they no longer drew crisp, neat lines. Ingrid had a fit and pushed her sister harder than she meant to, and she fell over and cried. Astrid went out and left the door open. Walt was walking by and stuck his head in the door.

"Everything all right in here?" He was greeted with Ingrid crying about pens, and she came over with a fistful of markers. And Fiona, sensing she was going to be the accused, went over to cry to her side, but louder. Poor Walt. He looked at Valerie, helpless. She came over, sent Ingrid to the bathroom to clean up, wiped the little one, cleaned her up and diffused the situation.

"We're just going outside." Ingrid came over and showed her mother her hands.

"Why do I have to clean up when I'm going outside and going to get dirty?"

"Good point. Go out and find your sister. I'll be right out with Fiona." She looked at her no-longer-a-toddler's hands. "Clean enough. You coming?" she asked Walt. "Unless you want to stay inside for some peace."

"No. When your kids aren't crying, they're kind of charming. I'll go out with you and keep you company."

They went outside, watched the kids, and sat on the grass in the shade. There was peace. Every once in a while, a child would yell out, "Look at me, Mommy!" Val would reply, "Good job there, sweetie."

"Do you have plans for New Year's Eve?" he asked.

"No. Do you, Secret Agent Man? You want to do something?"

"I'm not in the mood for the hotel. What if we went out to dinner and came back here to watch the fireworks? Get a sitter to put them to bed, and we come home and toast the new year from the balcony. Unless you want to go dancing?" Walter asked.

"You want to take ME dancing? You enjoyed that last year?"

"I won't deny the sole purpose was to get my arms around you."

"You liked dragging me around? It reminded me of the Weekend at Bernie's or Tom Petty's 'Mary Jane's Last Dance.'"

"Yes, I loved dragging you around. I'd drag you everywhere if people wouldn't complain."

"I can check with Jackie and see if she has plans."

"I already did. She's free. I made a reservation at this little out-of-the-way place."

"I'll have to look in the back of my closet for something to wear."

"You still have those shoes?" he asked.

"Yes. I will wear those shoes. Looks like you covered all the bases. Do you know that State Secret you told me? Is it still true?" Valerie asked.

"Depends. Is it still true for you?"

"Something like that doesn't just go away. It usually gets worse. Did it get worse?"

"Yeah. In a big way. How about you?"

"Same here. Why don't you just say it out loud? We had one encounter where we admitted we love each other, yet you don't say those three words. Or, haven't, since. I'm operating under the assumption that's still true, and you'll let me know if it changes, so please be kind enough to let me know if that happens."

"It's true. I do love you. I'm not sure you're in a place where you can love me back."

They had a quiet New Year's and were able to watch the fireworks from her balcony. Valerie leaned against his shoulder, and Ranger held her in his arms. They toasted at midnight and kissed. "To the New Year. May it be filled with blessings and joy." They clinked their glasses and drank to that, with the sky behind them lit up like the Fourth of July.

The new year didn't present itself any way different than the old one. Walt was on the road, Valerie still at Lambert. The predictability of it all was just fine with them. They managed to connect or reconnect as time dictated, and neither was unhappy. Time was a lazy river behind them.

Like most plateaus, it abruptly ended in a sheer drop. Caroline called to tell Val Ellin died.

"I'm sorry to hear about Ellin. She treated me like her own daughter. I'm glad the girls got to know her. And what about Greg? It would be a shame for him to backslide and start drinking because he's so sad he lost his mom," Valerie said. Concern laced her voice, but Caroline squashed that like a horsefly.

"Valerie, if you still care, he's making some big changes to improve his life, but we all know Greg's sadness will be worse than anybody else's. It's another chance for Greg to suck all the energy away from the real reason you're there. For fuck's sake, my mother died too. I'm grieving, too. We all are. But asshole Greg will take the company truck and disappear. Then it's all about Greg. Good lord, is he drinking and driving? Where did he go? Which is such a farce because we all know he's down at that dump O'Malley's with his other loser friends," Caroline said. It wasn't in her DNA to hold back.

"I think I'll bring the girls up. They should go. Your parents were a big part of their lives. I'll stay at my mom's. We all can."

***

Caroline met her outside of baggage claim. She took the kids from Valerie, which allowed her to return inside and get the bags. Once people and bags were securely stowed, Caroline started driving. She dropped them off at Valerie's mother's, but the heat had been turned down since Valerie's mom was away. Caroline would take the kids to see their Grandpa Dave, and they could stay for pizza, and when they returned, the house would be toasty warm.

"You go on ahead. I think I'm going to hang back. I'm thinking maybe Greg's grasp on sobriety might be tenuous at best, so I don't want to stress him out and be the cause if he relapses. I'm just going to stay here if you don't mind handling the girls. Tell your dad how sorry I am and that I'll miss her, too. I wish I could be there, but I think Ellin would rather her son stay sober. I don't know what got him to this point, but I hope he can hang onto it."

"If you want to go, you should go," Caroline said.

"You told me Greg manages to be in the spotlight, regardless of the occasion. I'm trying to prevent that. I don't want to be the reason he has a breakdown. I'm taking myself out of the equation. If he loses it, he can't blame me. Who does he blame now, Caroline? Whose fault is it now that he's not who he was supposed to be?" Valerie asked.

"I think he ran out of people to blame. He spent a lot of time with my mom. We all knew he was her favorite, but I think they talked a lot, and he finally realized he was better than that. He went to rehab on his own. I mean, I think he wants a better life for himself... Here's hoping."

Caroline returned. The house was warm, the kids full and sleepy. Caroline carried Fiona asleep. It was like carrying a fifty-pound bag of potatoes. The two older girls were awake and got ready for bed while Valerie firmed up the plan for the funeral the next day, and Caroline left.

The two girls were sleeping in the double bed in the spare room.

Val tucked them in, and they were talking about dinner at Grandpa's. "We saw Daddy," Ingrid said.

"Did you? I'm sure that made him happy."

"Mom," Astrid said. "Something is wrong with Daddy."

"I know. He's sick. That's why we had to leave. He wouldn't find a doctor to fix him, so we had to go somewhere else."

"No," Astrid said. "He looks awful. He's fat. His hair is all messy."

"I was glad to see Daddy," said Ingrid.

"I'm glad you saw him, too. Auntie Caroline thinks he's getting better. Daddy loves you both. Sometimes, it's hard to remember that. But he does," Valerie told them.

"If he really loved us, he would come with us," said Astrid with finality.

"I don't know what to tell you. I know your Dad better than he knows himself, and I know he was not good when we left. I didn't want him being sick and making the rest of us sick, too. That's why we left.

"I couldn't watch him get worse. Let's just pray that he finds his way back."

"But if he gets better, how will he know where we are if we moved? He won't be able to find us." Insisted Ingrid. "We need to move back so he knows where we are."

"Grandpa knows where we are. Daddy knows where to find you when he's healthy."

After she was sure the girls were in bed, Valerie took time to get ready herself. She turned on the bathroom light to brush her teeth and saw her reflection in the big mirror. It startled her. Valerie never took the time to assess her looks. She looked at the tiny wrinkles in her eyes. She looked the same as she did in high school, only older. It was her opinion that people who looked like they did in high school were afraid of getting older, afraid of changes. That didn't apply to her; all she'd done was roll with the changes.

She held up her hair with both hands. She kept it long because it was easy to manage. Ponytails, buns, braids. If she cut it all off, she wouldn't need to manage it. She decided her skin looked good, smooth, and absent of large pores. She should start using skin care products to preserve it, and maybe cut off all her hair. Her hair was still thick and its natural color, maybe a few gray hairs scattered here and there.

She turned off the light and went to bed. She needed to push Fiona, who liked to sleep in the middle of the bed, over to her side first. Once Fiona was settled, Valerie got in bed and went to sleep.

The next morning, the girls had breakfast and got dressed for the funeral. Astrid and, consequently, Ingrid gave Valerie a hard time about going, but they still got dressed. Fiona was easy to dress, if her sisters were doing something, she was going to do it too.

Caroline came and picked them up. She said they would be going to the luncheon afterward.

"Lunchtime?" Fiona said.

"In a little while," Valerie said as she buckled her in. "Be a good girl for Aunt Caroline. That goes for you two as well." She watched them drive away and went back inside. She took out her laptop and prepared to do some work. What she really wanted to do was talk to Walter, but he was out on a job.

She sent Walter an email saying, "Hello, checking in. All's well. Call me tonight."

She opened the ongoing program she was working on and got started. In the quiet house, she was able to get a good chunk of it done. She had a ton of emails to answer, so she waded into the mass of correspondence in an attempt to clear out her mailbox. So much of it was repetitive, everyone covering their asses with a digital footprint. She mindlessly looked over what would be spam in real life. She opened, looked, and deleted. Open, look, delete. It was boring as hell. Valerie was glad when she heard a knock on the door. She got up, opened the door, and had the shock of her life. It was Greg on the porch, in tears.

"Valerie...Valerie...help me," he cried.

Valerie froze. She didn't know what to do. She wanted to say, "Fuck off!" and slam the door in his face, but he looked so pathetic standing there. He looked wild and panic-stricken. Greg asked her for help, and being Valerie, she opened the door and invited him in.

"Come on in," she said. "Go sit on the couch. Would you like something to drink? No? Okay. I'll be right back." She went into the bathroom and grabbed a box of tissues. Valerie sat next to Greg. He had his face in his hands, weeping. She didn't know what he wanted. He just came from his mother's funeral.

What does he think I can do? Val thought.

She took her hand and rubbed his back. With a gut-wrenching sob, he turned towards her and ended up in her arms, his head in her lap, crying. She left him like that and figured he'd cry himself out, like the kids. He eventually stopped, sat back, and grabbed the tissues. Once he was finished, he cleaned his face. Valerie looked at him.

"I was sorry to hear about your mom. She was as special as they come." She waited for his answer.

"Val, I shouldn't have come here. I treated you horribly—"

"Now is not the time for that. Why are you here? What do you want?"

"I don't know. I was actually on my way to O'Malley's. I'm as low as I've ever been. I can't handle things without my mom. She gave me a reason to quit drinking. But she's dead. She died. I don't know what I'm doing here. I was going to O'Malley's and drinking myself into a blackout for the next month. I saw your house and thought maybe if I stop here, I won't go to the bar. I don't want a drink. I need a drink. I've never been sober enough to think about the difference."

"Huh," she replied. "Don't you have a sponsor? Is there a meeting somewhere? I don't know how to help you."

He took out his phone and selected a phone number. "It's my sponsor. Call him, please."

She hit send, and a man answered. "I'm calling for Greg Wilson. I'm his ex-wife, Valerie. I don't know the language of AA, but he is in a really weak moment. He just came from his mom's funeral, and he stopped here so I would talk him out of taking a drink. But he wants one desperately. Uh-huh. Uh-huh. Okay, yes. I will."

She stood and handed him his phone. "There's a meeting at St. Charles in twenty minutes. I'll drive. After the meeting, your sponsor wants me to take you to the Valley Diner. He'll meet you there. Let's go."

"But Valerie—" he started to say.

"Greg shut up. Just shut the fuck up and get in the truck."

She took his keys, and he got in the passenger seat. Out of the side of her eye, she could still see tears streaming down his cheeks. Valerie handed him more tissues. She pulled into the lot and parked behind the church. There were a number of people standing around the back entrance smoking cigarettes.

"Could you come in with me, Valerie? Please?"

"Is that allowed? Isn't it sort of personal?"

"Yeah, it is. I don't think you'll rat anyone out."

Valerie looked at him. "I will go in and keep you on the topic: the reason you came to my house. How to cope with grief without alcohol. Do not get into me or the kids, or anything related that happened in the past. This is about today. Got it?"

"Yes."

"Let's go." They exited his truck and went towards the group of people and entered the building. The meeting started by introducing themselves. Instead of asking the group if anybody had anything they wanted to discuss, the guy who ran the meeting looked at them. "You look like you've had a really tough day, buddy." Greg remained silent. He's not going to just sit here. He's not wasting my time like that, Val thought.

"My name is Valerie. This is my ex-husband, Greg. The reason I'm here is because he buried his mother today, and to cope, he was going to O'Malley's and drinking himself into a coma. Between the cemetery and the bar is my house. He pulled into my driveway to avoid going to O'Malley's. I'm helping him because he stopped before he went and got smashed and asked me to help him avoid drinking. He didn't know what to do.

"He has a couple of months of sobriety under his belt. This is just my observation, but right now, it's him and his grief. He needs to learn how to cope with these emotions without drinking. I really think he's trying, or he would have blown by my house and gone directly to the bar. I guess the question how does a person learn to cope with these heavy feelings when your first instinct is to grab a bottle? I'm sorry if I violated protocol by speaking. Greg is going to participate now."

She pulled out her phone and sent Caroline a text. I'm with Greg. I took his truck and brought him to a meeting, and after, he's meeting his sponsor at the Valley Diner, and I need a ride home. Can someone pick me up?

She sat while these people lay bare their most regrettable sins. The meeting ended, and they walked out, most only to stop and light a butt the second they hit fresh air. Some guy thanked her. He wished his ex-wife was so understanding.

"Understanding? He's got three kids to take care of. He needs to get his shit together and be a father."

Valerie drove to the Valley Diner. A local institution in the classic sense, every remodel kept true to the original. They walked to the entrance. Greg didn't like leaving her alone while she waited. She handed him the keys to the truck and turned him towards the door.

"Go immediately inside. I'll come in if it's longer than five minutes," she said and pushed him along. "Remember, you were a lemon wedge away from losing it. You hung on until it passed. Remember that. You can do this. Goodbye, Greg. Good luck."

Not five minutes later, Dave showed up to give her a ride, and she got in.

"I'm sorry you had to come get me. I'm sorry about Ellin. I loved her. She was always so sweet to me." Tears started to form in her eyes. "I hurt about this as much as the rest of you, but I can't even say goodbye. I can't grieve with anybody. I have to smile and hold it together for the kids. Then for Greg." The tears spilled out of her eyes and ran down her cheeks. "Dave, I'm sorry. You have so much to do, you don't have to take care of me. Just take me home."

Greg's father leaned over and hugged her. He opened the glove box and gave her some napkins that someone stuck in there a long time ago. She blew her nose. "Sorry."

"If you say you're sorry one more time, I'll...well, I don't know what I'll do. But stop. You have the least to be sorry about than anybody I know." He put the car in drive, but instead of taking her home, he drove to the cemetery. The canopy the funeral home set up was gone. All that was left was a mound of dirt covered in flowers. He parked the car and said, "Come on. I'll say goodbye to you."

They walked over to her grave. It was complete silence. Not a birdsong or a passing car disturbed the still air. Valerie looked down and saw the flowers were dying as well.

Ellin, sorry you weren't able to stay long enough to see how everything thing turns out. If Jesus isn't available, would you please be Greg's co-pilot? He needs help to keep him convinced he can do this. Enjoy your pain-free rest. You were a wonderful mother-in-law and a great Gramma. We have to go on now without you. If you have any pull in the universe, please push some good our way. I love you, Ellin, and I will miss you. Goodbye.

Valerie leaned on Dave. He put his arms around her and stood with her while she said goodbye.

She sniffled and blew her nose into an already saturated tissue. "I'm set, Dave."

They walked back to the car. He opened the car door for her and then got in the driver's side. He looked at Valerie. "You okay, Val?" he asked before he started the car.

"Yeah. I am now. I told her we would go on without her and be okay. We didn't want to, but we had to."

"That's right, Valerie. We have no choice. We need to enjoy the good right in front of us. It's hard to find at times like these, but it's there. I look at my grandkids and see the joy on their faces and try to soak it up. Speaking of the kids, they want to have a sleepover. All those screaming girls will take your mind off your problems. Can I stay at your house?" he joked.

"Sure, if you want." Valerie laughed.

"Valerie, I want to thank you for how you handled Greg. His mom's death hit him hard. I was sure he went on a bender, but he showed up at your house, and I guess you gave him a bit of stability until he could regain his footing. Thank you. You didn't have to do that."

"Yes, I did. He has three kids that need him. He needs to wake up. He has to!" Valerie said. "Sorry to be so emotional, but seeing Greg set something off."

Dave dropped her off. She went inside and checked the time. Valerie couldn't remember what the time difference was in order to call Walt, so she called Caroline to check on the girls.

"Please let them stay," Caroline asked. "They're having so much fun together. It's nice to have a little noise back in the house. Thanks for what you did today, Valerie. Greg came back okay. He's lucky he had an ex-wife who helped him. Most exes I know wouldn't call 911 if you were on fire."

"Look. I have three little girls that need a father. Their father. I'd do anything to help him get to the point where he wants to be their father. I don't know if he ever will, but I don't want my kids all fucked up with daddy issues because he's a selfish asshole," Valerie spat out. "Why don't people get that?"

"You're absolutely right. You have to try. There will be a point where you're going to stop trying. Once you cross that line," Caroline stated, "you won't come back. Personally, I think it was crossed a while ago. You're finally catching up."

"Maybe I romanticized this all, like Humpty Dumpty. Once it's broken, it's broken. No going back," Valerie said. "I'm not sure you can consider romance and Humpty Dumpty go together, but you get the idea. When I saw him at the door, I wasn't feeling 'oh, yay!' at the sight of him."

"I've got to go. They're trying to put a tiara on Dad. They already did his nails. This helps him so much," she said. "No time to talk or think, wrapped in a black boa, the queen is coming for tea, you know. Let's talk tomorrow when I bring the girls."

She hung up, looking at the phone. She found a number and hit send. Walt answered.

"Granger. What can I do for you, Mrs. Wilson?"

"Sounds like you're on the job."

"I am. I'll be tied up for about an hour. Can I get back to you then?"

"Yeah. Sure. I just need a friend right now."

"I'll call you as soon as I'm able."

"Okay. I just wanted to hear your voice. Call me when you can."

She turned on the TV to some travel channel about eco-tourism in the Galápagos Islands. She lay on the couch, listened to the murmur of the host, and fell asleep. Her phone rang and woke her.

"Hello? Turtles?" she said into the phone, her voice groggy with sleep. "Val? Val? Are you okay? What's going on? What about turtles?"

"Oh, hey, Walt. It was just a dream. How're you doing?"

"I've been worried since you called."

"Oh. That. I'm just ready to come home. The kids are at their grandpa's and a cousin's sleepover, and it's lonely here; my mom is at my brother's, so I'm alone. It didn't help that Greg showed up here."

"Greg? What did he want?" Valerie could tell by the edge in his voice he wasn't happy about it.

"He was out of his mind after they buried his mom, and he was on his way to the bar to get trashed. He's been sober three months now, and he pulled in here to stall getting to the bar because I think he's really trying to dry out."

"What did he expect you to do?"

"I'm not sure. I took him to a meeting, and to meet his sponsor. I believe he made it through the day and has a grip on it now. What were we talking about before? I'm not making any sense," she said into the phone.

"Greg showed up in a weak moment and asked you to push him the right way, and you did. I'm going to accept your version. I don't know why I love you, but I do. So that settles that. Anything to the contrary is someone else's delusion," Walt said firmly.

"That's a Beatles song. 'I don't know why I love you, but I do.' So there. But I felt sorry for the guy. He had his head in my lap, sobbing."

"That's not a Beatles song. But he had his head in your lap?"

"Sobbing, Walt. I couldn't kick him when he was down. Maybe that makes me a sucker. I talked to him for about thirty minutes. No past, no future. I helped him; I got him from A to B. That was it. I don't want to think about it anymore. I just want to fall asleep, go to the airport, and have you meet me outside baggage. Bring my car; Fiona's car seat is in there."

"Anything about your ex sucks you back in?"

"No. He was someone I loved a long time ago, no bells rang, no second thoughts."

"Second thoughts?"

"You're such a girl. He excited nothing. He pales in comparison to you," Valerie laughed. "How's work going? You almost done in Denver?"

"A few more weeks. I get in early and can pick you up. Will you be getting home in time for dinner?"

"We get in about four, so yes, we will be hungry. But please, no more pizza or macaroni and cheese. Make sure you bring my car. It has the booster seat in it."

"You got it, Val. Text me before you board so I'll be on time. Valerie, are you crying? What's the matter?" he asked her gently.

"Why are you so nice to me? I'm the nice one. I take care of things, not you. You take care of yourself; I handle everything else. I think I'm in a weak moment myself, that's all. Thinking for four people is enough. Now you throw some immature grown man-child in the mix, and I buckle. Too much weight," Val said, too tired to even pretend she had a handle on things, not to cry.

"Hey, you'll be home tomorrow. I'll take over for a bit, but I have to fly out early Monday. Take all day Sunday in bed if you want. I'll call Jackie to see if she's available to watch the kids. If you don't stop crying, I'll catch the first flight out of here and bring you home myself." He heard her blow her nose again.

"No, that's not necessary, Ranger. It's been a very heavy trip. I came all this way to say goodbye, and I couldn't even get anywhere close because I found out Greg went to rehab and dried out. I didn't want to jeopardize his sobriety and be the reason he fell off the wagon, so I stayed here the whole time. His sponsor said to take him to a meeting, so I did. When I left Greg with his sponsor, I left him his truck to get home, and his dad came to get me. He took me to the cemetery so I could say goodbye; that was nice. I feel good about that. The rest of me feels like I've been put through an emotional wringer."

"Val," Walt said, with tenderness in his voice. "Come on. It will be okay. Honest. I'm not happy about your ex-husband, I have to tell you. He's not in the position to dictate where you go or who you see. If you want to say goodbye to someone you love, do it. Be there. Fuck him. His emotional, medical, and mental health, or any other state of wellness, is of no concern to you. It's not your job. I know you are trying to preserve something for your kids, but is it even there to preserve?"

"It's about getting those kids what they deserve. They deserve a decent man to be their father. They deserve to be loved and respected, but if not by their dad, then who? Astrid already thinks he's useless, and Fiona doesn't even know him. It's for Ingrid. She's a child who still believes she deserves a daddy. Her own daddy. I know he's going to disappoint her; it's just a matter of time. I am just trying to hang in there enough so when he's finally gone, she doesn't think she drove him away. His choice to walk away will be because he's an inadequate human being, not because she wasn't worth sticking around for."

"I can beat the shit out of him for you like. Maybe not as far as a grease stain, but I could manage a bloody pulp." Walt offered.

"Oh, Ranger. You say the sweetest things." She laughed.

"That's my girl. He's history. I'm your future. No more crying. You just watch the Vacation Channel and enjoy the tropics. You'll be home before you know it, and things can go back to normal. It's been a tough trip for you. Promise you're done crying."

"I'm done. I think it released stress more than anything else. Thanks, Ranger. I mean Walter."

"That's my girl. Let me know if there's any change in your flights; otherwise, I'll see you at baggage claim. Goodnight, Valerie. Tell me you love me."

"What? Why?"

"I am not superstitious in the least, but if your plane goes down, I want those to be the last words I hear out of your mouth."

"Okay, you have to say it back because if my plane crashed, the last words I'd say would be 'Wheee, girls! Isn't this fun?' so they wouldn't know we are falling out of the sky towards certain death. I love you, Walter."

"I love you, Valerie. Have a safe trip home."

They boarded the plane when the overhead announcements called for parents with small children requiring a little more time. It's probably so the other passengers don't have to listen to kids fighting over who gets the window seat, Val thought.

A very perky stewardess asked for her boarding passes. She showed them to their seats in first class.

"I think there's been some mistake. I belong in the first class, but not these three heathens," Val said.

"These girls look like absolute angels, I'm sure first class is where they belong," she said in a voice honey-thick with a southern twang. Val asked to see the boarding passes. They were upgraded yesterday. She sat down and called Walt.

"Did you do this?" she asked. "Why?"

"You sounded like you could use a free drink. I used points, so it was no big deal. You can thank me later."

"Thank you. I think this is the best gift anybody ever gave me."

"That's what I don't get about you. You're so grateful for what most other people consider crumbs."

"How could people consider first-class tickets crumbs?"

"You'd be surprised by the number of people who think they deserve a Learjet. I'll see you at the airport."

She came through with those two Nordic gems holding hands in front of her, with Fiona keeping up behind them, mindful of the other two and making sure they were mindful of her. They ran up the ramp and waited.

Walter looked for them. He saw the girls but waited until Valerie met them before he approached.

"Mr. Stranger! What are you doing here?"

"He's our ride. He's got our car with Fiona's booster seat. What are you doing inside the building? They'll tow your car here or else boot it," Valerie warned.

"If you spent as much time as I do in airports, you make a few friends with the truly important people in airports: the parking guys. Now, girls," he said to Astrid and Ingrid, "how was your airplane ride?"

They were chattering and speaking over each other about how they sat with the pilot. "Well, behind the pilot. They closed the doors," Astrid said. Ingrid made a face. She was sick of how her sister always had to correct her. Ingrid was sick of her doing it the whole visit. Just thinking about it made Ingrid mad. She looked at her sister and couldn't control the impulse to shove her hard. It knocked her into Fiona, who fell over.

Fiona learned crying was a waste of time. People paid attention to her only to tell her to stop crying. They didn't do anything about what caused her to cry in the first place; they just told her to be quiet. While she was on the floor, she reached out and bit her sister's ankle. Astrid howled. Fiona thought, There. You cry.

"Hey, you guys, stop it. It was a long flight, and we were all cranky. Please. We're almost home. Mr. Stranger will leave us here if you don't stop," Valerie said. The three started screeching about who did what and who needed a time-out.

Valerie looked at Walter and said, "I need a time-out and a bottle of vodka." The luggage carousel started with the familiar sound they were waiting for, and bags slid down the ramp.

"Look! Our suitcases are coming. See if you can pick yours out." She directed them to the belt. Fiona found hers first, but she couldn't lift it and didn't let go. She somehow ended up on the belt, her hand around her Shrek suitcase handle. Astrid and Ingrid were speechless at the sight of their sister lying on the carousel, wrestling with her bag.

"MOM!" Ingrid yelled, "LOOK!" She pointed at her sister. Val's eyes widened. "Oh, shit!"

Walt sprinted over and plucked her off before the belt carried her away to the back. He managed to grab her bag as well. He gave it to her, curious to know what she planned after she had it. She knew enough to pull it behind her, but didn't orient the wheels correctly and tried to drag it anyway.

"Here," Walt said and fixed the wheels. "That should fix it." The little girl

looked up and smiled at him.

"Thank you very much," she said and headed towards her mom. He was momentarily stunned. She looked like Valerie 2.0. Everyone commented on the two blondes, but the little one was losing her babyish looks and would grow up and look just like her mother, a lucky girl. He went back and helped the rest of them get their things.

They exited the terminal and went to the car, parked right there. "Wow," Valerie said. "You do know people. These airport cops don't even let you stop to get out." After they got in the car, he pointed to the tag hanging from her rearview mirror. It was a special placard allowing parking. "I bought this off one of the parking guys for fifty bucks."

"Mommy! We're hungry. We want to go to Taco Bell!" yelled voices from the back seat.

"Taco Bell? Why Taco Bell?" Val asked.

"Because we're sick of pizza and macaroni and cheese!"

"Fine. But it's to-go. I want to go home."

Walt pulled into the drive-through and got their food. He didn't place Valerie's order other than her drink. When she questioned him, he told her not to worry about it, so she chose not to.

They pulled in, and it was like they never left. They put the girls with meals in front of the TV. Walt told Val to take up one load, and he'd get the rest and go out on her balcony and relax. He brought her a glass of wine and two covered plates. He took off the silver domes; they each had a filet with portobello mushroom sauce, mashed potatoes, and green beans.

"Eat," he demanded. "I hope it didn't overcook while we were at the airport. I think you ordered this on New Year's Eve, so I think you should like it. Some adult food."

"Taco Bell would have been good."

"I know, but I cooked this. You can have Taco Bell tomorrow." His voice was firm and sounded slightly annoyed.

"You did a very nice job with the sauce. It's delicious. The potatoes are a nice touch."

"Thank you," Walt said, his ego soothed. "You're lucky you turned it around. You would have forfeited dessert: cheesecake."

"You would have used plastic utensils if you thought that."

They sat back and enjoyed the evening with a glass of wine. "Sounds like quite a trip for you."

"The whole thing was incredibly sad. I couldn't sit there with my thoughts and mourn someone I loved and say goodbye. Instead, I had to bring her son to an AA meeting and go meet up with his sponsor. However, I think his mother would be glad someone helped and feel bad it was me, but grateful overall. I'm glad the girls went, and I do love Dave and Caroline. I guess it went well."

"Tell me about your husband. You didn't stroll down memory lane over a cup of coffee, did you?"

"Why? What are you talking about?"

"Nothing. Time and distance seem to take the sting out of things, and things that looked terrible up close aren't so bad from a distance."

"Are you trying to find out if okay? Now he's sober, and that's what I wanted, I'll take him back?"

"That sums it up," Walt agreed.

"Why, my mysterious stranger? Are you jealous?" she teased.

He frowned and looked at her, but didn't answer the question. Walt sat back and figured since honesty was the one thing she valued above all else, he wanted to see what she'd do with it.

"Suspicious, yes. Doubt, yes. Jealousy, sure. What of it?"

"I'm surprised. You didn't strike me as the jealous type."

"I never knew I was until I met you. Now, I worry about old boyfriends and ex-husbands dropping out of the sky when I'm out of town."

"If it's machismo driving this, get over yourself. If it's a concern because I have been waiting for him to sober up, the question is valid. Here's the thing. He's been drunk for the last ten years. Maybe he had good reasons that justified his behavior, but I don't care. Greg wasn't where he was supposed to be when I was there. I have no interest in a guy whose emotional development stopped in college." Valerie stood up next to him and put her arm over his shoulders. Walt put his arm around her waist.

"I know that. I trust you more than anyone I know, but sometimes the past has a way of showing up all moonbeams and stardust when all it is is rocks and dirt in space. It looks better than it was, and depending on what you never got, it suddenly appears, but it's a mirage. You're one of the smartest people I know. You would realize that, but still, even the best people get fooled," Walt told her.

"It's very strange how little I feel for him. He is not the guy I married," Valerie said. "Or maybe he is, and I've changed. I have no patience with drama. I'm pouring my energy into the kids. I can't be both parents; I know that. But what choice do I have? He's not some knight with a tarnished suit of armor. With some spit and polish, he'll be good as new, no. He's been a deadbeat dad. Who knows who he is now? Can we stop talking about him now? My involvement with him on this trip was minor. I don't want to think about him anymore."

Valerie peeked her head in to check on the kids. They had full bellies and were enthralled by the TV. She thought about making them pick up their trash and put on their pajamas, but decided she preferred peace right now. She grabbed Walt by the hand and pulled him to a corner of the balcony not visible from the doorway. She put her arms around his neck and looked at him.

"What are you doing?" he asked.

"Trying to figure out a scenario. Who are you? Why are you going to kiss me?"

"This one's easy. I'm your boyfriend, and I want to." He crushed her to him and kissed her like he meant to obliterate any thought of her ex and any other male from her head. He didn't stop until she was shocked and awed into submission.

He pulled back and looked into her eyes. He didn't like what he saw and kissed her again and again until he felt her press her pelvis into his erection. He pushed back against her, felt her sigh, and she collapsed against him. He stopped and looked into her eyes. He was satisfied with what he saw and stepped back. He smiled at her and sat back down. When she finally caught her breath, she spoke.

"What? You're just going to stop and leave me hanging?"

"Yes."

"Why?"

"Because I can, Valerie. It appeals to the machismo part of me." He laughed.

"You brute," she said. "You hairy brute."

"No, your hairy brute."

"That's a good fake name. Harry Brute. Next time you check into a hotel, use it."

"I wanted to play a doctor next time."

"You can be Dr. Harry Brute. Who am I? Not a nurse, please. That's so overdone."

"How about an X-ray technician? We could go into a closet and see what develops."

"That's funny. Obvious but funny. How about I'm a Russian operative trying to steal a serum you developed to cure cancer? I pretend to be a patient to throw you off the trail."

"Are you wearing one of those hospital gowns that open in the back?"

"Will it distract you to the point I can pick your pocket?"

He took a quick look at the kids and joined her. He pressed himself against her, and she could feel him hard through her clothes. He kissed her.

"I think you need to practice getting it out of my pocket. My front pocket," he specified. He looked at her; she gazed back at him. She suddenly shoved her hand into his front pocket. She took him by surprise, and he jumped a foot.

"Geez. You're gonna kill me." He took a breath. "You're off. A little more to the center. Yeah. You're definitely gonna kill me."

"You should be so lucky," she told him. "That's where we agree," he said. "Mommy?" Ingrid called. She was awake, which meant they all needed to be awake, time for potty to pajamas. Valerie and Ranger went inside.

"Ah, well, it was good while it lasted. Maybe next time. Thanks for dinner. It was delicious, but duty calls. Have a good trip," she said as she walked him to the door, and with a blink of a kiss, he said goodnight and left. "Okay, girls, time for bed."

No one had an argument for staying up, so bedtime was quick. She went out on her balcony to see if he was on his. She smiled when she saw him.

"Time for bed. I'm exhausted. Came to see if you were here, so I could thank you for your help and wish you a good night before I get in bed," Val said across the rail.

"Yes, I am, so goodnight. Glad you're home. Now go to bed. You're dragging."

"You're off to Denver tomorrow. Have a safe trip."

"I'll call you tomorrow night."

"Goodnight, Dr. Harry Brute."

"Goodnight, patient zero. Go to bed."

She went inside, ready to fall into bed with her clothes on, when she remembered her new skincare routine. She didn't have any creams or lotions to slather all over her face to erase ten years in one week, but she could at least wash it. As a compromise, she splashed water on her face, turned off the lights, and fell into bed.

✸✸✸

Eighteen

GREG

AFTER HIS MOTHER DIED, Greg felt alone and adrift. He still went to work with his dad, but afterward, he went to an AA meeting. After the situation with Valerie, he just wanted to die. After those years of nagging finally paid off, she wasn't here to reap the rewards. Only, she never nagged him.

What Valerie said was true. Greg couldn't cope when things went bad. He was the kind of guy bad things didn't happen to, which was probably why when he lost his football career, he couldn't handle it. Greg held on to the hope that it was only going to cost him time. He'd be out of commission for a while but would be back better than ever.

When he got the news, he was never going to be the same, he didn't believe it. It was going to take longer to heal; that's all. When the second surgery failed, the doctors were wrong. When he returned home after he lost his scholarship, he was alone. All his friends were away at school or doing things. Greg didn't have to pretend to be okay for them, they were gone. For his family, he put a big smile on his face and avoided them. And Valerie. He didn't know where to start.

He remembered when she got back from Italy, she didn't even go home. She rented a car from JFK and drove directly to him when she heard about his surgery, worried he was alone and depressed. She walked in on him with Missy, and she was pissed. Greg smiled at the memory of two girls fighting over him.

God, I am a miserable piece of shit, he thought. That was one of the first lies he told Valerie. Missy wasn't a football groupie. She was his groupie. Val wasn't gone half an hour, and Missy was back in his bed.

A few of the guys looked at him with disgust. Valerie made quite a big impression on them, but they weren't like Greg. They were regular guys, not preordained for greatness like he was.

Greg loved her and married her, just like they had planned. They were happy, too. She knew he had to be fucked up about the death of his dreams. Val also knew it had to affect him deeper than he wanted to admit. He wasn't going to admit it to her when he wouldn't admit it to himself. Greg felt he had to work in the field to avoid his father's scrutiny. Those guys had a beer at lunch, he didn't think it would matter. And then one at the end of the day, sometimes two. After a couple of beers, he felt loose and relaxed, not drunk.

Greg only drank to relax initially. A couple of beers never hurt anyone. He thought Valerie overreacted, it was just beer. He felt like all the edges of his life were as sharp as razor blades; internally, his guts were in knots.

A few beers blunted his emotions so he could manage them. And Valerie, Jesus. She bothered him with every detail. Her voice was like a dental drill without Novocain. Then, a baby. Another baby. He loved his kids, he did, but they were so needy. They cried and whined. With each one, a new set of responsibilities came, a beer or two more to cope.

It was the last baby that did it. Not her specifically, it was actually the idea she might be a boy that did it. He was a man who had no business having a son. Greg couldn't chase after him. How could he have a boy when all they did was jump and run, and climb trees? What was he supposed to say? "Here, son, put the football away. Let's play chess." That was the thing he could not face.

Greg thought he held things together pretty well. His process of emotionally distancing himself from a son applied to the rest of his family. He was too far gone to be reeled back in when the baby was born a girl. Greg had emotionally checked out on the rest of them, too. When he physically left, he was sure nobody even noticed, or so he told himself.

Greg couldn't believe he stopped at Valerie's after his mom's burial. He treated her badly. What word was worse than badly? Horribly? Terribly? Disrespectfully? Abysmally? All that and more, yet instead of coming outside and telling him if he was not off the property in five minutes, she was calling the cops, she invited him in. Valerie let him cry on her shoulder and took care of him. That's why he tried so hard to hate her. Why was she so good at everything? Being around her only highlighted what a fuck up he was. Valerie deserved better than him.

Despite it all, she did what needed to be done. Val held him like a baby, tenderly and with care, even though she probably hated him. He also knew she was fearless and did whatever the situation called for, regardless of her ability to pull it off. Like a surgeon, she cut quick and clean with little emotion, she excised him from her life. Or did he just convince himself of that so he could ease his guilty conscience for being such a shithead? No wonder he was jonesing for a beer.

One of the strategies that worked for Greg was instead of having a beer after work, when he really wanted one, was to go to a meeting. He wondered if the whole point of AA was to make your life about going to the next meeting, instead of the closest bar. They absorbed whatever reason you drank, and it was your job to find a meaningful life. Something unhealthy subtracted, and something positive replaced it.

In the meantime, you went to a meeting to prop you up if you felt weak, and to help the person that was you a month ago. Steps, as it were. Someone steps on your shoulders, and you step on the guy ahead of you. A pyramid, the higher up you went, the fewer people were successful, and most of the successful people were people who graduated from the program and worked there. He continued to work the program because his alternative was O'Malley's.

He had some really deep conversations with his mom about his purpose. She never mentioned his family, and he would bet she didn't because she knew he would never talk to her again if she did. Val and the girls were the highest rung of the ladder, and they didn't make it that far.

He spilled his guts to his mother, and she knew all his ugly truths and failures, his inadequacies as a husband and father, and his fall from grace to the gutter, and she loved him anyway. His vision cleared as he sobered up, and he realized perhaps Valerie loved him like that, too. Once. In fact, he was sure she did, and he felt unworthy of it, damage goods and all. If she wasn't smart enough to leave, his only option was to drive her away. Greg drove her halfway across the country, taking his kids with her. He could have fought for them, but in his alcoholic haze, he didn't. They were better off without him, too.

Greg went to a meeting every day after work to offset his previous happy hour two-for-one, and that's where he met Shannon. She was a faded kind of pretty.

He imagined much like himself, she once had a future. Potential. Dreams. All lost now, alcoholic roadkill. He could tell she made the choice to get sober, but did not have the luxury of the detox and rehab he had, and was hanging on by her fingernails.

She went to the same meetings as he, and he felt he might offer her hope, or at least perspective. Greg stood in exactly the same spot as she, and if he could make progress, however meager, she could too. He asked her if she wanted to grab a cup of coffee after a meeting, and she did. They were in the habit of having one a couple of times a week, after each meeting.

They got into the habit of grabbing dinner after an evening meeting. Greg thought that since alcohol wasn't involved, it wasn't really dating, or so he convinced himself. It had been so long since he had a conversation with a woman that he forgot how. He thought this was positive growth.

She was not as far in her sobriety as Greg and had a lot of anxiety. She suffered with anxiety her whole life, her posture taut, and she was hypersensitive to sound and bright lights. Greg tried to offer her a steady hand; her grip was dry and brittle. Shannon relaxed after a bit and wasn't so tense. She was funny, even. She laughed at his jokes. She was on the outs with her family and hadn't spoken to them in months.

Her program was court-ordered; it was one of several things from when her life spiraled out of control, including two totaled cars. Some other legal concerns about possessing stolen goods and drugs, but that wasn't her fault. Shannon didn't know that's what the people she was hanging around with were into. The DUIs were hers, and she would pay the price. He thought that was significant, her accepting the consequences of her behavior. She was making changes, too.

He felt confident they were pointed in the right direction, and they would negotiate the rapids of sobriety together. They formed an almost instantaneous bond. Greg thought she could help her, and Shannon saw Greg as someone she could cling to when life was too hard. When it got too hard before, she would disappear and party for days. Now, this nice, handsome man would come to her rescue. They became inseparable, spending all their free time together in an effort to keep each other sober. Even though he didn't want to leave his father alone in the house, he moved out and got a place, and Shannon needed a place to crash, so she ended up living with him.

He had six months of sobriety, she three. She ended up in his bed. Part of Greg felt uneasy. They were no longer going to meetings every day. He thought this process was to replace the source of his drinking with positive things, but she may not have been the best substitute. They had nothing in common except their alcoholism. She leaned on him, and he wondered if he had the strength to be her sole support, but Greg figured if they both stayed sober, that was the important thing.

Greg came home from work one day and found Shannon excited, happy to see him with some wonderful news. "You're not going to the meeting?" he asked.

"Greg," she called from the couch, "come in here! I have something to tell you! Sit here, next to me."

He took a seat next to her. "What's up?"

"You won't believe it! I'm pregnant!"

Greg was stunned. One of the feelings he drank to numb away was intimacy. After he left Valerie, all he really wanted was to be left alone. He wanted to drink or stay out or not come home whenever he felt like it. The only responsibility he was required to keep was his job. He felt invisible when he was out with the crews, just one of the guys in Carhartt jackets and steel-toed boots. They kept a cooler with them on every job, stocked with beer, available at lunch or quitting time or any other time somebody wanted one.

As the insulation that kept him emotionally removed from his feelings was no longer being supplied, he felt things he hadn't in a long time. One of them was the basic human need of connection. He had a longing for companionship. Shannon was a warm body in his bed, and one night, it happened. He reached for her, and she reached back. He knew he didn't love her. He never told her he did. This tsunami of emotions threatened to derail the hard work he had done to get this far.

"Greg. What's the matter? Aren't you excited about having a baby?" Greg sat mute.

"Greg? Are you okay?" Shannon asked, alarmed.

"Uh, I guess I'm shocked. I thought you were on the pill," he finally choked out.

"I was, but I didn't get it refilled the last couple of months, I needed to see the doctor. I must have forgotten," she explained.

"Oh. You need to see a doctor now, right?"

"I made an appointment for next Monday at the clinic. It's at ten. You can take time off from work, can't you?"

"Probably. If you don't mind, I need to talk to my sponsor. This is pretty big news, and I think I need a drink to steady my nerves, but I don't want to start that again. I can't start that again. I won't."

"But, Greg, this is great news! Why aren't you happy?"

"I am," he lied. "It's a huge responsibility. I need to talk to my sponsor about it. You understand, don't you? I mean, about the need to drink in the face of such big news." Here I go again, with the lies, he thought. First, I started missing meetings, now lying. Fuck. I went from one mess to another. He decided he was not going to walk away from this one. He'd face it clear-eyed and level-headed. And dry.

He met with the sponsor, who was not thrilled at Greg's situation. He talked about how the odds of success with two addicts having a baby so soon after getting clean were slim at best. He asked Greg if he could handle being a father this time when he couldn't do the job last time. Greg wanted to punch the guy.

"You can get mad at me if you want," George said, "but think about it. You didn't have the resources to be a father before. Have you gained enough to be one now? Because babies don't change. Babies are tough. Not only will you be required to meet the baby's needs, but Shannon's too, as well as her sobriety, and your own sobriety. I've got to tell you, Greg, things don't look good. It's too much too soon, but we're here to support you."

They talked it out and left as friends. George was doing his job, giving a reality check, one Greg needed to hear. It was one he needed to hear years ago. If he only sought help earlier, all their lives might be different. He needed to tell his father, something he dreaded. Part of the process of releasing alcohol's grip on him was doing what he dreaded sober and paying the price. Then it was off the list, and he did not need to worry about it. Greg needed to let go of the guilt. He needed to quit crying "poor me" into a beer bottle and man up. His other kids had Valerie. This little baby had only him, and he was going to get it right this time if it killed him.

The lie, or false truth, that Greg used as a way to justify his behavior, was the foundation on which he built his house of sand. He used more lies to keep it together. Even when he was knee deep in empty bottles rolling around the floor of the passenger side of his truck, he told himself they weren't all his was a lie. His promise to Valerie never to drink and drive with the kids in the car was a lie.

The way he rearranged Valerie in his mind to be this unreasonable bitch of a nag was a lie. She tried everything in her power to keep his family together. Calling him out on his drinking was something she had to do for the safety of his kids and the state of their marriage. The lie he told himself was that she always blew things way out of proportion. After all, it was just beer.

Greg had to admit to himself that all the lies did one thing. It served him to sit on that bar stool and avoid dealing with the negative feelings of his life not going as planned. He didn't have to deal with the overwhelming guilt he felt if he wasn't numbed by booze. Greg was inadequate as a husband and even more so as a father. He let everyone who loved him down. He was going to honor his mother's wish that he pull himself out of the gutter and get sober.

When he finally dried out and saw the wreckage of his life and everyone around him, it took everything he had not to crawl back inside the dark comfort he got he got from both the booze and the bar. He had to deal with the guilt of it all. Greg fucked up big time. It was time to face the consequences of his choices and actually feel what he tried to hide from all these years.

His failure to come back from his injury was the root of it all. Rather than mourn that loss and get on with things, he remained stuck there in disbelief that this happened to him. Bad shit like this happened to other people, not him. The fact that it did turned him upside down and inside out, shit like this didn't happen to people like him.

God, I was such an asshole thinking life owed me a pass because I got hurt. I remember when Valerie accidentally got pregnant with Fiona…And now, my worst fear of being inadequate as a man who shouldn't have a son came true, he thought.

His father was picking him up for work, Greg thought bad news might go down easier with eggs, so he asked if they could stop for breakfast. They went to the Valley Diner, took a booth, ordered, and over coffee, Greg started the discussion. His father wasn't fooled that Greg had something positive to say, as much as his son smiled and acted pleasantly. He waited for Greg to serve up whatever was on his plate.

"Dad. I need your help and your advice," Greg started.

"Why? What's up?" his father said.

"I made a mess. A big mess, and I don't know what to do about it. I don't know if you ever met Shannon, but I know her from AA. She didn't have a place to go, her family isn't talking to her. I let her crash at my place; it was supposed to be temporary. It doesn't look like that's going to be anytime soon. She's pregnant."

His father sat back and took a sip of coffee. "Yeah, that sounds like a big mess," he agreed.

"That's it? That's all you have to say?"

"No, I have plenty to say. The question is, are you ready to listen? Some of it might be painful and ugly."

"I know, Dad. Six months ago, I would have said fuck it and gone to O'Malley's. I wasn't interested in painful and ugly. I would have walked away and let it be somebody else's problem. But I'm sober, and it's hard to look back at the wreckage I caused, but it's there. I can't avoid it. I can't fix that now. I have to make sure I don't cause anymore."

"That's good to hear, to try to get in front of it. A baby is no joke. This Shannon, do you love her?"

"No."

"Does she know that?"

"No. She hears what she wants. I don't remember asking her to move in, yet there she is. She told me she was on the pill. She was, once. Shannon lied about that, I think, but I don't think she thinks so. She looks at it as something she never got around to doing. I haven't had a drink in six months, and I don't want to start now. The feeling that life's collapsing around me is making me want one, bad, and it's not getting better. I need to go to a meeting after work, to settle my nerves, and she wants me to come home instead. I can't go home. I need to go to a meeting. My sobriety is the most important thing. I can't be a good father if I'm not sober. She disagrees. She thinks I should be home with her."

"Is she sober?"

"She stopped going to meetings when she found out she was pregnant. I don't know if she talks to her sponsor. She might be involved with people, I don't know. The only thing I can think of is to take the next six months off to protect the baby. Shannon can't be left alone. She has to be watched 24/7. She is an addict in the worst way. She sucks the life out of everyone in the room. After she leaves, everything looks dull and lifeless. I can't believe I'm saying these things. I want to judge her, but I can't. You probably felt all these things about me."

"Son, do what you have to do. I can come out of semi-retirement for the next six months. Take her to meetings three times a day if you have to. She might get off on being the poor pregnant girl desperate to drink, and the group will focus on her. Maybe if staying clean becomes the center of her world, we can use it to protect the baby. I don't know if it will work, but honestly, you barely know her. Manipulate the meetings so they always come back to her. You could try that," his father suggested.

"That makes sense. If I start to make her the reason I fixed breakfast, it's because

I'm taking care of her, but what I'm really ensuring is the baby is getting adequate nutrition. If she asks me why I'm not at work, I'll tell her I took family leave to take care of her. That's not a lie," Greg said. "As long as you'd be willing to not expect much out of me, work-wise."

Greg started the next morning, over breakfast in bed. She was flattered and worried because he didn't go to work, but it was because he could spend all his time with her. After breakfast, they went to a meeting, and then to the store for nutritious food. They went back, and she rested, only to go to a meeting after dinner, followed by home for the night. Greg managed to do this for a month or so. Sometimes Shannon would sneak out. Greg went to great lengths to keep her preoccupied as the apple of his eye, and she couldn't get enough. Shannon was an empty well, a bucket with a hole; she could never get enough. Greg went to all her doctors' appointments, and the baby was growing fine. Baby boy Wilson was right on schedule.

Right around the seventh month, Shannon started to chafe under Greg's adoration. She still enjoyed his attention, but she was getting bored. Having this baby made her wholesome in a way that wasn't natural. She was sick of all the meetings, but she loved the way strangers approached her to talk about the baby. Earlier, people asked about her, but now it was all about the baby. People still made caring comments about her, but once she began to show, and people focused on the baby, she got sick of the whole thing.

Greg took her to all her doctor appointments. One day, she ran into a few old friends on the corner.

Greg had to park far away from the doctor's office, and she waited for him to pull up. They were the kind of people she developed bad habits with, not good influences at all. Even they, however, wished her to stay clean for the baby's sake. She had an itch that needed scratching, awakened by seeing her old friends.

Greg had a bad feeling about that. He noticed the clues maybe a non-user might overlook. He could tell by the evasiveness of her answers as to who those people were and how she knew them. Greg could tell being pregnant bored her, and she wanted this baby out soon. He doubled down on his "obsession" with her, keeping her in his sight always, determined not to have his son born damaged by her behavior.

On December 13, three weeks earlier than his due date, Trevor Joseph Wilson was born, seven pounds, one ounce via C-section, perfectly healthy and substance-free. Shannon, however, seemed more concerned with pain management.

She was more interested in her next dose of Oxy than her son, which was okay. The baby was healthy. Shannon was not.

The birth of her son gave Shannon another opportunity in the spotlight. She tried to stay an extra day because of intractable pain, but the tide had turned away from pills being dispensed at the patient's request. They gave Shannon a few extra to cover her, but Tylenol should have been enough after discharge.

Greg's dad gifted them an agency nurse to help Shannon learn the mechanics of new motherhood. She arrived at seven forty-five a.m.; Greg left at eight. Initially, Shannon couldn't get up because of her surgery, so Greg got up, fed the baby, and got him ready for the day. He put him in with Shannon and got ready for work. Connie, the nurse, was there when he left. She left at three, and Shannon had him until Greg got home. Sometimes she was still in bed when he got home.

After a few weeks of lying around, Shannon got up. Connie was concerned about her. In her experience, new moms fell in love with their babies. Maybe not all at once, but little by little, they would be enchanted by what a marvel of nature a baby was, but Shannon exhibited none of this. She had visitors during the day, but the minute the boy fussed just a little bit, she called Connie to take over. Connie couldn't help overhearing bits of conversation, things like the Wilsons were loaded and Greg was a sap. She couldn't help but relay the information to Mr. Wilson.

Trevor was three months old when Shannon fired the nurse. She found Connie's presence intrusive. Greg still did the morning bottle and got him ready for the day. He never knew what he would find when he got home. Shannon was lazy. He wondered if she even changed him once during the day, causing Trevor a painful diaper rash. He was such a good baby. Even if his butt was on fire, he hardly fussed, but in Shannon's words, "He was miserable all day long." Greg needed to bathe the baby because Shannon always ran out of time.

Greg stopped home one day at lunch to pick up a contract, and Greg walked into a living room full of strangers, his son crying in his crib a room away. He went in and changed the baby, and gave him a bottle. He called Shannon into the kitchen.

"Look. I don't know who the fuck those people are, but they have to go. Now," Greg told her. "You need to take care of Trevor."

"Fuck you," said Shannon. "I can have anybody I want here. I get sick of watching that kid do nothing but cry all day."

"Get those people out of here. Go with them if you want, but get them out. I'm not kidding. If you've started drinking again, things are gonna go bad real quick."

"What are you going to do about it, anyway?"

"Get you back into treatment."

"Relax. I'm out and taking everyone else with me. Good luck," she laughed and left.

Greg was alone with Trevor. He grabbed the diaper bag and car seat. Remembering the contract, he hoped his new diaper and full belly would put Trevor to sleep so he could get the contract signed and bring in some business. He could use a big win. Greg's ego was stretched as thin as it could go without snapping and heading him face-first into a blackout drunk, his go-to strategy before rehab. He didn't, and he couldn't. His son deserved better, and Greg promised his mom to do better.

He took the baby with him and went up to the boardroom. Greg was early for the meeting, which was rare. He usually walked in a minute before, unprepared and ready to wing it. If Trevor stayed quiet, he could review the contract beforehand and spot any oversights or mistakes. As soon as Greg checked in at the front desk, Gail, the receptionist, saw Trevor and said, "Aww."

It must have been a sound at a frequency only women could hear. They left their desks and collected up front. Greg had his briefcase and the car seat. He put the baby on the reception desk, and they gathered around him. They all offered to watch him while Greg was busy, but Trevor slept like the baby he was, so Greg decided to bring him in. He was sure his competitor didn't bring a baby with him; maybe it might sway the two women he knew were on the panel.

Greg was called into the conference room. He brought his briefcase containing the professional-looking proposal and his sleeping baby. He put the car seat on the table, opened his briefcase and got ready. He looked up to see the confused faces of the committee and smiled. He'd bet this was the first time a baby was entered under "attendees."

"Good afternoon. My name is Gregory Wilson, for those of you who I haven't had the pleasure of meeting yet. I'm with Conover Properties and here to present our bid for the Brookside Corners project. This is my son Trevor; I know you've never met him. You'll have to excuse me for bringing him with me today. My sitter was ill and unable to watch him this afternoon, so I picked him up on my way here. I didn't have time to scramble around and find someone to watch him. I do have a contingency plan; if he gets fussy, Gail will take her break early and watch him. So, let's get started."

Greg glanced at his son and said, "You. Sleep like a baby." He looked down at his papers, took a deep breath, and exhaled. He looked up, smiled widely, and began his pitch.

Greg finished, satisfied he did his best. Trevor also did his best and let out not a peep. When the meeting was over, it wasn't the ladies who flocked to Trevor; although they did, it was a couple of guys. The older man pulled Greg aside.

"You got balls, I'll give you that. It was pretty gutsy to bring a baby to a meeting where the decision was riding on it. It also showed you think quick on your feet. I'm not supposed to say, but once legal signs off on it, it's yours. You won the bid." The gentleman shook his hand. It took a minute for Greg to realize he was the CEO.

"Thank you, Mr. Alamanda. You won't be disappointed."

"My first grandchild is due at the end of the month. I hope he's as cute as this one."

He left, and the others filed out afterward. Greg grabbed his things and his son. He stopped by the front desk on the way out to get the diaper bag Gail stowed under her desk.

"Thanks, Gail. I couldn't have done it without you."

"Anytime, Mr. Wilson." It took a minute for Greg to realize she was referring to him.

Greg left on a natural high; he knew his habit was to have a beer to keep it going; that's what he used to do. He knew he had a weakness in this area. Nobody liked the way they felt once the high faded, but non-alcoholics expected it would fade, and the rest of their lives were enough to compensate. Greg hated to lose that feeling, and he thought drinking was a way to preserve it. Another lie he told himself; it never gave his good mood legs, but it numbed him, so he didn't have to experience its loss.

He drove right over to share the meeting recap and the CEO's news with his dad. He figured Trevor was due for a diaper change and a bottle. He was making noises in the back seat. He brought his son in and found his father watching TV.

"Great news, Dad. It's not official, but Mr. Alamanda told me we won the bid. I think Trevor's a good luck charm. If I change him and get his bottle ready, could you watch him for a bit? I'd like to go to a meeting. I'll call you after I'm done and pick up dinner."

Greg needed to learn how to celebrate sober. He still wanted a beer, just one, for a job well done. It never was only one, he knew that about himself. Greg was surprised how booze clouded his mind now that he'd been dry. Greg thought in his beer-blurred haze that was who he was, when in reality, he was so much more. It wasn't easy for him; at times, he wished he still was at O'Malley's, talking about whatever game was on with an ice-cold beer in his hand. Greg made a promise to his mother, and he'd be damned if he broke it.

After his meeting, Greg headed back towards his father and his son, food waiting on the passenger seat. He set the table and put Trevor back in his seat on top of the table to watch them eat. He gurgled every so often and kicked his feet, but otherwise entertained himself.

"The meetings, they help you quite a bit," his dad said. "I am so proud of how you've handled the baby and the hard work it took to make sure he's healthy. Look at the little guy. Reminds me of you as a baby. So happy and interested in everything."

Greg blushed at the compliment. The baby was here, happy, and healthy. He put his face near Trevor, put a burp cloth over his face, and played peek-a-boo. Trevor thought it was the best game ever.

"Greg. We have to talk about a few unpleasant things. I hate to bring it up since you had such a great day, but we have to talk about Shannon. I think we should sue her for sole custody. She can visit as much as she wants, but with supervised visitation. While you two are still together, document any reason that highlights her as an unfit mother. Like the people she hangs out with. Drug paraphernalia. Nights she doesn't come home. How many times you see her feed him, dress him, bathe him. Document everything. Take pictures. Your lease? It's done the end of next month. Have your exit planned, and then tell her it's over."

"We'll have all the legal stuff in place. If she wants to see him, have her hire a lawyer. Let her prove she wants him back. We are reasonable people; nobody wants to take her baby, but if she has no interest in motherhood, somebody has to step in. Better us than Child Protective Services."

"I know. She has other legal issues more pressing than custody. Shannon had to go to AA as part of her sentence, but she hasn't gone since I dragged her. Her sponsor can talk about that better than I can. George, my sponsor, can vouch that I am still going to meetings voluntarily. I reach out to him before I have a drink, and he talks me through it. I successfully completed rehab. If she tries to paint me with the same brush as her, I did what I had to provide for him. I demonstrated my commitment to sobriety. Let her do the same."

"I'll talk to my lawyer to see if he can recommend a good attorney who handles these types of cases and get the legal ball rolling. You get your head straight. You and Trevor can stay here."

"Thanks, Dad," Greg said as he packed up. "It's time to get Trevor home and ready for bed."

Greg got home and noticed several cars in the driveway; he was forced to park on the street. He went to unlock the door, but it was already open. He was greeted with a cloud of smoke. Cigarettes, mainly, but the more pungent odor of weed wafted through. He entered and saw strangers on his couch watching cartoons. Shannon was nowhere to be found. Greg stood in the kitchen; he placed the baby in his seat on the table. He heard laughing and saw Shannon exit the bathroom with some sketchy guy.

"Shannon? Can I talk to you?" Greg asked. She turned to the sleazeball, said something, and turned back to Greg.

"What is it now?"

"Now? For starters, everyone out. Now. What the hell were you thinking? The baby can't be in a house full of smoke, and I don't like it either. Your attitude is pissing me off. We got together to keep each other sober. I'm still committed to it. Are you? It doesn't seem like it."

"I can have friends over. It's my house, too, you know."

"Actually, it's not. Your name isn't on the lease. Get those people out now. And look at your baby. You haven't seen him all afternoon. Don't you want to say hello? He's happy to see you."

"I can't. I have to send my friends home," she said, like a snot and left the room. Greg followed her to make sure they all left, including Shannon. "Greg opened the windows to air the place out, wishing he could air her out of his life.

Later that night, Shannon came home in tears. "I'm so sorry, Greg. I haven't been a good mom. I wish I had a better excuse, but I don't know how." She put her arms around Greg and sobbed into his chest. "I'm sorry." Greg put his arms around her and rubbed her back.

"It's okay, Shannon. It's okay. You can learn. Nobody taught me, but I figured it out; you can, too. We can get the nurse back for a few weeks and help you."

"Not the nurse. She made me feel bad. She was always watching me."

"Yeah, but that was to see if you needed help. She wasn't here to criticize you."

"You don't trust me with him."

"It's not that. I have no idea who is even here when I'm not home. You can't smoke around a baby. Maybe your friends have never been around babies before, and they don't know how to behave. He's so little, and we have to make sure he's safe. It's our job. He can't tell us if he's hurt."

"I know. Teach me," she sniffled. "Let me take care of him tomorrow. I can do it."

"Are you sure you want to tackle it tomorrow?"

"Yes. I'll call you at lunch to check-in."

"You don't need to. I'm in the office, so I'll be able to stop by. This is good, Shannon. He's such a sweet little guy. You'll get the hang of it."

The next morning, Greg heard the baby as he was getting in the shower. He stuck his head out into the bedroom.

"Shannon. Get Trevor. He's up." He stepped out of the shower and still heard him. He quickly dried off and stuck his head out of the door to see where she was. She was in exactly the same spot, only now she was awake.

"Shannon—"

"Can you get the kid? I need a few more minutes."

He went and got Trevor and propped him up with Shannon so he could finish getting ready for work.

When he was finished, he saw Trevor had eaten, and Shannon was still in bed.

"Are you going to be able to handle this? I haven't found another sitter. I'm counting on you."

She sat up and rubbed her eyes. "I'm good." She looked at the baby. "Well, hello, little man," she said as she sat with him on the bed. Greg looked at her and relaxed. She seemed intent on being a mom.

"I have to go," he said. He kissed the baby on the head and, on impulse, kissed her too.

Shannon fell into motherhood, and while she was no Mary Poppins, she did her best. She liked Greg to give him a bath, but he was clean and happy. When Greg got home, they had dinner he picked up, Trevor sitting on the table between them. It was almost as if they were a little family. Shannon loved this. Greg took care of them both. Little moments like this stitched together are poignant but are not meant to be the solid foundation upon which one could build a family, and sooner rather than later, cracks appeared.

Greg had taken the twin bed in Trevor's room, leaving the double bed they shared before. Like he told his dad, she was a creeper. Always looked at the benefit to her first, she slowly and methodological carved out a niche for herself in his life. Once entrenched, it would take a lot to get her out.

Greg went to bed as soon as Trevor did. Greg was having the most incredible dream, like he was held down and hands were touching him everywhere. His hands focused below his waist and started to establish a rocking rhythm. Slowly at first, but firmly and expertly, the hands coached him to be fully erect. Greg could feel the urgent need of his body. He had avoided physical contact with anybody since the news about Trevor, but this dream felt so real. When he came, he immediately sat up.

"What the fuck? Shannon, get out of here! What do you think you're doing?" he said as he pushed her away.

"Oh, come on. You know you liked it, I can tell," Shannon said. "I can make you feel good. Real good."

"No. It's not like that anymore. That was a mistake."

"We belong together. The last few weeks proved it."

"No. The last few weeks were about you learning how to be a mom. Not how to be a wife."

"If you want me in that kid's life, you better want me in yours."

"Look, Shannon, you've walked away from AA. You're hanging around your old party friends. Nothing good is going to happen to you."

"Nothing good is gonna happen here if you don't let me in your life," she threatened. "You should marry your son's mother."

"Why? We aren't compatible. You still get sucked into the old life; you aren't done with it. I thought we could work together to help each other stay sober, but you don't want that. Instead of propping each other up, I'm afraid you'll drag me down. I can't do that. I have to stay sober for that little boy. He's more important than either of us."

"That so?" she said as she stomped away. "We'll see."

No mention was made of the night before. Greg got the baby up, changed his diaper, prepared his bottle, and brought him in with Shannon while she was still in bed and took a shower. He got out of the shower, and he went to check on why Trevor was crying. He dropped the bottle out of reach, and Shannon had made no move to help him; she had made no move at all.

"Hey. Shannon," he said as he tried to shake her awake. She mumbled in response but didn't open her eyes. He shook her harder. "WAKE UP!"

"What the fuck is wrong with you?" she said, her eyes squinted at the daylight. "Get up and take care of Trevor. Now. I have an appointment I can't be late for," he said as he dressed for work.

She sat up and gave him his bottle back, propped up by pillows. "Can't you at least hold him?"

"He's fine," she said, and went into the bathroom. She came back out and pointed at him. "See?"

"He has clean clothes on the changing table. You can dress him after you change his diaper. I have to run. I'll pick up dinner before I come home."

He got home shortly before dinner, placed the food on the table, and looked for his son. He was on a blanket placed on the floor, batting a play gym Shannon set up. She was asleep on the couch. He woke her. She seemed groggy and out of it. When he asked her if she was all right, she said, "You'd be out of it too if you just woke up."

"Does he need his diaper changed? Never mind. I'll take care of it." He grabbed Trevor like a football and carried him to the changing table. Greg frowned. The diaper was soaked through, his little bottom looked red and angry, and he was wet through his sleeper. He bent to pick up a clean one and noticed the clothes he set aside that morning were clean and in a pile on the floor. He wondered if he had been changed at all since he left that morning.

One of the emotions he was trying to learn how to handle was rage. It had its roots in anger never expressed after his injury, he knew that, but years of denial and pretend had it pretty well cemented in his psyche. The condition and total neglect of his son had him ready to strangle Shannon, but his exit plan was almost in place, and he didn't want to tip her off, so he said nothing. He knew Shannon liked it when she was the focus, so he played her vanity. He put Trevor back in his seat and sat the table. He went to find Shannon sacked out on the couch.

"Hey, baby, are you feeling okay? Are you coming down with something?" He could barely disguise his anger as concern, but managed to spit it out.

"Maybe you need to eat something. I have dinner."

She looked at him with blurry eyes. "I probably need to eat. I don't think I ate today."

He took her by the hand and brought her to the table. Greg wanted to look at her up close under the light. He made a display of fixing her plate and getting her a drink. He took a good look at her up close and did not like what he saw.

Shannon's eyes were glazed over and bothered by the light. He thought he smelled stale smoke on her. He was an alcoholic, not an illicit drug user, but he thought she was under the influence of something. She kept tripping on her words or trailing off in the middle of a sentence. Shannon was on something, no doubt. After dinner, he brought her back to the couch and tucked her in. He put Trevor down on a clean blanket under his play gym. He was afraid if he gave her the baby, he would slip right out of her grasp.

"Are you good for a few minutes? I need to put the trash out."

Greg pulled the bag out of the can in the kitchen and went out the back door to place it in the big can. He happened to look down and noticed some cigarette butts by the steps. He looked further and found a hypodermic needle sticking out of the grass, needle up. Greg was lucky he looked; he wasn't wearing shoes. He picked it up and put it underneath the stairs, safely out of the way. He saved it in case he needed proof if things got difficult.

He put a new bag in the can and checked on them both; neither had moved. Greg told her he was going to throw a load of clothes in the laundry downstairs, but he'd be right up.

Over the noise of the washer, he called his dad. Greg didn't want Trevor alone with her at all. He wanted to bring him by in the morning, and the two of them would move in over the weekend. Greg planned to tell her the landlord needed to work on the pipes, and Trevor was going to his dad's.

The landlord said he had to turn the water off, and banging on the pipes would bother the baby. He figured she would leave if the landlord was in and out, creating noise. If she were out, the landlord would change the locks to prevent her from coming back in.

Shannon over time, had stolen money out of his wallet, he never called her on it. But she was a thief, a liar, a junkie, and an alcoholic.

At least I'm just an alcoholic, he thought. If I think being a drunk was better than being a druggie, I'm also a fool. For just being a drunk, he sure tore through one family.

Greg wondered how his kids were, how Valerie was. Greg deserved to burn in hell for that chapter of his life. Once again, he was making it about him, and he didn't have the right to do that. Greg had to sit there, shut up, and eat it.

***

Nineteen

GREG AND VAL

GREG WOKE up and, as usual, he took care of Trevor before he got into the shower. He woke Shannon and asked her to watch Trevor while he got ready. She mumbled something and turned away. He placed the baby on a clean blanket with his toy. Shannon didn't even pretend to be interested in him or getting up. Greg behaved as usual and packed a number of things in a backpack as well as the diaper bag. He had no plans of returning and had a running list of items he would need scrolling through his head. He didn't worry about his own items, there were still things at his dad's. Anything Trevor needed, he could buy. Greg just had to get out of the house without causing Shannon to get suspicious. He got everything ready and packed it in the truck. Greg just needed to grab Trevor and get out.

"Hey, Shannon. We're leaving now. Don't forget the landlord is coming and the water will be turned off. If you want to shower, you'd better get in there now."

She rolled over and looked at Greg and Trevor through barely opened eyes. "You're taking him?"

"Yeah. To my dad's. Remember?"

"Good."

Greg turned and left without saying goodbye. He hoped he never saw her again. Once the baby was secured, Greg started the truck, took out his phone, and blocked her number. He put his phone away and drove off with a smile on his face.

***

Valerie's company, Lambert Development Corp., was sold to a much bigger company, APEX Holdings, Inc. Mr. Lambert was presented with an offer he couldn't refuse, much to the surprise of his employees and customers. APEX immediately implemented a leaner, get more from less strategy that meant nobody's job was safe.

It was to everyone's surprise except hers, Valerie was the sacrificial lamb. She was the first to go. If Ms. Wilson, whom everybody loved, got the ax, an undercurrent of fear rippled through the company. Would they be next?

Valerie's job required her successful use of soft skills with everyone, which translated into an extremely high retention rate. Employee morale was high; people loved working at Lambert. It had the highest employee satisfaction rate in the industry, but that was something not easily quantifiable. Her VP position of Corporate Communication Relations was viewed as expendable. The board felt what she did could easily be absorbed by Human Resources.

Valerie Wilson accepted a very generous severance package and a few other concessions. She would make a graceful exit, and if ever asked about her departure, her answer would be a "changing marketplace." She could have gone out bitter and verbally slashed and burned the company to the ground, but she chose not to. Val personally thought there was no way she lasted as long as she did and wasn't surprised. The job market was such that they could deplete a whole pool of candidates and never run out of new college grads. She wasn't surprised the first ax that fell was on her neck. Lean and mean, indeed.

They gave her until six to pack up her things. They loaded the boxes into her car, took her keys and access cards, and sent her on her way. She drove home after stopping to get a bottle of wine.

As soon as Valerie was out of the building, Marvin from building maintenance came up with a screwdriver and took the brass plaque off her door. He had it in his hands and went over to Jackie's desk.

"Wow. The body's not even cold, and they send you up here to remove any trace of her," Jackie said.

"Nobody told me to do it. When I saw her escorted outside, I came up and removed it myself. I knew they'd put somebody else's up and probably throw hers out, and Mrs. Wilson deserved better than that." He passed the plaque to Jackie. "If you see Mrs. Wilson, you can give it to her. Tell her I'm real sorry to see her go. She was the only bigwig up here who bothered to learn my name."

Walter wasn't home. Valerie forgot his schedule, but she knew he wasn't in town. She looked around and saw nothing that needed to be done, and burst into tears. Val left the unopened bottle on the counter and decided to wait until later.

She pulled herself together and met the school bus as well as the preschool mom dropping Fiona off. Valerie had them change their clothes and offered to take them out to dinner for chicken fingers. They ate them at the restaurant, something Valerie was loathe to do but would rather they clean up after the kids. They came home, did their homework, washed up, and got ready for bed. The girls asked for some TV time. She said yes if they were all set for bed; otherwise don't even ask. They settled in.

"I'm going out to use the phone," she told them, but they were already residents of Bikini Bottom.

"Granger."

"Wilson."

"My favorite girl. Are you okay? You sound funny."

"I'm unemployed."

"You're kidding me. How are you doing?"

"Okay, I guess. Marcus, my friend who really did have the corner office, gave me a heads-up about what was going to go down. He made sure I wasn't surprised and took any package I was offered, so I was ready with what I wanted if they wanted me to go out quietly. The separation package was very generous. When are you coming home?"

"Do you miss me? Want me?" Walt teased.

"Ah, never mind, I called. I can find comfort anywhere. The clubhouse is still open," Val teased back.

"I'll be home tomorrow. Wait for my comfort. It's the best."

"I can wait. I hope. I don't even need to get ready for work. Work is no more. I can spend all day in my pajamas. In bed. The sky's the limit."

"Well, that settles that. I'm taking the red eye, and I'll be back to spend tomorrow in bed with you."

"Are you kidding?" She heard the phone being passed around. "Hello? Is this Valerie? My name's Bob. Yes, Ranger is taking the red eye home. It's his company. He can do what he wants." Ranger got on the phone. "It's true. See you." He hung up.

The next morning, she got up and had coffee while the girls had breakfast. She didn't run after them screaming, "Hurry! You'll miss the bus!" She got them on the bus and looked at Fiona.

"You and me, girl! Let's go." They went back inside. "We have a little bit of time. Let's play." Fiona looked at her, confused. Her mom wasn't a player. She was a supervisor, an overseer. She drove. Fiona figured out what was wrong with this picture. She pointed at Valerie. "No work?"

"Right. No work anymore. Let's play with Play-Doh before you go to preschool. Now, where do we keep it?"

They had a few hours where it was just the two of them. Fiona liked to tell Valerie what to make, and Valerie tried her best to make a dinosaur, a girl, a pair of glasses, a dog, and the Time flew by, soon her ride to preschool came. Valerie told Maddy's mom, the driver, she was now available to be on the carpool schedule. As they pulled away, another car pulled up, and Walter got out as the driver went to get his bags.

"Ranger!" she said, threw her arms around his neck, and greeted him with a kiss. "Perfect timing!"

He kissed her back. "You need to let go so I can pay the guy." He tipped the guy twenty dollars in cash.

"I'll bring this up," he said about his luggage. "Do you want to follow me?" He started toward his unit, and she followed him with a little skip in her step. He opened the door, and they entered his condo. He dropped his bags, shut the door, and tackled her onto the couch. "You seem happy. Is it unemployment or me?"

"It's you. I haven't thought about my job yet. I'm in denial, so you have my complete attention until five o'clock."

"An afternoon with no interruption? Let's go in here," he took her hand a pulled her towards the bedroom. He picked her up and tossed her on the bed, and jumped on next to her. He stopped and stared down at her. It was rare to see her still, undistracted, her mind not on the clock or the kids. He could not believe how beautiful she was.

Without worry, her eyes were clear and untroubled. Bright, even. Her face unlined and youthful. He never realized everything she was responsible for ran quietly in the background of her mind. No longer having the pressure of her job freed her. Val stared back at him with a slight smile, waiting. For the first time, there was no next time.

Val said, "I'm happy to see you, Ranger."

"I'm happy to see you, too." She slid over and kissed him. Walter kissed her back. She ran her hands through his hair. He hated when she did this. His hair was fragile. He needed to hang on to every strand.

"Please be delicate," he said.

She made her touch light, she kissed him without touching his lips. Walt was under her spell, absolutely enchanted. Walter felt her lift her leg and throw it over him. He reached down and grabbed behind her knee and hiked her leg up higher. She rolled on top of him, opening his mouth with hers. He put both hands on her bottom and used it to push against him.

"Let's take our clothes off and get under the covers."

"Okay, but no covers. Just you and the bottom sheet."

"Okay, but you drive a hard bargain."

"Hard? Definitely. Bargain? Absolutely not. You're in for top shelf loin' tonight. Or this afternoon. But top shelf all the way."

They sat up and helped each other undress. Walt grabbed the covers and flung them in the corner. He gently laid her down and made love to her, looking her in the eyes the whole time. Valerie decided he could look at her all he wanted, but she closed her eyes and felt it all. She could feel his insistence that she look at him, so she opened her eyes and held on.

Walter was strong and physical. He had this sexual energy that ignited with hers. He didn't mind if she wasn't as available as some; Valerie was worth the wait. When they crashed together, they met as equals and opposites. Valerie could leave it all up to him. He took charge, he took care of her, he took care of them. Walt brought his mouth down and kissed her. When he was sure she came at least once, he plunged into her and let go. He missed her too much to deny himself any longer.

"Three more hours of peace. Want to do it two more times?" he asked.

"Maybe once. I'm just going to lie here and let you adore me."

"I can do that. That's easy," he said. "I could do that in my sleep."

"I miss you when you go away. I like you," Val told him.

"You just like me? Not like, like me?

"No, I like, like you. Maybe I like, love you."

"How do I get you to love, love me?"

"Not much. You're only a couple of letters away."

"I don't need them. Because I already love, love you,"

Valerie started processing her career at this point in her life. She called Caroline to talk about relocation. Caroline's advice was to move next door to her, never mind the house wasn't for sale.

"I'm not sure I want to go back home, but I feel like my mom needs me. I think she wants to go into an assisted living place; it's not right she's in that house alone. She deserves a social life. If she's still hung up on my dad, maybe she can't let go. I'm sure she has a story for every square inch in that place. Maybe if I buy it, she'll move because she'll be happy it's in good hands," Valerie mused.

"That's an idea. Have you heard about Greg?"

"No. I've talked to your dad a few times, but I don't ask and he doesn't share. The last time I saw him was after your mom died."

"Well, you won't believe what that idiot did now."

"What did he do? Fall off the wagon and disappear down a well?"

"No, he's still not drinking, if you can believe it. He met this woman at AA and had a fling. And a baby boy. She was all messed up; drinking was the least of her problems. They sued her for sole custody, but they couldn't find her to serve her the papers. She ran out on a number of legal things. If they ever find her, I think she's looking at jail time. Custody is the least of her concerns."

"Huh. Who has the baby now?"

"He does. They live with my dad. He's back working in the office, done with working with the crews. My dad is finally semi-retired. Greg's taken over a lot and seems to be doing okay."

"Huh," Valerie repeated.

"Valerie, this is the first you're hearing all this. Are you okay?"

"Yeah, I'm okay. Stunned, but okay. Who knew he had it in him? At least the baby is safe. What's his name?"

"Trevor."

"Trevor. My girls have a half-brother."

"I never thought about it, but yeah, they do. How are you supposed to explain that?"

"That asshole can't be a father to my kids, yet he can dry out and be a dad to somebody else's? I had to move because of him. He treated me like I didn't exist, and I couldn't bear the fact he got over me just like that. He took me out and dumped me on the curb with the rest of the trash."

"He's really turned his life around. Greg knows the anniversary of Mom's death is coming up, and he'll be sober. He talks about stuff like that with his therapist. The stuff he knows will trip him up. He's still going, still going to AA. He's grown up a lot. He's Greg. But different. Older. Softer. Bigger."

"Huh," Valerie said again, but spoke no further. Walt went out for work, and she carpooled. They still had donuts and coffee on.

Sundays. Due to his schedule, he was always on the road during the week, and she was alone quite a bit. He wanted to make it up to her on weekends; he decided to take her out on a date.

Astrid hung around while Valerie got ready. Kids grew up quickly, and she was on the cusp of tweenhood. She knew about dates and grownups kissing. She still imitated vomiting at the idea of kissing.

Still, it had an aura about it that kept her curious. She watched her Mom put on makeup. Ladies who put on makeup at night usually meant that they were going out. Out with friends. Out on dates. Valerie never had any friends, so it had to be a date.

"Mom, are you going out on a date?" she asked. Valerie was glad she wasn't applying mascara when Astrid spoke, she might have poked her eye out.

"Why do you ask?"

"When it's Saturday night and a girl puts on makeup, it's usually because she has a date with some dude."

"You are a very smart girl. I am going out on a date with a dude."

"Oooh," said Astrid, feeling grown up knowing about such things.

"With who? A boy?"

"No, I'm too old for boys. Guess who."

"Mr. Stranger."

"Why do you think him? Is he a dude?"

"I see him look at you when you don't know it, and his eyes look all moony. He's so into you."

"Yup. Him."

"Are you going to kiss him?" Astrid asked bravely.

"Depends," Val answered.

"On what?" Astrid looked like Valerie was passing great knowledge onto her.

"What he has for dinner. If it's gross, no way." Valerie laughed. "Go find Jackie, and let me finish getting dressed." On her way out, Astrid ran into Walter, who had just exited his unit.

"Hi, Mr. Stranger," Astrid called on her way by him. "Have fun on your date!"

"Thank you," he answered and walked through the open door.

He went inside and called for her. "I'll be right out," she yelled back. Soon, she entered the room, fixing her earring. He loved her look. She borrowed from different eras and looked a bit like a hippy. She had on a blue dress and gold bangles up her arms. She wore Birkenstocks. Walter looked at her feet and frowned. Corporate Ms. Wilson was no longer in the picture. "Not tonight, Walter."

Her old admin, Jackie, still wanted to watch the kids. They were older now, Astrid, eleven; Ingrid, ten; and Fiona, five going on six, finally losing her baby fat. She was tall like Valerie was, all arms and legs. Jackie was a well-paid playmate. The girls were working on cheerleading moves when they left.

He arranged for a reservation at this place on the edge of a ridge for the windows facing west to see the sunset. They ordered and enjoyed a drink while they waited.

They made small talk, his latest job in Nashville, her loose and unstructured days.

"Okay, Valerie, spill it. What's on your mind? You aren't going to enjoy dinner if you're already chewing on something else. Tell me," Walt said.

"I want to talk to you, but I don't want you to take this the wrong way, because you're one of the most important pieces of the puzzle," Val started. "Do you remember a long time ago you said you'd follow me anywhere, that it didn't matter where, as long as you were there with me? That's why you kept the condo next door rather than leave?"

"Yes, I remember saying that," he said, sipping his drink. He knew he should pay closer attention to what she was saying, but his eyes kept going to her neck. She wore her hair down, and her neck was obscured from his view. He was trying to figure out why it was so fascinating, but his eyes were drawn to her lips and the way every once in a while, the candlelight shone off her white teeth as she spoke. He then got caught up in the way the warm light shone in her eyes, flashing and gleaming.

"Walt, where'd you go?" she asked, confused.

"I just got lost looking at you. I think you are the most gorgeous woman I've ever seen."

"Well, stop that. You need to pay attention and help me figure out what I'm doing unless you want out. Then it doesn't matter what I do or where I go."

"It matters, or really it doesn't because I'm behind you, whatever you choose," he said.

"You can't do that. You have to participate. You have to be aware of what you sign up for." Valerie took her hands and pulled her hair back so that the neck that so infatuated him was fully on display.

Walter nodded. He'd rather go back and study the hollows of her neck, but since she asked, he did have something that bothered him about her. Walt needed clarification on that before anything else got decided. It nagged at him, occasionally rising like a bubble but popping before he could put words to it.

"Since I've known you, your main goal has been to unite the kids with their dad. Is that what you're going to do? Chase him for the next twenty years? Now that he's sober, or sober right now, is it time to realize that this wasn't about kids at all? Is it about reconciling with him so you can have your family back together?"

He could see her eyes water at the idea. I sure struck a nerve there. I have to be close to something painful, he thought.

"I'm not sure I ever told you what happened that made me leave in the first place, but it wasn't so he could chase me around and beg me to take him back," Valerie explained. "It wasn't that big a deal, really. I was sitting at a traffic light when I noticed his company truck stopped opposite me. I was so excited; if he could see me, if he could only see me, he would realize what a big mistake it all was, and we'd work it out.

"When the light changed and traffic started to move, he looked up and saw me. He made eye contact with me and turned away. He turned away. Like I was nothing. I felt like he stabbed me right in the chest, aiming for my heart. When I think about it now, it hurts just as much as it did when it happened." She picked up her napkin and wiped her nose.

"Then I got really pissed. I decided right there he could go fuck himself. He could hurt me and reject me all he wanted; I could take it, and someday, I'd pay him back in spades, but right then, I had to protect my girls. No man, including their father, would ever hurt them like that.

"So, I took the promotion at work because I wanted the girls safe from that selfish asshole. They weren't going to be around for him to ignore.

"We relocated. It wasn't a mistake. He has an obligation to those girls. That's what I can't let go of," she explained. "Now he has a son. If he can stay sober and raise that kid, he has a responsibility to my kids. His kids. Does that help answer your question?"

"Yes. I knew you had unfinished business with him, but I wasn't exactly sure what that entailed. I believe you have no romantic fantasies about him. Take me out of the equation, though. If I wasn't here, what would you do?"

"That's easy. I'd move back and be near my mother."

"That's the answer, then. That's what you should do."

"What about you, Ranger? What do you want?" Valerie asked him.

"I told you. I'll follow you wherever you go if that's what you want me to do." He set his glass down.

"There has to be more. You have to want more."

"Yeah, but you'll probably think I'm nuts. Here's what I want: shared custody. I want my life back, or at least 50% of it. I've had 100% of the parental duty for a long time. I'm getting tired. Here's the plan. It's kind of out there, but I think it might actually work. I buy a two-family house. He gets upstairs with Trevor, I stay downstairs with the girls, and when you're in town, you live in my mom's house.

"I think it's the healthiest option. My girls didn't do anything. Why do they have to split their lives in half because of their parents' divorce? And why my kids? Why are they on the outside making all the concessions? This way, they just go up or down the stairs depending on whose turn it is. When it's his turn, I'm yours. If you find it appealing, I could go with you when you have a job in Miami. Or California. He'll finally pick up his end of the deal, and I'll get some freedom.

"During the week when you're traveling, I stay with the girls. What do you think?"

"I think you've put a lot of time into this, and what's best for the girls. I'm not crazy about you guys sharing a house, but I understand your thought process. I have two conditions. One, I need to meet your ex and see for myself it's over, if he's going to rise up and be kind to the girls and follow through and be their dad. And two, you need to marry me."

***

Twenty

VAL

VALERIE WAS STUNNED. "What are you talking about? We never talked about getting married."

"Why didn't we?" Walter asked her.

"You never brought it up. I figured your experience with marriage and family growing up left a bad taste in your mouth, and that's why you stayed a bachelor all these years, to avoid a connection with someone. That's why you picked a career that deliberately made a relationship impossible. Meeting my ex is one thing. You all should meet with the kids someday, bring a pizza, and do the two dogs circling around each other thing and get it out of the way. But marrying is a topic for another day."

"It's a topic for today," Walter insisted. "Everything you've ever done was to minimize any damage to the kids. How are you going to explain the concept of morality to the girls when their mother's shacking up with some dude? I want to be more than that. Maybe I want to be their stepdad, did you ever think about that?"

"Can we get married on a beach at sunset? By a shaman?"

"Yeah, if you can find one."

"I might like that. We go away to get married. We come home with rings. We have everything but a license. We have a ceremony at sunset. Take pictures. Are you going anywhere? No. Me either. So, we have a commitment ceremony. At sunset."

"I'd like that. I'll probably not be married for the rest of my life. Why can't I get a make-believe wedding and a fake wife?" he asked her.

"Let me work on it. Maybe I'll call you my husband anyway. There has to be something you can't be. You can't be an in-law. How about this? You can be my faux husband."

"I'm confused," he confessed.

"I just want to be with you."

The school was out, and the girls had some free time. Valerie figured now was the best time to introduce them to their new life.

They knew she lost her job. The school was like that; kids appeared and disappeared all the time because of the transient nature of their parents' employment. Astrid was angry.

"I don't want to move. I have friends here. A life. I'm not going," she said and stomped off to her room.

"There's more news. If you don't come down, Ingrid and Fiona will know it first," Valerie played her.

She stomped back into the room.

"So, what's the big news?" Astrid asked. Her tone said that unless it was the keys to the lost city of Atlantis, it wasn't worth her effort.

"Well," Valerie grabbed Walter's hand. "Mommy has a boyfriend." All three gasped together.

"Who is it?" breathed Ingrid.

"Mr. Stranger!" said Astrid. She pointed at the way they were holding hands.

"Very good," Walt congratulated her.

"There's more," Valerie said. She looked at their excited faces. Astrid couldn't help her "poor Ingrid" sigh. Second again, it meant. Val took her hand and turned Ingrid towards her and shoved the ring right in her face.

"We're getting married!" Ingrid screamed as she looked at the ring. "Look! Look! Mom has a ring!" They squealed. Three girls of various ages screamed, "OH!" and "YAY!" Ingrid yelled, "'We're getting married! We're getting married!" They danced around. Ingrid, mostly. Fiona, too. She started to mimic Ingrid, much like Ingrid used to copy Astrid.

Valerie stood and went into the kitchen, motioning Walt over with her head. He left the girls undisturbed in the celebration and walked over to her.

"Look," she whispered, pointing her chin at her daughters. "I think they're happy."

He kissed her. "I have four girls now."

"Is that a bad thing?" Val asked him.

"Honestly, it's the best thing that ever happened to me. 'Yeah, that's my stepdad. He was marine.' Has a nice ring to it. 'Have her home by nine.' It's a whole life I never imagined for myself. It's a whole lot more of a life than I deserve. I'm honored you want me to be a part of it."

"That's where you're wrong. You deserve every hormonal, crying, boot-stomping, door-slamming minute of this, and I'm not talking about the kids."

He laughed. "Like I said, bring it on."

"Okay, girls, you can go out and play. Ingrid, you have to swim at four o'clock. Don't go too far away. Walt will go with you. I'd like to talk to Astrid alone."

"Yeah, Mom?" Astrid said once everyone else was outside.

"Astrid, I can tell something's bothering you. What is it? I want the truth." Val reached out and stroked her daughter's arm.

"You want the truth? Okay, I'll tell you the truth. I'm mad. Why do we have to move again? I like it here just fine. Now you're getting married. I have to switch schools again. Make new friends again. Why does everything always have to change?"

"I can understand your point. Things are always changing; that's life, honey.

Things are always changing like the sun. It doesn't shine every day. Sometimes it rains. That's why you should always have an umbrella in your car. Even if we stayed, we'd still have to move because this place is owned by the place where I no longer work. Yes, you will have to change schools. Do you know what else will change? No uniforms. You get to go back to school shopping."

"Shopping?" Astrid sounded like she was warming up to the idea. "Yup. Sometimes, change is good. Or bad. Or exciting and scary, but things are always changing. For everyone."

"I guess," said Astrid. "I'm going outside."

"Would you please send Walter up?"

"You wanted to see me?" he asked as he returned.

She laughed. "Look at you. Soon to be a stepdad. My husband. Did you ever in your life think there would be so many people in your life? I mean, when I met you, you were a regular rolling stone, living out of a suitcase. Never anywhere long enough to set down roots."

"Just for the record, I didn't live like a monk before I met you. I was around enough to get familiar with the cheap floozies. Those were some messed-up chicks with a lot of daddy issues. I was considered a fly-by; I could make them feel special for a night, but I was not the solution to their problems. There was no future with me.

"I have a confession to make," he added. "The first time I saw you was at one of those launch meetings, and I decided 'her.' I don't know why. Well, I do know. There were all kinds of people in that room, and you didn't say anything other than your name. Meanwhile, everyone in that room is sucking up to someone to gather some political cache for future use. It was a feeding frenzy, and you rose above it all. I thought you must be a secretary to take notes, but most secretaries don't make enough money to afford the suit you were wearing. You had your hair in one of those fancy braids."

She laughed again. "When I had meetings like that, I got there early so Heather in accounting could do my hair. Nobody talked to me because my communication was downward, to the staff. I made that clear early on so they'd leave me alone. They believed I had no power to get them to the corner office when, in fact, I had lunch with the CEO every other Friday. Marcus and I go way back. He promoted me. He was hired at the same time I was. He was in management. I was a grunt in the stacks. He came looking for me once, he thought I got fired. I was back there working on my two-foot pile of accounts. He asked me why I never went up front and increased my visibility among management.

"'Management? Nobody in management knows my name, and I'm keeping it that way. Most of them are morons and don't know their left from their right. They show up, manage us for an hour, and go to lunch. and we don't see them again for months.' He told me I was wasting myself back there."

"You said management was a bunch of morons to someone in management? You're the one with the brass balls."

"Yeah, and they promoted me anyway."

She watched her kids grow up playing here. It was Friday, the night of the neighborhood cookout. It was a warm night, the air humid with natural bug repellent many of the moms used for a holistic, chemical-free solution to bug bites.

There was no way Walt was going to do a communal cookout. He cooked upstairs, assembled the burgers per Valerie's directive, wrapped them in wax paper, wrote their names, and put them in a Valerie-supplied basket. She made a chef salad for a side dish and purchased a fruit salad. He got a cooler full of lemonade for Ingrid and Fiona, Arnold Palmer for Astrid, and some bottled water for them. He scored a major win with parking. It was essentially a giant tailgate party. Everyone mixed and mingled. The evening culminated with fireworks over the golf course. She would miss this, the sheer volume of people in a state of flux. The people were constantly changing. Always changing. Walter, Valerie, and the girls were next.

She needed to visit her mom and thought she might look at houses at the same time. Her mother offered Valerie the family home and was glad Valerie wanted it. Mrs. Reynolds wanted to relocate to something more manageable, but felt it was the family home, and they'd get mad at her if she sold it. Mrs. Reynolds didn't care if Valerie sold it. Let them be mad at her. She was glad it was settled so uneventfully.

Val thought she'd look at two families and found one that would work perfectly. Parking in the back for four cars and a swing set. The realtor was willing to come back in two hours if Valerie was sincere. Val called Grandpa Dave.

"Valerie! How nice to hear from you."

"Guess what? We're moving back! I'll be back by the time school starts. I left Lambert and came home to be near my mom. I know this is short notice, but could you get a hold of Greg and have him meet me at two-thirty at 415 Auburn Ave? Call me back if you can't get ahold of him. I'll come over for coffee tomorrow morning. I'll bring the donuts."

She sat on the front steps and waited. Shortly, a Conover Properties truck pulled in, newer than the one she last saw him drive. He got out and unbuckled a little boy, his son. Where the fuck was this guy when I was dragging his kids around, she thought, but immediately chastised herself. This wasn't going to work at all if she didn't adjust her attitude.

Greg carried his son, but he was kicking his legs like he wanted to walk, so Greg put him down. He immediately went limp. Valerie laughed when she heard him say, "You'd better get up, or I'll leave you here." The boy got up and took his father's hand, and they walked over to the steps where Valerie sat.

"Valerie. Hi. This is a surprise," Greg said.

"Who's this little charmer?"

"That's my little boy, Trevor. Trevor, can you say hi to Valerie?" He handed her a stick. She found another stick and gave it to him, and he laughed and handed it back.

She looked up at Greg and said, "Cute kid."

"Valerie, I have to be honest. I'm scared to death. I don't know what to say."

"Good, because I want to do the talking. For reasons I don't want to get into,

I'm moving back with the kids later in the summer. I understand you quit drinking."

"Over three years ago. It hasn't been easy, and I have done some really fucked up things quitting," he looked at Trevor gathering sticks. "Well, you remember me at my mom's. I've come a long way since then."

Val looked at him and nodded. "You look good."

"Thanks, Val. It's just me, Trevor, and my dad. It's a regular bachelor's paradise."

"That's what I want to talk to you about. I have a number of things I've been thinking about and trying to create a plan. I'm not working anymore, and I'm moving back with the kids. First, I'm buying my mom's house. She wants to move into Greenbriar, that assisted living place."

"That's nice. She should be happy there," he said. "But why did you want to want to meet here?"

"I guess this is part two. My kids need a dad. Your kids need a dad. I can't be the sole parent anymore. These past five years have been really hard. I'm exhausted. I want you to share custody. That's why we're here. I want to buy this house. You and Trevor live upstairs. The girls and I live downstairs. That way, there's no driving them back and forth to two separate homes. When it's your turn, the girls go up the back stairs and stay with you. My turn, they come back downstairs. This way, they have stability.

"Every decision I've made, I had to ask myself, how will this impact the kids? I want my girls to feel settled, and I'm scared of what kind of men they'll be attracted to. Assholes who view them as disposable? Will they see themselves as worthless? After all, their own father doesn't want to see them. He has a new kid he does stuff with. Why not me? What was wrong with me that he left? Why doesn't my Daddy love me?"

"Geez, Valerie—"

"Shut up. Do you know why we left? I don't know if you were aware of this, but after you left, I held out hope we were worth more to you than a bottle of Bud, and you'd miss us and come back to—"

"Valerie," he said, as he interrupted her again.

"I told you to shut up. Just shut the fuck up and listen. Give me that much. Anyway, I saw you at a red light, coming the other way. I remembered being really happy and excited, we could talk and try to figure what went wrong if I could only get your attention. Okay, there I was, holding the steering wheel, leaning forward so you would see me. You did. You made eye contact and looked away.

"You looked away. From me. That was the day I lost all hope. The way you rejected me crushed me. It crushed me." Valerie started to cry.

"Val—"

"I said shut up. Shut up. You're going to listen to me. I'm not done."

He got up and fetched Trevor, who was wandering around looking for more sticks, but had both hands full. He gave Valerie the sticks, and Greg brought him closer to a new spot. "Sorry. Go on."

"Okay. I was scared the girls would be riding their bikes and you'd drive by, they would wave at you, only to have their own father turn away from them. I could barely cope with it. They would not suffer the rejection I did," she said, pausing to wipe her nose on her shirt. "Anyway, I took a promotion and moved away. I sent them to see your parents, so they still had a connection with your side. That brings us to why I'm here today." He remained silent.

"Astrid. She's at that stage where she's questioning everything. She'll give you a ton of shit for leaving. It's going to take a long time; she already has trust issues. Ingrid, sweet Ingrid. She is so hungry for a dad. She still asks me if you're sick. I'm afraid she'll end up seeking a father figure as an adult and be a doormat for any guy because she's so desperate to be loved. And Fiona. She doesn't even know you." She stopped talking and took a deep breath.

"Can I talk now?" She nodded.

"Valerie, all I can offer for the past is an apology. It will never be enough. I am so sorry I hurt you like that. I was, and still am, an alcoholic. I'm not sure if I was a bigger alcoholic than I was an asshole. I behaved horribly to the people I love. I'm sorry I was so cruel to you, but I'm sober now. I want to salvage some sort of relationship with the girls. Maybe even take them to therapy with me."

"You still go?"

"Yeah. Another reason I was cruel to you was because you were right about my leg. It was the root cause. I never accepted I had to reinvent myself. I was scared, I didn't know how, and I had no idea who I was if I didn't play football.

"I had no plan B. I should have figured that out before we got married. You were always right, and it used to make me so mad. I hated you for it. I had no place to put my rage, so blaming you was easy. I don't anymore. That's the first thing that came up in therapy."

"My denial was not your fault. Nothing was your fault. I think I wanted to drive you away so you were safe. When you got pregnant with Fiona, someone said maybe it's a boy, and I freaked. I had no business having a boy. What kind of father could I possibly be? I can't run, jump, climb trees, nothing. I pulled away deliberately."

He stopped, and they both looked at Trevor and laughed. He shrugged and continued. "I cannot make up for any past events. When we found it was a girl, it didn't matter. I had separated myself so far from you I figured it was better just to leave. How could I have kids? I didn't want you and the girls there to witness my collapse. Or maybe because I was a drunk who wanted to drink in peace, and you always had something you needed me to deal with. More likely the second, but I'm a drunk, like I said. I'm glad you left.

"Things got ugly when my mom got sick. I'd gotten really bad. I told her everything I did and how horrible I was. She brought up you and the girls, how they deserved the very best. I couldn't stop crying, and I just lost it." He looked at her and continued. "I'm not looking for sympathy. I don't deserve it. I guess I heard your side, and I'd like to share mine."

"That's okay. I'd like to hear the rest."

"I promised my mom I'd stop drinking. I'd do it for her, and she said don't bother. The only way it was going to work was if I did it for myself. I knew I could be better than some bum on a barstool. I went that night and detoxed, and I did everything they told me to, right down to AA. I came out dry and haven't had a drink since. There's been plenty of times I wanted one so badly, but if I distracted myself, it passed. You saved me the day I buried my mom.

"I was so sad. I wanted to drown myself in a keg of beer. Who gave a fuck whether I had one beer or twenty? My mom just died. She'd say, 'Don't use me as an excuse. Man up.' When I drove by your mom's, I knew you were there. I didn't plan on stopping. I was on a mission to get to O'Malley's as quick as possible.

"Maybe my mom took the wheel and turned into your driveway. As much as I deserved you telling me to fuck off and slam the door in my face, I prayed you wouldn't. I hoped you'd help me. You did. You got me to my sponsor, and the moment passed, and I stayed sober. I still go to AA.

"This part of the story is embarrassing, but I have to own it all. I met Shannon at an AA meeting. I thought we could help each other stay sober. I was lonely, and she was there, and next thing you know, she's pregnant. I talked to my dad. I said I was afraid she'd use and hurt the baby, so he gave me an extended leave. I rode her ass the whole time.

"He was born three weeks early, but perfectly healthy. She had a C-section. The way she kept asking for more Oxy kind of sent up a red flag as to the extent of her addictions. The tox screen was negative on Trevor, though, and that's all I cared about. We bring the baby back to my place, and things turn bad quick. In the beginning, she had surgery, so she couldn't move around much, and I took care of Trevor and her. She loved being waited on. She stopped going to meetings and meeting with her sponsor. When she was pregnant, I dragged her to at least two a day just to keep her occupied.

"After he was born, I would get up, feed him, dress him for the day, and hand him to her while she was in bed. I'd get ready and go to work. She'd bother me all day long. Is the bottle supposed to be hot or cold? He pooped all over. What do I do? He was so little I couldn't leave him with her. My dad gave me two more weeks off so I could care for him.

"She was a horrible mother, and an even worse person. I was planning on moving back in with my dad when the lease was up. The last straw was when I found a hypodermic needle by the back stairs. I called the landlord and said that I'd pay what was left of the lease, but he needed get that girl out because she brought drugs into his house.

"We made a plan, Trevor goes to my dad's, I go to work. The landlord showed up and said he needed to work on the plumbing. He banged on the pipes for a bit, and she left. He moved her stuff out onto the porch, changed the locks, and she was done. I haven't seen or heard from her since. I filed for sole custody, but can't find her to serve the papers."

Greg stopped and looked at Valerie, sadness in his eyes. Another person to explain his deficiencies to, just one more on the road to recovery. Such was his life. She looked back at him and said, "I'm proud of you."

"What?"

"I said I was proud of you. You had a few false starts, mostly because you were doing it to shut someone up, usually me. But you committed to it this time. A lot of shit went down that could have caused you to stumble, even fall. You got up and tried again. Here you are, and there is still time to build something with the girls. Even Astrid. She'll punish you, but now you know you're strong enough to take it. She'll come around."

Trevor came back with more sticks for Valerie. He helped her build a pile, and she whispered to him, "When your dad isn't here, I'll teach you how to light a fire with a magnifying glass."

"Hey," he said. "Don't teach him that." Trevor went off in search of more twigs. "He's got your blue eyes," Valerie told Greg. "My cerulean blue eyes?"

Valerie looked at him and suddenly let out a wail. She started crying, great, big, rib-cracking sobs. She put her face on her knees and wept. Greg sat there and watched. He knew he was the source of her pain and felt like crying with her, but didn't. He let Valerie feel her pain. He had to let her be. To involve himself took the focus off her, and she was entitled to her feelings. Greg would forever feel guilty he caused her such anguish. Valerie deserved so much better than what she got from him. When she finished, he handed her a burp cloth. She looked confused, and he pointed to the diaper bag.

"Oh my God, I can't believe I lost it like that. I remember that day like it was yesterday. Some memories, I guess, will never fade," she said. "I hope they don't.

You were my first boyfriend. I loved you. There was an awful lot of good before it went bad. I don't want to forget that."

"Thank you, Valerie. It means a lot you can look at it that way. That's exactly how I look at it, until I start to feel like a shit, that I ruined it all."

"Circumstances ruined it. Your leg. Maybe you didn't handle it so great, but you were young. We both were. How the hell were we supposed to deal with that? How the hell were we even supposed to know we had to deal with it? Take whatever guilt you have about us and let it go. It serves no purpose."

"Are you sure you can forgive me just like that?"

"No. I'll say I've forgiven 80% of it, but that last twenty, I'm not sure I'll ever get over. You never even tried to work it out with us. You never gave us a chance, and that I can't get over. You were supposed to love me. If you really loved me, it wouldn't have been so easy to just let me go. I'm not sure I can get over that, either."

"The only thing I can say is I was an alcoholic. I wasn't in my right mind. That negates nothing, but I will regret what you went through for the rest of my life. I loved you with my whole heart. I know I shouldn't say this, but it doesn't matter because you've already moved on, but you were the best. I know we were young and didn't realize what exactly we were facing, but if I had been honest with you, we might've had a chance.

"You never gave a shit about football, and it was my whole identity. I was really mad at you because you never valued what I considered my whole life, but it was just a stupid game. You were so smart, I couldn't face what you already knew. I loved you then, and I always will. I don't think I'll ever fall in love again." He looked at Trevor. "I didn't love his mother, and look what happened."

Valerie had stopped crying and looked at him. "You got him. You love him. He's the girls' half-brother. They have a brother. I know when Fiona was born, the girls expressed vehemently, "No boys allowed," but they might change once they see him, and Fiona will be overjoyed, she'll have somebody younger to boss around.

"I have to tell you, though, I'm with somebody else. If we enter into this arrangement, you have to know there is no way we will ever be together again. It's too late for me, but not the kids. It won't be easy with Astrid, but love her and she'll come around."

"I understand about us. I respect that you are with another man and wish you the very best. I'll put my efforts into repairing my relationships with the girls," Greg said.

"The realtor is coming soon. Will this work? Is it realistic to think you can live upstairs over us? It's not going to put too much stress and anxiety on you and cause you to relapse, is it? An instant family? All those girls? They can be tough. There are benefits. Built-in babysitters. The kids are together, sorta, and if you feel the need to go to a meeting, send Trevor down. I'll watch him."

"It feels like I won the lottery. I need to get out of my dad's, he helps with Trevor, but he's getting old. He raised his kids, he shouldn't have to raise mine. I would love to spend time with the girls. I have missed you all so much. I've missed so much. I've gone to many meetings to come to grips with the fact you left because of me. That me, my own actions, cost me my family. This feels like a second chance, and I want to grab it with both hands and not let go."

"Well, that settles that. When the realtor comes, she can show you the upstairs. Wait a minute. Are you going to be able to manage the stairs? It won't be too much on your knee? You mentioned you went off the rails because Fiona might be a boy. Well, now you are the sole provider of one. How are you doing?"

"I knew he was a boy early, so I had some time to prepare. When he got here, I was so concerned about his mother. She wanted nothing to do with him. I didn't have the time to worry or obsess because I had to take care of him. When I saw how badly she let his diaper rash get, I knew I had to rise up because he had nobody. The best way to take care of it was to leave, so we went to my dad's. I understand how difficult it was living with an addict. It must have been so hard for you to love one on top of it."

"Well, thanks for that. Some days, it was really hard to love you. How's your knee? Still nervous about having a boy?" Valerie wanted to know.

He hiked up his pant leg and showed her his brace, or the bottom of it. "Once

I got used to wearing it, it gave my knee stability. I'll never run a four-forty, but I don't need to. I can trot, so I can get a bad throw. I can walk upstairs. I can do mostly everything, just slower. With the brace, I don't have to worry about it giving out. That's a blessing. He doesn't seem to mind."

"He'll never know you any other way. You're just his dad. He won't love you any less than if you had two good knees. So, you are my new upstairs tenant, correct?"

"Yes. What's the rent?"

"I don't know. Talk to your dad. He set up college accounts for the girls. Put money in there periodically, and we'll be square." Valerie stood up. "I wish she'd get here. I need to get to my mom's."

"I thought you were keeping it. Are you renting it out?"

"It's for Walt. I'll be living in the flat. He travels a lot for work, so I'll be here during the week, and the two weekends you have them, I'll stay with him there. He's a lifelong bachelor, the concept of family is foreign to him, so I have to break him in easy. Plus, he felt uncomfortable shacking up with me; what kind of message it would send to the girls?"

"Sounds like a good guy, worried about sending the wrong message to the girls. How'd you meet him?"

"At work. He was one of the contractors we used. He had the condo next to mine. After the job was done, he stayed next door. He wants to meet you. He's sort of old school. Walter wanted to make sure we were safe. That you weren't a real loser, the girls shouldn't be around."

"Sounds like a real stand-up guy."

"He is. He's not sure what his role would be as a stepfather. If you are healthy and willing to share custody, he was going to step back and let you figure it out. If you weren't, he'll step in and be there for the girls. He'll be there for them anyways."

"His name is Walter? He's a contractor who's never been married? Does he do electrical?"

"Yeah. Why?"

"Because if his name is Walter Granger, we've met before. I know him. Nice guy. This industry has the same players. They may work on a number of different projects, but we always run across each other someplace or another. I don't know if you know this, but his single status made him a hot commodity among single women, or among mothers with single daughters and divorcees. He's probably marrying you so he'll can say he's off the market and be left alone."

"Huh," Val said. "Oh, look. The realtor's here." Valerie introduced the two stayed on the porch, and wrote a check. Once he took a look, she was going to sign it.

∗∗∗

Twenty-One

VAL

THEY WERE MOVING NEXT WEEK. At the Friday night tailgate party, many people in the complex came over and said goodbye. Valerie didn't know she knew so many people there, but she had been there a while. For the new tenants, they got their grills out and fired up as pit masters, while people like her, the long-timers, brought sandwiches.

Valerie arranged to have dinner at the new house and wanted both Walt and Greg there. She wanted to see if they could be a little bit friendly. Greg already told her he was cool with Walter. Walter, as long as he accepted Greg's motive was not to get Valerie back, had no problem.

"Are you concerned about meeting Greg?" she asked Walter.

"No. Should I be?"

"No, but he already knows you. He's seen you occasionally at work if the two of you were in the same spot at the same time. He said hearts are breaking everywhere because you're off the market. Single women, young and old, are weeping in gyms everywhere."

"What are you talking about?" Walt was irritated, concerned Greg was already causing problems.

"Greg said a single guy your age is a hot commodity. Lots of attractive, interested females seeking a partner find that you have infinite possibilities. You can't tell me you don't know chicks are after you. He said by marrying me, your life will be easier because you'll be off the market."

"Greg? I can't place him."

"Have you ever done work for Conover Properties?"

"Yeah. Plenty. Why?"

"His mother was a Conover. His dad bought it and runs it now. Greg's last name is Wilson. He grew up working on sites."

"Greg Wilson. What does he look like?"

"Like he'd be very popular in prison. He was very pretty, beautiful even before alcohol ruined his looks."

"Your two older girls. Do they look like him?"

"Yes. His mom was Swedish. They all look like her."

"You're right. He is very pretty," Walter agreed.

"He was. His looks have faded, and he's gained about fifty pounds. Alcohol was hard on him. I'm not sure you'd recognize him."

Walter sat next to Valerie and held her hand. He looked her in the eye. "Now, Valerie, I believe you. I may not say it enough, maybe because I didn't grow up hearing it, but I love you. I trust you completely. So much of this is out of character. It seems strange that I'm so comfortable with it. We have all these people now. Please tell me we count as one vote. We're more than roommates. Tell me we will always discuss whatever comes up and come to a consensus. That's what I need to know. After your kids, it's me. After they're gone, it's still me."

"I'm not used to you being so insecure, Walt. Come here," she said, opening her arms to him. She wrapped herself around him and gave him a big hug. "I know your views regarding a future with a woman. I understand when you were growing up, things looked ugly; relationships were toxic. I had the exact opposite. My father worshipped my mom. He never raised his voice, let alone his hand, at any of us. We both come from extremely opposite home lives, so what if 'I love you' doesn't roll off your tongue? I don't need to hear it. I feel it.

"I grew up in a house where we said 'I love you' every time someone left the house. I don't say it because I think it makes you uncomfortable, but I think you need to hear it. You don't have to tell me; I know you love me. You're it, baby. The end of the road. Mine. I love you. If you want a real ceremony and a traditional wedding, I might do that. Let me know. Now, let's go pick up the food and go over to Auburn. We're having a mixer. Let's see how everyone gets along."

It was a fine night for a party. All the doors were open, and Valerie watched the kids run around, up and down the front and back stairs. She had Trevor inside with her, toddling around the empty rooms.

Greg and Walter had some peace out in the backyard.

"So, Valerie tells me we've met before?" Walter started. "On one of the jobs. Do you remember the project?"

"The Art Walk, I think."

"Yeah. I guess some of it could be considered art. The rest, I don't know what it was. I have to ask this question because, although I believe what Val thinks, I'm asking as a guy. What's your opinion of the situation? What do you want to get out of this?"

"You mean Valerie? Am I going to use our close proximity to try to win her back?"

"Yes."

"No. I wish I could, but it would never be what it was; too much time has passed. Plus, Valerie is not the girl for me, or more like I'm not the right guy for her. I love her. I always will. Even if I get married again, I won't love her like I love Valerie. I can't not love her. Valerie is strong. Determined. She needs someone as brave as she is. A Marine might be man enough. If you wash out and she'd let me, I'd make a play for her. Otherwise, no. She's your girl now."

"Thank you. I think if I described this setup to most people, they would think I'm nuts. You and Valerie will be playing house while I'm on the road. Maybe it's love, but I believe her. And you. So, I hope this works. Those girls deserve a sense of permanence, of home."

The girls came running out of the house, and Val brought Trevor outside. The noise level went up too loud, and Walt walked down the sidewalk to check the noise; yes, the neighbors had something to get used to. He walked down the street to look around and started talking to the man next door, who was out watering his plants. Walt was interested in the history of the neighborhood.

Next door, arrangements were made for move-in day, next Saturday. "No! Sooner!" they yelled.

"Okay," Greg told them. "I thought you might like to pick out paint colors for your rooms, but I can paint them white." The screams got louder. "Okay, okay, we can go to the paint store tomorrow." He looked around at the crowd of kids and swallowed.

"When you come in to get the girls tomorrow, I can keep Trevor," Val offered.

"Thanks. I'll see if my dad can keep him. The best thing about a day off is not having to get him ready on time."

"That's true. I'll ask Astrid to help you with the other two. Don't worry. She has a superiority complex. She loves to be in charge. Use it."

"Thanks. I'll be by around eleven. Goodbye, girls, see you in the morning. Walt." He nodded, picked up Trevor, and got in his truck.

"Okay, girls, pack it all up. Time to go back to Gramma's."

The girls were excited about getting to pick out paint colors. "I call purple!" Astrid yelled.

"No! I want purple!" Ingrid wailed. "Mom!"

"No! I want purple!" Fiona yelled, mostly because Ingrid did. "Pink!" screamed Astrid to be heard over the other two. "I want pink! The color of cotton candy!"

"No!" yelled Fiona this time. "Pink! The color of bubble gum!"

Ingrid, sensing an opening, said loudly, "That's it! You heard them, Mom! They want pink. I get purple."

"I want pink!"

"No! I do!"

"Stop it, Fiona!"

"I want pink!" came from the back seat. Valerie looked at Walter, sensed he was getting flustered by all the drama behind him, and asked him to pull over. He did and looked at Valerie for guidance. She put her index finger against her lips and mimed, "Shh." They sat there in silence while the kids argued in the back seat. Finally, a voice popped up.

"Hey!" said Ingrid, who had already won her choice of color. "Why are we stopped?"

Valerie turned around and looked at Ingrid, but said nothing. She pushed her sisters. "Shut up, you guys! We're parked on the side of the road. Mom's mad!"

They settled down, and soon, no noise came from the backseat. Only then did Valerie speak.

"Knock it off back there. Mr. Stranger is going to make us walk home if you don't stop. You can pick out whatever color you want. Do you know how many shades of pink there are? Be quiet, and when we get home, I'll give you some magazines and pick out what you like. Have Daddy bring it to the paint store, and they'll match it. Deal? Okay, Walt. Take me home before I lose my mind." Walt started the car and pulled out.

"Is that the key to successful child-rearing? Losing your mind?" Walt asked Valerie.

"No, but it helps."

"Mom!" called Astrid. "Ingrid said, 'Shut up!'"

Valerie turned back around and stared at Astrid. Astrid sensed she better be quiet. She frowned at her mother and whispered under her breath, "But she did."

After Valerie made them help empty the car and put everything away, she called them to the den, where Gramma Mary used to watch TV. There was also a basket filled with all kinds of magazines, many for home decor and design. Before she gave them each a pile, she said, "You are only looking at paint colors. No furniture. I don't care if you find the bedroom of your dreams, paint color ONLY. Got it?" She handed out the magazines only after they all agreed. "You guys sit here and watch TV and look at the magazines. Mr. Stranger and I are going to have a glass of wine on the porch."

Finally, when everything was managed, Walt brought her a glass of wine and sat in the chair next to her. They watched small-town life pass by for a bit and enjoyed the silence. After a while, Walt spoke.

"Does it bother you? Not drinking around Greg?"

"Not really. I never was a big drinker. It seemed like I always got hungover before I got drunk. I do like a glass of wine now and again, but I don't really care when I have it. Now, I have a question for you after listening to them argue all the way here. Do you think you can handle it? Do you even want to handle it? You can say no."

"Valerie, I'll say this," Walt started. "I had a rule never to date complicated women. If a woman came with three kids and an ex-husband, those are complications. If you were all alone and expected me to solve every problem or come up with all solutions, I guess you'd be an uncomplicated woman, but you'd also be a bore and a pain in the ass." He took a sip of wine, looked at her, and smiled. "Speaking of asses, you are one fine piece of ass. Who gives a shit about complications if you're standing next to me?"

"The ride here wasn't even that bad. They can get so much worse, especially at home. They argue about who gets the red bowl or the special spoon. Ingrid blinks too loud, you know. They don't even realize they have bedrooms in my half of the house; they'll need to paint. Their heads would have exploded if they knew they got to pick colors for six bedrooms. Sure, you don't want to cut and run?"

"I'm not too worried. If it gets to be too much, I can go home."

"Stay. Hide in the downstairs bathroom. That's what I do. Is my mom's house too far away? It's kind of a drag. If you wanted to go home and pout for ten minutes, it takes ten to get there and then back. It's thirty minutes for a small snit."

"Why am I having a snit?" he asked, perturbed. "Anyway, while you were working out some details, I took a walk around. It's a nice neighborhood. I was talking to your neighbor, the old guy next door, watering his plants. Nice guy. Widower.

He said he wanted to move to his brother's place in Tampa. Remember when I said you could live any place you wanted as long as I could be near you?"

She nodded.

"I hope you meant it. Your mother's house is too far away. I need to be closer, so I'm buying the house next door. I talked him into moving to Tampa. We'll be next-door neighbors, just like before."

The End

Acknowledgments

To my friend and beta reader, Judy Hentges.
To my daughter, Moira King, my coach and excellent advisor.
And my daughter, Monica King, who handles so much and makes it look easy.
And to Ameena Dye, Monica's sister from another mister.

About the Author

After retiring from Corporate America, she spent her free time volunteering until Covid-19 made those activities obsolete. Not one to sit around and watch Days of Our Lives, she decided to write a book. She wrote a couple, so depending on which one hits the shelf first, this could be her debut novel. She is an empty nester with two adult daughters. One husband, a dog, and a cat remain.

Regarding any questions or comments you might have, feel free to reach out at cynthiaakingbooks.com.

www.ingramcontent.com/pod-product-compliance
Lightning Source LLC
Chambersburg PA
CBHW042028050526
44107CB00103B/742